SITĀR TECHNIQUE IN NIBADDH FORMS

PERFORMING ARTS SERIES

General Editor
FARLEY P. RICHMOND

VOLUME VI

Sitār Technique in Nibaddh Forms

STEPHEN SLAWEK

MOTILAL BANARSIDASS PUBLISHERS
PRIVATE LIMITED • DELHI

First Edition: Delhi, 1987
Second Revised Edition: Delhi, 2000

ISBN: 81-208-0200-4

Also available at:
MOTILAL BANARSIDASS
236, 9th Main III Block, Jayanagar, Bangalore 560 011
41 U.A. Bungalow Road, Jawahar Nagar, Delhi 110 007
8 Mahalaxmi Chamber, Warden Road, Mumbai 400 026
120 Royapettah High Road, Mylapore, Chennai 600 004
Sanas Plaza, 1302 Baji Rao Road, Pune 411 002
8 Camac Street, Calcutta 700 017
Ashok Rajpath, Patna 800 004
Chowk, Varanasi 221 001

Printed in India
BY JAINENDRA PRAKASH JAIN AT SHRI JAINENDRA PRESS,
A-45 NARAINA, PHASE-I, NEW DELHI 110 028
AND PUBLISHED BY NARENDRA PRAKASH JAIN FOR
MOTILAL BANARSIDASS PUBLISHERS PRIVATE LIMITED,
BUNGALOW ROAD, DELHI 110 007

To ANITA,
CHARU and
DEEPIKA

Lord *Śiva*, omniscient husband of *Pārvatī*, is pleased with music. *Kṛṣṇa*, in his endless concert of the *Gopī*-s, enchanted them with the sound of his flute. The Creator is engrossed in the chanting of the *Sāmaveda*. *Sarasvatī* dwells in the *vīṇā*.

In the shadow of these, what to say about others, creatures such as demons, gods, demigods, and men.

The child crying in bed, who does not yet know the taste of attachment, is overjoyed by the nectar of music.

The brindled fawn grazing on the forest grass is entranced by the music of the hunter and relinquishes his life.

Who is capable of correctly evaluating the song which causes all this, the greatness of that music which is the only means of attaining *dharma*, *artha*, *kāma*, and *mokṣa*?

Saṅgīta Ratnākara
verses 22-30
Svarādhyāya

FOREWORD BY SERIES EDITOR

India is one of the great repositories of performing arts, particularly those of the classical, folk/popular, devotional and modern traditions. The sheer enormity and diversity of its cultural expressions in music, dance, dance/drama and theatre are the envy of many nations around the world. This series intends to assemble some of the best books now available on these subjects.

Without exaggeration, a series such as this would not have been possible twenty years ago when I first began writing about Indian theatre. At that time little more than a few dozen books comprised the entire field of scholarship in the English language, not to mention the paucity of materials in regional Indian languages. Today that picture has radically changed. Numerous publishers have devoted precious press time to volumes of well-illustrated, detailed and, yes, sometimes even esoteric works on the multiple aspects of this fascinating subject. Comb any bookshop in Delhi or Madras, Bombay or Calcutta and you will regularly find new works appearing on the shelves. This represents a real area of growth! It is to the credit of Motilal Banarsidass Publishers Private Limited that there is now the potential of assembling numerous volumes together under one umbrella.

It is rare that a book attempts to uncover the root of the creative process of performance. Stephen Slawek, a creative artist trained in the *sitār* at the feet of great twentieth century Indian masters, has given readers a taste of Indian music from the inside of the creative process. His scoring of the music for western readers and those who follow western musical notation is insightful and allows those who are versed in this field to "hear" the music in their mind and to examine its intricacies on the printed page. The excursion is well worth the effort to all who examine this fascinating work.

FARLEY P. RICHMOND

CONTENTS

LIST OF TABLES

LIST OF FIGURES

FOREWORD

I congratulate Stephen Slawek on his well researched thesis 'Sitār Technique in Nibaddh Forms".

This work should prove useful to students of north Indian music and sitar, both in theory and in practice.

Teaching and performance of European Classical music is now firmly based on a written tradition whereas music of India relies mainly on our long and complex oral tradition. Since, outside India, performers, composers and scholars are eager to know more about the forms, techniques and improvisational processes that are so unique to our music, there is a growing need for efforts such as this publication.

Interpreting an oral art tradition through writing can be confusing, unsatisfactory or even misleading in spite of the seriousness and competence of the writer. I am happy to say Stephen's thesis does not seem to have any such flaws.

I hope this work will encourage publication of other similar scholarly works on the art of sitar playing.

95 Lodi Estate, New Delhi-3
(*India*)

2nd August, 1984

PREFACE

The study of improvisation is a topic of increasing popularity among ethnomusicologists. What I find so attractive in this area of concern is that it provides a fertile field for studying music as process, not product. The choices a musician makes while performing in an improvisational tradition can tell a researcher a great deal about musical values in that tradition. The means by which he executes those choices may provide clues to the basic principles by which the culture of which he is a part organizes its affairs. One might even venture that a study of musical improvisation may some day further our understanding of the processes by which the human brain receives, stores, interprets and retrieves information. However, before we can approach any of these broad problems, it is necessary that we first understand exactly how improvisation takes place in individual systems of music.

This study attempts to provide a basic understanding of improvisation in the instrumental music of North India in general, and in music idiomatic to the *sitār* in particular. The approach of this study is severely descriptive. In effect, I derive what ultimately may be viewed as an "emic" oral theory of the music, and then use that theory as the basis for the analysis of selected examples drawn from material I learned from my teachers of Indian music and of one extended performance by *Paṇḍit* Ravi Shankar.

The reader is advised that quite some time has intervened between the original writing of this study and its publication. The major part of this book comprised a thesis submitted to the Graduate Division of the University of Hawaii at Manoa in partial fulfilment of the requirements for the degree of Master of Arts in Music (Ethnomusicology) in August, 1978. I have continued my study of the *sitār* with *Paṇḍit* Ravi Shankar since then and have learned a great deal more concerning his methods of improvisation. To incorporate this material here would have required additions and revisions of a magnitude beyond what could be deemed practical. However, I have made minor corrections and additions when possible that reflect changes in my own thinking and recent developments in the study of Indian music in general.

This book is not a complete study of improvisation on the *sitār*. I have not touched at all upon improvisation in the *ālāp-joṛ* sections of a performance of a *rāg*, nor have I discussed at length the genres grouped together under the rubric "light-classical." Much of what I have written here is, by extension, applicable to improvisation in these forms; however, there are significant differences of procedure and content that differentiate the *gat śailī*, the focus of the present study, from the *ālāp-joṛ* and *ṭhumrī/dhun aṅg*-s of instrumental music in North Indian music.

Another major issue not discussed in this study is the role of the *gharānā* in defining musical style. Though the term *gharānā* originated with the various schools of *khyāl* singing that developed since the mid-nineteenth century (see Neuman 1978 for an extensive study of the rise of the *khyāl gharānā*-s), it has since been appropriated by instrumentalists as a means of identifying and legitimatizing one's musical style. There are distinct stylistic differences that differentiate musicians of different *gharānā*-s. For example, *Ustād* Vilayat Khan rarely resorts to the technique of *tihāī* to close his improvisations whereas *Paṇḍit* Ravi Shankar has exploited the use of the *tihāī* to an incomparable extent. As I have shown in a paper recently delivered before the American Musical Instrument Society, these two musicians, representing two of the most influential instrumental *gharānā*-s of the twentieth century, are diametrically opposed in practically every aspect of their musical styles. The approach I have followed in this study lays the groundwork for future studies of a comparative nature.

Some readers may feel that I have given short shrift to matters of cultural context in this study. There are excellent publications available that have addressed the issue of *Hindustānī* music as a cultural system (see, e.g., Neuman 1980 and Wade 1979), and the interested reader may refer to these studies to fill in contextual gaps as needed.

Chapter I outlines the thesis, background research and methodology of this study. In Chapter 2, I discuss the prominent theories regarding the origin and development of the *sitār*, describe its structure and briefly review the historical development of the repertory of the instrument. Chapter 3 is rather speculative in nature as I attempt to trace the sources from which modern *sitār* playing techniques have been derived.

In Chapter 4, I begin the "inside-out" development of a descriptive theory of improvisation on the *sitār*. I define the basic "building blocks" of left- and right-hand playing techniques and describe how these are combined and concatenated to form larger structures. In Chapter 5, I show how these techniques come into play in the process of musical instruction in the traditional manner. Chapter 6 consists of a short discussion of the variables of musical performance in improvisation followed by a detailed transcription of a performance by Ravi Shankar. The analysis of this performance, based on and compared to what has been derived in Chapters 4 and 5, comprises Chapter 7. A brief summary concludes the main text.

I am indebted to many individuals for many kinds of help in bringing this study to fruition. Without the exacting instruction given by my *sitār* teachers, *Paṇḍit* Ravi Shankar and the late Dr. Lalmani Misra, this study would never have been begun. Dr. Lewis Rowell and Miss Barbara B. Smith aided tremendously in the original drafting of the manuscript as did Dr. Rama Nath Sharma, who assisted in the translations of the Sanskrit terms included in this study. I am also obligated to those who read the manuscript at various stages of completion for their comments and suggestions: Dr. Bruno Nettl, my mentor at the University of Illinois; Dr. Charles Capwell, University of Illinois; Dr. Lawrence Gushee, University of Illinois; Dr. Alexander Ringer, University of Illinois; Dr. Harold S. Powers, Princeton University, to whom I also owe thanks for leading me to the study of Indian music.

CHAPTER I

INTRODUCTION

The idea for the topic of this study resulted from my realization that the practice of technique on the *sitār* creates a substratum repertory, a template, so to speak, upon which an infinite number of variations can be formulated by the selective imposition of the musical constraints that comprise the system of *Hindustānī* music: *rāg* (melodic generative structure) and *tāl* (rhythmic cycle) at the broad level; archetypal forms and stylized formal elements at the specific level. These latter constituents are the determining factors in defining music idiomatic to the *sitār*.

1.1 Objective and Approach

The main objective of this study is to make evident the abovementioned substratum repertory and to examine its relative importance in music as it is performed on the *sitār*. The approach in achieving this objective will be a series of analytical descriptions of technique at increasing levels of complexity culminating in the analysis of the technique in music at the performance level. The analyses at the higher levels of complexity will focus primarily on the techniques and formal elements that constitute the *vilambit gat* (H. 'slow composition') and its *vistār* (H. 'expansion', 'development'). A detailed study of the *vistār* of the *vilambit gat* will reveal practically every aspect of improvisation utilized in *sitār* playing. The majority of contemporary *sitār*-ists have adopted the *vilambit gat* as the compositional form within which the complete *rāg prastār* (H. 'spreading out') is realized.[1] A greater variety of improvisational procedures occur in the *vilambit gat vistār* than in any other *gat* form. In contemporary styles, the only improvisational procedure not found in the *vilambit gat vistār* is *jhālā* (H. onomatopoetic?), the closing section usually played at the end of a performance of a *drut gat* (H. 'fast composition').[2] In view of these aspects, the *vilambit gat* is the logical choice to fulfill the objective of gaining as much information as possible from a limited investigation.

The results of the above investigation should lead to a determination of the extent to which an architectonic approach is utilized in *gat vistār*, and the extent to which technique influences *gat vistār*, and *vice versa*. In addition, the results should afford insight into the processes involved in the art of improvisation as exemplified on the *sitār*. Improvisation is a vital element in North Indian music. A proficient artist will improvise anywhere from fifty to ninety per cent of a performance of a *rāg*. When one considers that the performance of a single *rāg* may last over one hour, and a performance by a single artist may last as long as six hours, the amount of time spent in the extemporaneous production of music is impressive, if not awe inspiring. Moreover, the *rāg prastār* and *gat vistār* are realized in such a logical progression, maintaining the integrity of the *rāg* and *tāl* throughout, that one must infer the existence of a preconceived structure underlying the course of the improvisation, providing a unifying force to the diverse influences on a performance. Although only one performance by one particular artist is examined in this study, it is my personal opinion, based on years of listening, learning, and performing experiences, that the observations drawn from this particular example are widely applicable to the performance practice of the majority of *sitār*-ists adhering to the traditional constraints of *Hindustānī* music. However, it is necessary to remember that the present study is limited to the *nibaddh saṅgīt* (H. 'bound music' [set to a rhythmic cycle]) of classical styles. The improvisatory processes of light-classical music[3] will not be dealt with, nor will the use of *sitār* in non-classical music (e.g. George Harrison et al.) be examined.

1.2 **Background Preparation**

The background knowledge utilized in undertaking the present study was obtained through a study of the performance practice of the *sitār* beginning in 1969 at the University of Pennsylvania and continuing at the Banaras Hindu University in *Vārāṇasī*, *Uttar Pradeś*, India, from 1971 to 1976. During this period, I learned primarily from Dr. Lalmani Misra, Head of the Department of Instrumental Music at Banaras Hindu University. In June, 1977, I was initiated as a disciple of *Paṇḍit* Ravi Shankar while on a field study grant from the East-West Culture Learning Institute in Hawaii.

The traditional manner of transmitting knowledge through the ages in India has been the *guru śiṣya paramparā* (H. 'preceptor disciple tradition'). The relationship between the *guru* and *śiṣya* is considered by orthodox *Hindu*-s to be of a spiritual nature. The *guru* is likened to a god, and the disciple must submit fully to him. In return, the *guru* accepts responsibility for the *śiṣya*, treating him as a blood relative, and passes on his knowledge to him in as thorough manner as possible. Because of the economic and social conditions in India, the *guru śiṣya paramparā* is in a state of decline, and educational institutions are resorting to conservatory-style training. However, the majority of teachers of music at institutions received their own education in the traditional manner, and traditional attitudes prevail towards the teacher-taught relationship. Thus, regardless of the fact that most of my training took place within a university setting, I was still able to experience many facets of the *guru śiṣya paramparā* while under the guidance of Dr. Lalmani Misra.

My training at Banaras Hindu University was geared to a predetermined syllabus that had to be completed before appearing in a final examination. The syllabus contained both a performance repertory requirement, and a non-performance requirement consisting of selected topics to be covered in a lecture situation. The topics were usually musicological in nature, with a heavy emphasis on the history and philosophy of Indian music. The repertory requirement was defined in terms of *rāg*-s and compositional forms. Thus, a certain group of *rāg*-s were to be learned in each academic session (July-April). A number of compositions were taught in each *rāg*, most of which were set to *tīn-tāl*, a rhythmic cycle sixteen *mātrā*-s (H. 'durational limit' [the basic durational unit of a *tāl*]) in length. However, a specified number were taught in *tāl*-s other than *tīn-tāl* (e.g. *rūpak, jhap-tāl, ek-tāl*, etc.). The examinations were conducted by a team consisting of one faculty member from the department and a faculty member from another university. The examinations consisted of a public performance lasting at least one hour, an oral examination during which the external examiner asked questions regarding the cumulative material taught up to that time, and three written examinations covering the material taught in the non-performance section of the syllabus.

The idea for the topic of the present study was a result of my training in India; however, in outlining it, I felt that certain aspects of my approach needed clarification and reinforcement. I was fortunate to undergo an intense training period with *Paṇḍit* Ravi Shankar during May and June of 1977, in Santa Monica, California, during which we concentrated on refining my own *sitār* technique and also discussed certain aspects of my thesis. The most important event of this training session was my initiation as his disciple. The initiation ceremony symbolizes the binding for life of the *śiṣya* to the *guru*. The ceremony takes its name from the most important part of the affair—*gaṇḍā bandhan* (H. 'thread tying')—in which the *guru* and *śiṣya* tie red sacred threads around each other's right wrist, after which the *śiṣya* makes a small offering to the *guru* and touches his forehead to each of the *guru*-'s feet. This action is an expression of humility and submission to the *guru*-'s omniscience, and is re-enacted (slightly modified in that the *śiṣya* touches the *guru*-'s feet with his hands and then his own heart and forehead) at every meeting and taking leave of the *guru* (Shankar 1968: 185). The teaching sessions with Ravi Shankar were very productive, and many of the music examples to be presented in this study will be drawn from those lessons.

1.3 Previous Studies

Although there is a voluminous amount of literature available on Indian music, very little of it deals with instrumental music. There are no studies of instrumental music that have taken the approach utilized herein, that is, the analysis of music through the techniques employed in producing it. The literature on *sitār* written in Indian languages is primarily of a practical nature, intended for use in conservatory style training in music schools. These books (e.g. Vandyopadhaya's *Sitār Mārg* , Khan's *Sitār Darpaṇ*, Sharma's *Sitār Mālikā*, etc.) are useful as references for historical background and, to a limited extent, musical examples; but, the approach is purely prescriptive, and no semblance or intention of analysis is to be found. There are no analytical studies of instrumental music as performed on the *sitār* in Western languages. There are a few introductory manuals on *sitār* technique, the most notable being the one included in Ravi Shankar's autobiography, *My Music, My Life*.

One may ask why Indian musicians and musicologists have neglected to develop an analytical approach to music structure. Part of the answer is that music theorists and musicologists in India have persistently avoided to examine the contemporary music of their own times in its own right. Instead, they usually summarized the concepts embodied in previous literature, and then proceeded to mold the existent music practices into these concepts, instead of molding the concepts to contemporary music. As a result, one finds an abundance of literature dealing with concepts, but no analyses of actual examples of music. On the other hand, musicians talk a lot about music (after all, it is an oral tradition), but rarely write anything about it, and never attempt to transcribe a performance for the purpose of analysis (to my knowledge). The reason is that the music tradition is one of improvisation and retains its vitality by means of the transient, ephemeral nature of the music that comprises it. Musicians recognize that modern technology is already wreaking havoc with the accepted ways of maintaining their traditions, and are reluctant to contribute to the damage by creating volumes of descriptively notated performances of music which could be memorized and performed by students in general. One can readily imagine how such practices on a large scale would adversely affect a tradition based on improvisation (even though it is a highly structured improvisation). For my own part, I offer my apologies to those practitioners who may consider this study to be exactly what Indian music does not need. In my defense, I offer my belief that all artists strive to be creative, and their creativity is based on a firm grounding of understanding. I feel that the present study makes a positive contribution to that understanding.

1.4. Translation, Transliteration, and Glossing of Foreign Words

Translations of Hindī (including Arabic-Persian derivations) and Sanskrit words are given in instances where a translation helps clarify the usage of the word. The translations are mine, made with the assistance of Dr. Rama Nath Sharma. All words are transliterated as they appear in *Devanāgarī* script. (see Appendix A).

Foreign words are pluralized according to English usage, but with a hyphen inserted to isolate the original word.

The glossary includes foreign words that recur throughout the study. Some words occurring only once, or recurring in close, proximity, are included at the discretion of the writer.

Notes to Chapter I

1. It should be noted that the complete *rāg prastār* is also effectuated in the *ālāp*, the non-metered solo section played at the beginning of a performance. However, in this study, only forms set to *tāl* will be examined.

2. Prior to the contemporary format (c. 1940) in which a *vilambit gat* and a *drut gat* in the same *rāg* are played in succession, musicians specialized in one or the other of the *gat* types. It was the practice then to conclude a performance of either with *jhālā*. With the joining of the two *gat* forms, *jhālā* has become restricted to the *drut* gat.

3. Indian musicians are fond of distinguishing between classical and light-classical music. The essential difference is that in light-classical music, the integrity of the *rāg* is allowed to be broken, whereas in classical music it is strictly upheld. In addition, certain *rāg*-s and *tāl*-s have come to be considered as particularly appropriate for light-classical music.

CHAPTER II

THE *SITĀR*: ORIGIN, CONSTRUCTION, AND REPERTORY

The *sitār* is the most popular stringed instrument in India today. However, its popularity is rather recent when viewed in historical perspective. The first references in literature to the *sitār* were made in the early eighteenth century. Some scholars have tried to prove that the history of the *sitār* extends as far back as the thirteenth century. The evidence they offer to substantiate this is inconclusive, though, and the early history of the *sitār* remains speculative and incomplete.

2.1 Theories of Origin

The various opinions about the *sitār*'s origin may be considered in two broad categories: (1) those which maintain that the *sitār* is indigenous to the Indian subcontinent; and (2) those which consider the *sitār*, or its prototype, to have been borrowed from West Asia.

2.1.1 *Indigenous prototype*

A traditional story, especially favored by Muslim musicians, credits Amir Khusrau with the invention of the *sitār*. Khusrau's life is surrounded with legend, and it is difficult to separate the facts from fiction. He is remembered primarily as a poet in the court of the Delhi sultan 'Ala-ud-din Khilji (1296-1315), and there is some evidence that he introduced the *ghazal* and *kavvālī* vocal genres to North Indian music. However, there is no empirical evidence that he invented the *sitār*, nor is there any evidence that he modified a pre-existing instrument and named it *sitār*. Many musicians refuse to give up their belief in this myth, and it appears that the legend will persist.[1]

It is generally accepted that the instruments in existence before the tenth century A.D. known as *viṇā*-s were comprised of harps, short-necked lutes, and stick zithers. According to Marcel-Dubois, the long-necked lute appears for the first time in a tenth-century sculpture at *Paṭṭadakal* in South India (1941: 89). This is of interest, because if the long-necked lute were to have arrived from West Asia, it would be expected that it would have appeared first in Northwest India and then later diffused to the southern portion of the peninsula. It is known that there were sea routes connecting ancient India with the cultures of Rome, Greece and Constantinople; however, according to Basham, India wanted little other than gold in return for the goods it shipped to these areas (1954:229), so it is improbable that the long-necked lute arrived in India by sea. The lute depicted at *Paṭṭadakal* may have been some sort of hybrid of the early stick zither and short-neck lute. Of course, we can not entirely discount the possibility that these early Indian long-necked lutes were modeled upon an importation from West Asia that managed to penetrate into the subcontinent without leaving a record of itself in the plastic arts or written literature.

The first depiction of stick zithers with gourd resonators is seen in a seventh-century work known as "Descent of the Ganges" or "Arjuna's Penance" located at *Mahābālipuram* in *Tamil Nādu*. The stick zithers depicted in this bas-relief are held diagonally across the chest, with the gourd above the left shoulder. The lute depicted at *Paṭṭadakal* is held similarly; and, except that the standing posture has now changed to a sitting one, the North Indian *bīn* and *sitār* are held likewise. These instruments also employ gourds as resonating chambers.

A fretted *vīṇā* is first seen in a tenth-century sculpture at *Ābāner* in the *Harsat Mātā Mandir*. The instrument is a stick zither with notably raised frets, much like those of the modern *bīn*, and may be considered the forerunner of the *kinnarī vīṇā* described by Śāraṅgadeva (Misra 1973: 8, plate 19).

Misra contends that the *sitār* is a descendant of the *vīṇā*-s prevalent in India during the twelfth century. He cites the raised frets, broad bridge and presence of drone wires as purely Indian innovations. In addition, he states that the *sitār* was previously known as *tritantrī vīṇā* or *jantra*. He maintains that the *tritantrī vīṇā*, described by Śāraṅgadeva as a fretless instrument, acquired frets at a later date and was known as the *jantra*. He supports this contention by citing a passage found in the fifteenth-century treatise *Kalānidhi*, Kallinātha's commentary on the *Saṅgīta Ratnākara*, in which the *tritantrī vīṇā* is said to be known as *jantra* by the populace (Sastri 1951:248). The following description of the *jantra* is found in the *'Ain-i-akbarī* of Abul Fazl-i-'allami (c. 1598):

> The *Yantra* is formed of a hollow neck of wood a yard in length, at each end of which are attached the halves of two gourds. Above the neck are sixteen frets over which are strung five steel wires fastened securely at both ends. The low and high notes and their variations are produced by the disposition of the frets.
>
> (Fazl:268)

From this description, the *jantra* appears to have been a stick zither with movable frets. As such, it can at most be considered as some type of intermediary between the medieval *bīn* and the modern *sitār*. Barring some other evidence describing the *jantra* in more detail, Misra's hypothesis must remain inconclusive.

According to Roach, the *sitār* is first mentioned by name in a court document of Farouk Shah (c. 1719 A.D.) describing the musical activity in the Delhi court of Muhammad Shah Rangila. The *sitār* is described as having either six or seven strings (1971:16).

A more recent reference to the *sitār* occurs in the *Saṅgīta Sāra*, a treatise compiled by the Maharaja Savai Pratapsinha Deo of Jaipur around the end of the eighteenth century. Here, a passage describes an instrument termed *nibaddh tānpūrā*, but commonly known as *sitār*, as having a cut gourd attached to one end of a wooden neck with frets tied to the neck in the places of the *svara*-s (H. 'tone'). This instrument had four, five or six strings (1910: Vadhyādhyāya, p. 6-7).

According to the opinion that the *sitār* evolved from indigenous prototypes, the family tree depicted in Figure 1 may be constructed. In this scheme, the *sitār* is derived through a hybridization of an unfretted long-necked lute with a fretted stick zither having gourd resonators. The evidence available in the visual arts indicates that unfretted long-necked lutes were fairly popular in India as early as the tenth century. By the end of the sixteenth century, the *tānpūrā* was fully developed in its modern form. Many depictions of the *tānpūrā* are found in the miniature paintings of the Moghul period (see, e.g., Khandolavala 1960:49, plate E). The structural similarities of the modern *tānpūrā* and *sitār* suggests that these two instruments share a related history.

2.1.2 *West Asian prototype*

Sachs, Solis, Roach and other Western scholars have written that the Indian *sitār* is an evolved form of one or another of the many long-necked lutes of West Asia. For example, Sachs states:

> Broad-necked lutes are a distinct and exclusively Indian variety of the Southwest Asiatic tanbur-sitar family. With the tanbur, they share the small and pear-shaped body covered by a perforated wooden soundboard, the long straight neck with a flat, fretted fingerboard, the wire strings and the mixed frontal and lateral position of the button head pegs. Contrary to the tanpur, they have a disproportionately wide neck and shiftable wire frets which, before each piece, are placed in the position necessary to produce the tonality required.
>
> (1940:231)

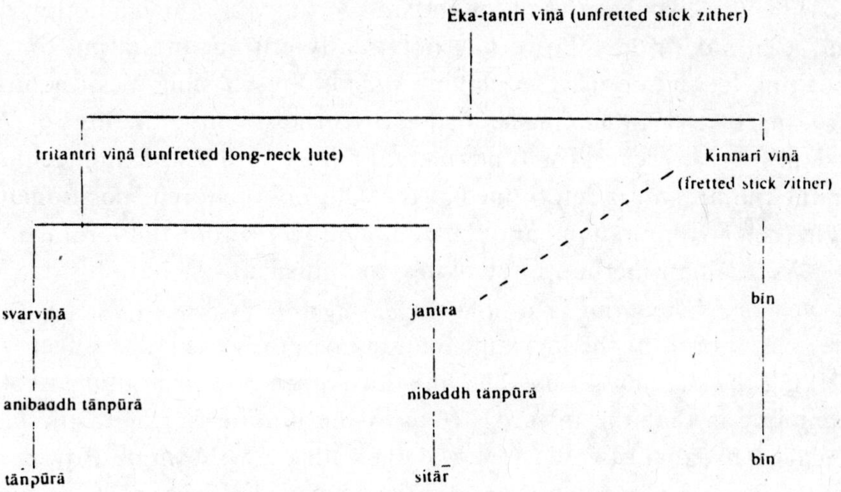

Figure 1: Evolution of the *Sitār* from Indigenous Prototypes

Solis, in support of the view that the *sitār* had its origin on West Asian soil, implies that the *sitār* evolved from the *tanbur* of Afghanistan (1970:59). Slobin states that the earliest attested date for the existence of the Afghani *tanbur* is 1821 A.D. (1976:56-57). He also relates that Afghani instrument makers tend to copy the North Indian *sitār* in making *tanbur*-s (1976:239). Such statements detract from the argument that the *sitār* is a derivative of the Afghani *tanbur*.

Powers has recently outlined a plausible account of the development of the Indian *sitār* and *Tañjorī vīṇā* in which both these instruments are regarded as conflations of some West Asian long-necked lute and the South Asian stick zither (*bīn*).

> The sitār and the south Indian *vīṇā*, in detail, both seem to be mixtures of the south Asian stick zither and the western Asian long-necked lute, but in opposite ways. To the arrangement of strings, the name, the tuning and the plucking technique of the medieval *vīṇā*, only a wooden lute bowl, replacing one gourd, has been added to make the south Indian *vīṇā*. The *sitār*, conversely, has the nucleus of strings and tuning, the arrangement of strings, the name and the basic plucking technique of a western Asian long-necked lute, perhaps a collateral ancestor of the Persian *setār* and a cousin of the plectrum instruments *rabāb* and its descendant *sarod*. Yet the *sitār* has several essential features of the stick zither *bīn*: high frets, side strings for drone and a gourd bowl instead of a wooden bowl.
>
> (1980: v.9, p.130)

To these *bīn*-like features of the Indian *sitār* may be added a hollow neck and a broad bridge. Powers is not totally correct in stating that the plucking technique used in playing *sitār* is West Asian. Yes, the in-out stroking of the index finger is similar to the stroking method of West Asian lutes; however, the fundamental nature of the stroking technique on the Indian *sitār* is determined by the "thumb-anchored" position of the right (i.e., stroking) hand and the unified movement of all four fingers. In the West Asian method of stroking, the musician anchors his hand by placing his thumb, ring and little fingers against his ring or index finger the soundboard of the instrument and moves only the index finger when striking the playing string. The only difference in *sitār* and *bīn* stroking technique is that the inward stroke of the middle finger on the *bīn* is replaced by an outward stroke of the index on the *sitār*. Powers has commented in more detail on stroking techniques in another pertinent passage:

> It seems most likely, however, that the sitar was in fact originally a three-string import that was gradually modified in the direction of the *bīn*. One strong argument against its having originated from some variety of *vīṇā* is that the sitar has the main playing string (*bāj*) at the bottom of the fingerboard, farthest from the player, whereas the *vīṇā* pattern has always had the main playing string (the *nayaki* on the Hindustani *bīn*) at the top of the fingerboard nearest the player. The sitar is plucked with the forefinger only, moving in and out, while identical plucking patterns on the *bīn* are made by the two first fingers in alternation plucking only inwards; in both cases patterns of *dā* and *rā* are the basic alternations making up the formulae, although they are applied differently. The sitar movements suggest those of a plectrum, like that of the *rabāb*, transferred to a finger; the *bīn* movements are *sui generis*.
>
> (1980 : v. 9, p. 129-30)

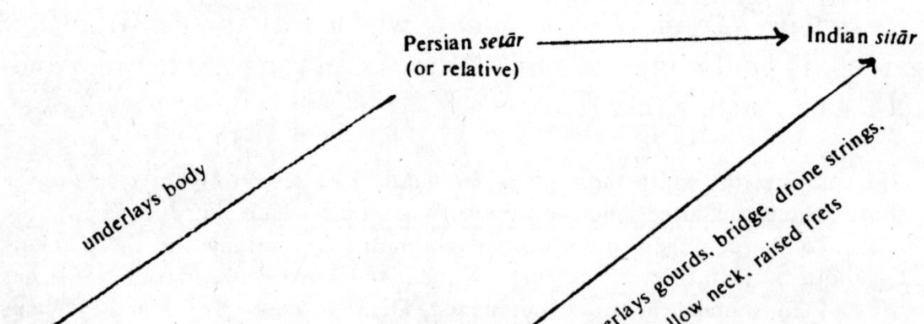

Figure 2: Hybridization Processes Leading To Fretted Long-necked Lutes in India

As we shall see in the next chapter, *sitār* stroking techniques have been derived from both the *bīn* and the *rabāb*. The hybridizations described above are summarized in Figure 2.

Regardless of how it arrived, the *sitār* was definitely present in the musical scene of North India in the eighteenth century and evidently existed in several variants dependent upon its shape, number of strings, and number of frets. Tagore, writing in the middle of the nineteenth century, states that most *sitārs* were made with five strings; however, some in West India had three strings and others had up to seven, depending on the addition of the *pārśva tantrī* (i.e. drone, or *cikārī,* wires). Tagore also mentions a variant known as *kachuā* (H. 'tortoise') *sitār*.[2] In this instrument, the gourd is cut horizontally, forming a shallower bowl with a round face (1879:3). This form of the *sitār* disappeared from popular practice c. 1950 (Misra 1973:59). The addition of the *taraf* wires appears to have occurred after Tagore's writing. Day states that: "Sitars, called Taraffedar, with sympathetic strings underneath those played upon, are sometimes found" (1891:18). He gives the following tunings for three-, four-, five-, six-, and seven-stringed *sitār*-s (Day's order is reversed to conform to the ordering employed in this study.).

number of strings	*tuning* (from instrument's left to right)
3	f c G
4	f c G c^1
5	f c G c^1 c^2
6	f c c G c^1 c^2
7	f c c G g c^1 c^2

Since c. 1940, the seven playing wires have been tuned by most *sitār*-ists as: f c G C g c^1 c^2. It should be noted that these are relative pitch values and are subject to fluctuation.

2.2 Structural Form of the *Sitār*

As shown in the preceding section, the *sitār* has existed in various shapes and sizes in the past. Also, different numbers of frets and strings were in simultaneous use. Although this situation still persists, the *sitār* used for concert performance has become fairly standardized. An artist may customize his *sitār* to some extent to suit his particular style of playing, or adjust the timbre to his taste, but these are usually minor adjustments such as changing the curvature of the bridge.

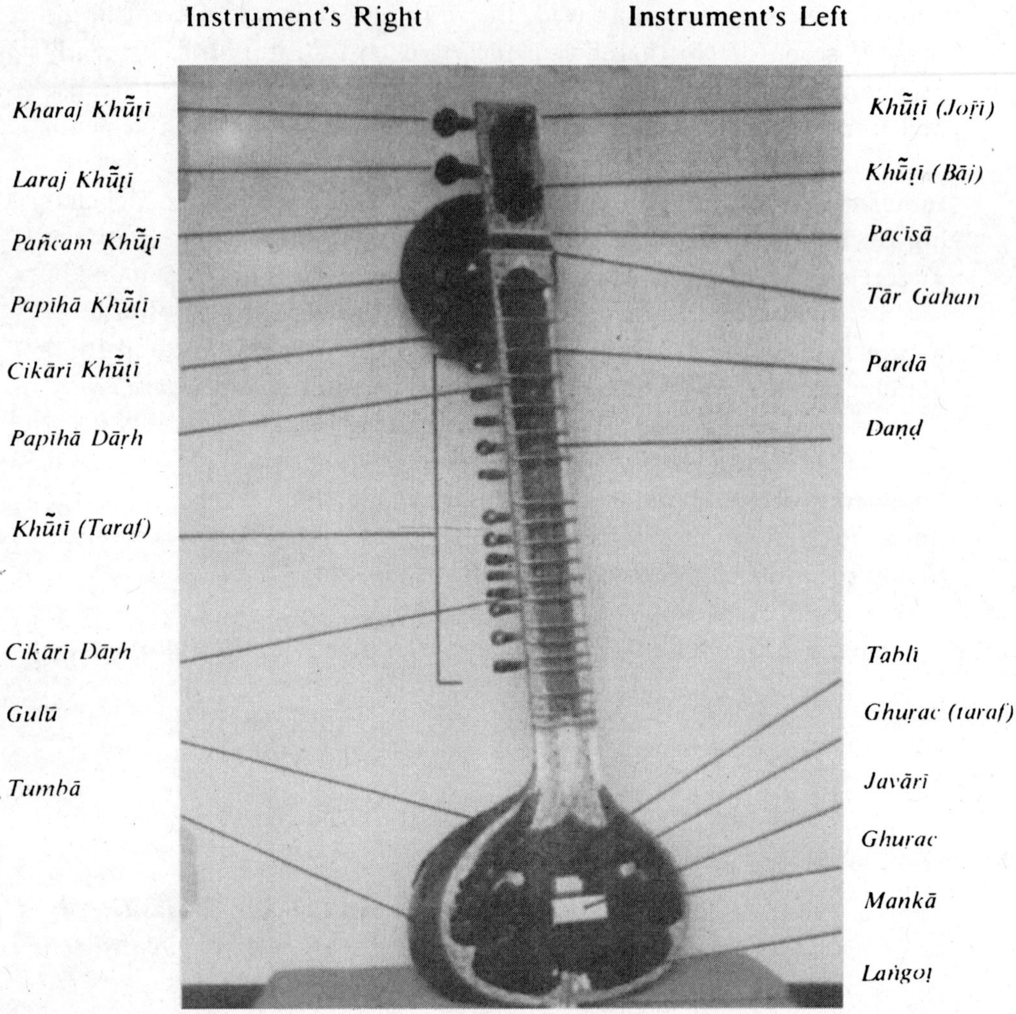

Figure 3: The Cal Ṭhāṭ Tarafdar Sitār (Ventral View)

What may be considered as the standard *sitār* of professional-level performances is depicted in Figure 3. This instrument is specifically termed *cal ṭhāṭ tarafdār sitār* because it incorporates a set of sympathetically resonating wires [*taraf*] under the frets, and because the frets need to be repositioned for certain scale types [*ṭhāṭ*]. Details of the construction and functional use of each of its parts follows. In the descriptions, the directions of the instrument are given according to the player's viewpoint. Thus, the right side of the instrument appears to the left side of the illustration (Figure 3).

(a) *Daṇḍ*: This is the neck of the instrument. It is usually made of *tun* wood (mahogany), but Burmese teak is considered superior because it is stronger. Its length is c. 34″. It is constructed of two separate pieces. The dorsal part, curved and hollowed out, is c. 1.25″ deep. The flat ventral part is c. .5″ deep and is glued on to the hollowed out portion, thus forming a hollow tube with a flate side. The ventral portion is slightly carved out to form a trough which houses the *taraf* wires. The neck is c. 3.5″ wide. The *daṇḍ* is attached to the body of the instrument by means of a dovetail joint. This joint must be precisely made in order to insure that the *daṇḍ* lies in the plane of the face (i.e., ventral side) of the instrument. The joint is made semi-permanent by using wheat paste as an adhesive, reinforced by screws driven from the inside of the instrument.

(b) *tablī*, *gulū* and *tumbā*: These three parts form the main resonating chamber of the instrument. The *gulū* and *tumbā* form the rounded bowl, the *tablī* forms the face. The *gulū* is made of *tun* wood; the *tumbā* is gourd. The main structural function of the *gulū* is to provide a strong base through which the *daṇḍ* may be indirectly joined to the gourd resonator.

The *tablī* is the sound-board. At the widest point, it is normally c. 14″. The *tablī* covers the cavity formed by the dovetailed portion of the *daṇḍ*, the *gulū*, and the *tumbā*. It is slightly convex in shape in order to make it more resilient, and to increase the force of the tension of the wires against the bridge. The *tablī* must be thin enough to provide adequate resonance, but thick enough to withstand the pressure of the strings transmitted through the bridge.

(c) *khū̃ṭī*: A standard *sitār* will have twenty wooden tuning pegs (*khū̃ṭī*) fashioned from *śiśam* wood (Indian rosewood). Four of these pegs are for the main playing wires, three for the *cikārī* (drone wires), and thirteen smaller pegs for the *taraf* wires. Two of the large pegs are inserted from the ventral side, near the end of the neck. The remaining five large pegs and thirteen smaller ones are inserted laterally along the right side of the instrument. Each peg has a small hole drilled through it through which the corresponding wire is looped and secured.

(d) *laṅgoṭ*: The *laṅgoṭ* is a triangular piece of deer horn affixed to the bottom of the *tumbā*, flush with the *tablī*. Its function is to provide an anchor to which all of the playing wires are attached.

(e) *tār gahan, pacīsā*, and *dāṛh*: These three parts function to keep the wires in alignment with their respective positions on the bridge. They are all made from camel bone. The *pacīsā* is located c. 7.5″ from the end of the *daṇḍ*. It is c. .75″ high, and measures the width of the neck. It has five holes in it through which the four main wires and one *cikārī* are guided to their respective *khū̃ṭī*. The *tār gahan* has the same shape and dimensions as the *pacīsā*. It is located c. .75″ from the *pacīsā*, towards the bridge. The *tār gahan* is notched to seat the same five wires that proceed through the *pacīsā*. The lower position of the holes in the *pacīsā* insure that the wires fit securely into the slots of the *tār gahan*.

The *dāṛh* are two small posts made of horn that are inserted ventrally into the *daṇḍ* on the instrument's right side. These posts support the *cikārī* wires and guide them to their respective *khū̃ṭī*. One *dāṛh*, supporting the c^1 wire, is located in between the fourth and fifth *pardā*-s (frets); the other, supporting the c^2 wire, is located behind the thirteenth *pardā*.

(f) *pardā*: The *pardā*-s (frets) of the *sitār* are made from a thick brass (sometimes bronze) wire, c. .13″ in diameter. They are tied to the daṇḍ by silk or nylon string and are movable, thus allowing for perfect tuning. The best string for tying the frets is a silk fishing line manufactured in Āssām known as *muṅg*.

Sitār-s have been classified into two types according to the fret settings. The most popular is the *cal ṭhāṭ* (movable-fret setting) *sitār*. Until the turn of the century, *sitār*-s of the *cal ṭhāṭ* type had either sixteen or seventeen frets. If named according to the note produced on the *bāj tār* (main playing wire), and equating *madhya* (H. 'middle') *śaḍja* (tonic pitch) to c, they would have the following arrangement:

1	2	3	4	5	6	7	8	9	10	11	12	13	14	15	16	(17)
$f^{\#}$	g	a^{b}	a	b	c^1	d^1	e^1	f^1	$f^{\#1}$	g^1	a^1	b^1	c^2	d^2	e^2	(f^2)

A more recent arrangement of the *cal ṭhāṭ* type has twenty frets.

1	2	3	4	5	6	7	8	9	10	11	12	13	14	15	16	17	18	19	20
$f^{\#}$	g	a^{b}	a	b^{b}	b	c^1	d^1	e^{b1}	e^1	f^1	$f^{\#1}$	g^1	a^1	b^{b1}	b^1	c^2	d^2	e^2	f^2

A less popular fret arrangement on the *sitār* is known as *acal ṭhāṭ* (stationary fret setting). There are twenty-four frets in this less common arrangement. They are tuned in half-steps from f# to f^2.

(g) *ghuṛac* and *javārī*: The *ghuṛac* is the bridge of the *sitār*. The top part is fashioned from deer horn, the bottom from *tun* wood. It is c. 3″ x 1″ x 1″ in dimension. The top part of the bridge is known as the *javārī*. The *javārī* has a crucial role in maintaining a pleasant sound. Because of the large width of the bridge, the strings do not have a fixed point of contact. This enables their vibration to spread out over a portion of the width of the bridge. In order to produce an even, rich sound, the *javārī* must be filed to a precise curvature. The filing technique is a highly specialized craft, and there are only a few *sitār* makers in India who can produce a good *javārī*. It is not uncommon for a *sitār*-ist to travel great distances to have his *sitār*-'s *javārī* refiled.

(h) *tār*: The modern *sitār* has seven main wires (*tār*) and thirteen sympathetic wires (*taraf*). The following terminology and tuning (given from left to right) are fairly standardized for the seven main wires.

Wire	*Material*	*Gauge* (mm)	*Name*	*Tuning*	*Range*
1st	steel	.300	*bāj*	f	f - $f\#^2$ (-c^3)
2nd	brass or copper	.400	*joṛī*	c	c - g
3rd	brass	.550	*kharaj*	E F F # G A^b A	G - e (in standard tuning)
4th	brass	.700	*laraj*	C	C - c
5th	steel	.250	*pañcam*	e♭ e f g a^b	collectively known as *cikārī*
6th	steel	.230	*papīhā*	c^1	
7th	steel	.200	*cikārī*	c^2	

The tuning of both the main and *taraf* wires varies according to the *rāg*, but a standard *śuddh svar* (H. 'pure tones', i.e. unaltered) setting would be as follows for the *taraf* wires:

1	2	3	4	5	6	7	8	9	10	11	12	13
c^1	a	b	c^1	d^1	e^1	f^1	g^1	a^1	b^1	c^2	d^2	e^2

(i) *mankā*: Oval-and swan-shaped pieces of camel bone are used for fine tuning. The *mankā*-s on the *bāj* and *joṛī* wires are located between the *ghuṛac* and *laṅgoṭ*. Sometimes *mankā*-s are applied to the *kharaj* and *laraj* wires between the *pacīsā* and *khū̃ṭī*.

(j) *mizrāb*: The *mizrāb* (H. [from Persian] 'to beat') is a triangular-shaped wire plectrum that is fitted to the right index finger. It is also known as *nakā* ('nail') and *trikona* (Sk. 'three-cornered').

(k) *decoration*: The *sitār* is highly ornamented with inlay and wood carving. All of the joints of construction are covered with inlay engraved with various motifs. The *gulū* is sometimes plain, but on more expensive models it is decorated with carvings of grape vines. This decoration extends down to six triangular leaves that are shaped to the *tumbā* and applied flush with the joint of the *gulū* and *tumbā*. The *tablī* is decorated with carvings of flowers, vines, and leaves along with inlays of doves, one on either side of the ghuṛac. A large piece of bone or white plastic inlay covers the joint of the *daṇḍ* and *tablī*. This is both decorative and functional in that it protects the wood of the *tablī* from getting marred by the *mizrāb*.

2.3 *Sitār* Repertory

The historical development of the repertory of the *sitār* can be viewed in three phases: (1) pre-*gat* period (c. 1500-1750), (2) *gat śailī* (H. 'style') period (c. 1750-1900), (3) *svatantra* (H. 'free form') period (c. 1900-1986).

2.3.1 *Pre-gat period (c. 1500-1750)*

If one accepts the *jantra*, mentioned in the *Āīn-i-Akbarī*, to be an earlier form of the *sitār*, then it can be surmised that the instrument was used in an instrumental ensemble complementing the *bīn* and *rabāb* (a short-necked lute prevalent in India during the Moghul rule) that accompanied female singers in the royal courts of the late sixteenth and early seventeenth centuries (Fazl:273). Thus, the musical repertories for the *sitār* were based on vocal music. Solis states that prior to its incorporation by members of the *Senī gharānā*, *sitār*-s were used to accompany *kavvālī* and *ghazal* songs (1970: 59). Day states that small *sitār*-s (incorporating a coconut shell resonator) produce a "tone singularly sweet and plaintive" and are generally played by women (1891: 116). It is probable that simple songs of a lighter nature rather than the *gat śailī* of the classical *rāg* system were played on these instruments.

During the seventeenth century, the *sitār* achieved a higher status in that it was adapted as a solo instrument for playing in the *dhrupad* style. The pre-composed music in this style was based on *dhrupad* vocal compositions, while improvisations were based on the rhythmical accompaniment of the *pakhāvaj*, a barrel-shaped drum that accompanies *dhrupad*. These improvisations were known as *tār paran* (see 3.2).

2.3.2 ***Gat śailī period (c. 1750-1900)***

Instrumental compositions in North Indian music are referred to as *gat*-s (from Sanskrit *gati* 'movement'). The *gat śailī* is said to have had its beginnings in the second half of the eighteenth century. The creation of the *gat śailī* is credited to members of the *Senī gharānā* (H. 'house'), the musical dynasty that extends back to, and takes its name from, Tansen, the master musician of Emperor Akbar's court in Delhi (c. 1555-1606). The *Senī gharānā* consisted of two schools: (1) descendants of Tansen's son, Bilas Khan, who were known as *rabābiyās* (*rabāb* players), and (2) descendants of Tansen's son-in-law, Misri Singh, who were known as *binkār*-s (*bīn* players). The *rabābiyā* branch gradually lost favor because of limitations inherent in the instrument. The *binkār gharānā*, however, incorporated many of the techniques of the *rabābiyā*-s and flourished. The *binkār*-s, a tightly knit family taking pride in their ancestry, were very reluctant to pass the technique of their instrument on to anyone other than blood relatives. According to most Indian scholars, the *binkār*-s began to use the *sitār* and *surbahār* (an instrument similar to *kachuā sitār* in shape, but much larger) to teach music to students not belonging to their family. On *surbahār*, they taught *anibaddh saṅgīt* (music not bound to *tāl*) such as *ālāp* and *joṛ-ālāp*. On *sitār*, they taught compositions that were based on popular vocal genres of the time. These compositions were called *gat*-s (Misra 1973:57)

During the first half of the eighteenth century, Nyamat Khan (Sadaranga) began to popularize the *vilambit khyāl* style of vocal music. Shortly thereafter, Masit Khan, a *binkār* residing in Delhi, created compositions to be played on *sitār*. Misra contends that Masit Khan was inspired by the *khyāl* style of singing to compose these compositions (1973:57). They were to be played in a *vilambit lay* (slow tempo), and used a predominance of *mīṇḍ* (portamento) and *gamak* (H. 'shake'). They were said to be very pleasing to the ear, and the *gat* clearly manifested the *rāg* in which it was composed (Vandyopadhyaya 1957:94). The compositions were based on a fixed *mizrāb* pattern that has survived until today (see 5.1.1) and were known as *Masītkhānī gat*-s (H. '*gat*-s of Masit Khan'). This style of composition was also known as the *pacchvā* (H. 'western'), or Delhi, *bāj* (H. 'instrumental style'). Masit Khan's son, Rahim Sen, was also a famous *sitār*-ist of his time (c. 1825) who added profusely to the repertory of compositions in the *Masītkhānī bāj* (Vandyopadhyaya 1957:94).

Some authors relate that sometime in the past there was a type of composition known as the *Amirkhānī gat*; however, according to Nigam, this was identical to the *Masītkānī gat*, excepting that it was played in a faster tempo (1964:25-26). Misra states that the *Amirkhānī bāj* is no longer extant (1973:57).

The other major *bāj* popular among *sitār*-ists of the nineteenth century was the *Razākhānī bāj*, created by Gulam Raza Khan.[3] This style is believed to have been modeled on the *ṭhumrī* and *tarānā* styles of vocal music. These styles were very popular in the royal courts of Lucknow during the nineteenth century (Shankar, personal communication: June 6, 1977).

Misra, quoting from *Kanun -e- Sitār* (written in 1870 by Saiyad Safdar Husen Khan), gives the following information about the *Masītkhānī* and *Razākhānī bāj*-s as they existed in the nineteenth century:

> "The gats of the *Razākhānī bāj* are very difficult because they use *āṛī mizrāb bol*-s [a stroking pattern syncopated with hemiola] and are played in a fast tempo. Because of this, they are played in *addhe tāl*.[4] The development of these gats is also difficult. In *Masītkhānī*, every type of style can be played and its capacity for development is so broad that one can continue to play as long as he wishes. It was *Miya Bahadur* Khan, the son of Masit Khan, who began playing the *toḍā*-s of the *bīn* on *sitār*. In Masītkhāni, toḍā ḍhāh, dun, jhāṛ, and *kivāṛ*,[5] *gamak*, *sūt*, *tān*, and *mizrāb*[6] are played."
>
> (Misra 1973:58)

One other type of *gat*, known as the *Sitārkhānī gat*, was developed by *sitār*-ists of the *Razākhānī bāj*. Misra states that these *gat*-s were performed after the *Razākhānī gat* as a medium for expressing more colorful and romantic themes. They were usually set to *addhā tāl* and began from the seventh *mātrā* (beat). The development of these *gat*-s consisted of *ṭhumrī* style techniques, including *bol-banāv* (H. 'to make [on] words') and short *tān*-s (fast passages) (1973:60).

2.3.3 *Svatantra period (c. 1900-1986)*

The styles of music played on the *sitār* today are derived from the following sources: (1) the *ālāp—joṛ ālāp dhrupad aṅg* (Sk. 'limb') of the *binkār*-s, (2) the *Masītkhānī* and *Razākhānī bāj*-s, (3) the *sitārkhānī gat*, (4) the *khyāl śailī* of vocal music, and (5) the light-classical vocal styles including *ṭhumrī, tappā, ghazal, dādrā, bhajan,* and *lok-gīt*.

2.3.3.1 *ālāp; joṛ ālāp*

Ālāp and *joṛ ālāp* (H. 'join') are both *anibaddh* forms. *Ālāp* is non-metrical while *joṛ ālāp* (usually shortened to '*joṛ*') is structured around rhythmic groupings regulated by a specific rhythmic pulse. Prior to the twentieth century, the *sitār* was not favored for playing *ālāp* and *joṛ* because of its limited range and inferior tonal quality compared to the *bīn* and *surbahār*. During the twentieth century, the *sitār*'s construction was improved to create an extended range and more pleasing timbre (Shankar, personal communication: May 21, 1977). With these developments, artists began to play *ālāp joṛ* on the *sitār*, and the *surbahār*'s popularity declined.

2.3.3.2 *gat styles*

In today's repertory, one still finds that *gat*-s are referred to as being a *Masītkhānī gat* or a *Razākhānī gat*; however, even though the *gat*-s performed today are based on the same principles as those of the last century, factors such as tempo, *tāl*, and *gat vistār* (H. 'to spread out') have changed so much that many prominent musicians prefer to classify *gat*-s according to *lay* (H. 'tempo'), *tāl*, or style of rendition. Thus, one hears of the *vilambit gat* (H. 'slow composition'), *drut gat* (H. 'fast composition'), *madhya lay gat* (H. 'medium-tempo composition'), *khyāl aṅg gat* (H. '*khyāl* style composition'), etc. Lalmani Misra prefers the term "*kūṭ-bāj*" (H. 'integrated', 'complicated') *gat* for *gat*-s that are composed in *tāl*-s other than *tīn-tāl*.

Vilambit gat-s in *tīn-tāl* normally incorporate the *bol* pattern of the earlier *Masītkhānī gat*. However, the modern *vilambit gat* is played at a tempo that is approximately half the speed of an authentic rendition of a *Masītkhānī gat*.[7] *Gat vistār* is also more systematic and intricate in modern playing. Ravi Shankar credits 'Ala-ud-din Khan and Rameshvar Pathak' with the development of today's style of playing the *vilambit gat* (Shankar, personal communication: June 1, 1977). 'Ala-ud-din Khan, the disciple of the famous *bīnkār* of the Rampur court *gharānā*, Wazir Khān, is well known as the father of Ustād Ali Akbar Khan and teacher of Paṇḍit Ravi Shankar. Rameshvar Pathak was an early twentieth-century *sitār*-ist. He received his musical training from his father, Paṇḍit Apuch Pathak, a *sitār*-ist and dhrupad singer. Rameshvar Pathak passed most of his musical life at the Unnav court under the patronage of Maharaja Ray Bahadur Ram Sumaranprasad Agraval (Vandyopadhyaya 1957: 110).

The *drut gat* of today has its origins in the *Razākhānī gat*-s of the nineteenth century. However, these *gat*-s have diversified so much in the recent past that it is illogical to classify them all as belonging to the *Razākhānī bāj*.

Musicians sometimes designate performances of *gat*-s as being in a *dhrupad aṅg, khyāl aṅg* or *ṭhumrī aṅg. Gayakī aṅg* is another term commonly used to indicate a liberal adaptation of vocal idioms to instrumental forms. These terms have yet to receive standardized interpretations, but each does convey certain meanings among knowledgeable musicians. For example, a performance of a *gat* in the *dhrupad aṅg* would certainly be preceded by an *ālāp* and *joṛ*, and would preferably be accompanied by a *pakhāvaj*, rather than a *tablā*. The *gat* would be set to a *tāl* associated with *dhrupad* singing such as *cau-tāl, śūl-tāl* or *tīvrā tāl*, and the musician would be expected to emulate the severe and stately ornamentation of a *dhrupad* singer. Conversely, a *khyāl aṅg* gat played in *vilambit lay* would not be preceded by an extensive *ālāp*. In the manner of a singer performing a *baṛā khyāl*, the instrumentalist would incorporate the *ālāp* within the framework of the *tāl*-bound section of the performance. Most *baṛā khyāl*-s and many *choṭa khyāl*-s are set to the twelve-beat rhythmic cycle, *ek-tāl*, Instrumentalists usually retain the favored *tīn-tāl*, though, when playing a *vilambit gat* in the *khyāl aṅg. Choṭā khyāl aṅg gat*-s are set to *madhya* or *drut lay*-s and usually attempt to reproduce faithfully a particular *khyāl bandiś*, basing right-hand strokes on the syllabic durations of the *khyāl cīz* (text, from H. 'thing') rather than on a stock *mizrāb* pattern.

A controversial term implying some kind of connection to vocal forms is *gayakī aṅg* (h. 'singing style'). The famous *sitār*-ist, Vilayat Khan, uses this term to describe the style of *sitār* playing associated with his family and presumably created by his grandfather, the legendary Imdad Khan. Many instrumentalists object to the monopolization of this term by musicians of the *Imdādkhānī bāj*, though, because, as has already been shown in this study, so much of the general repertory of all *sitār*-ists is so heavily based on vocal forms (and *gayakī* means singing in general) that it is not really accurate for one group of *sitār*-ists to claim that theirs is the only style that can be termed as *gayakī aṅg. Gayakī aṅg* is a useful term to describe the style of the solo repertory of those instruments traditionally regarded as vocal accompanying instruments (such as the *sāraṅgī* and violin) or to refer to those instrumental repertories that are direct reflections of vocal models such as the *ālāp-joṛ-jhālā-dhrupad* format of the *surbahār* and *bīn* or the *bandiś*-derived repertory of the Indian bamboo flute (*bānsurī*).

The term *ṭhumrī aṅg* usually implies a performance in a "semi-classical" style. However, the term has also been liberally used to indicate a performance of any *gat* form, but in a lighter vein.

At this point, a few words are in order on the distinctions between classical, semi-classical and light music. If one imagines a continuum with classical music on one side and light music on the other, the following criteria may be placed at the poles of this dichotomization:

classical	*light*
strict adherence to *rāg*	no intentional adherence to *rāg*
strict adherence to *tāl*	simple metrical rhythms or short interruptable *tāl* cycles
complex developmental techniques	little or no development techniques
music dominates text	text dominates music

For sure, exceptions do exist. Two examples that readily come to mind are the *sargam*, a classical form (not usually performed) that has no developmental techniques associated with it, and many film songs (generally considered as light music) that are set to particular *rāg*-s. On the basis of these criteria, the one overriding factor that distinguishes semi-classical music from light music is the inclusion of some developmental passages in the former. *Gīt, bhajan* and *ghazal* are strophic vocal genres normally accepted as light forms. *Bhajan*-s and *ghazal*-s, though, are sometimes performed in a semi-classical style.

Ṭhumrī, dādrā, kajarī, horī, ṭappa and others are distinct vocal genres usually admitted as falling within the semi-classical category. The identity of many semi-classical vocal genres is heavily dependent upon the thematic content and dialect of the text. Thus, instrumental renditions of these different vocal genres sometimes can not be differentiated on the basis of musical criteria alone.

Musicians trained in a traditional classical system recognize the distinctions in the classical—light continuum and will proceed only so far towards the light side in their musical performances. Classical instrumentalists often close their performances with a semi-classical piece drawn from any of the above mentioned vocal genres or with a *dhun*[8]. The term *dhun* is often used by village people in the context of folk music in the same way that Westerners use the word tune. This may be why *dhun*, in the context of a classical instrumental performance, implies some reliance upon folk melodies for tonal materials. However, the terms *ṭhumrī* and *dhun*, when used instrumentally, are not mutually exclusive. This is because a vocal *ṭhumrī* (or for that matter, a *kajarī, horī* or *bhajan*) may

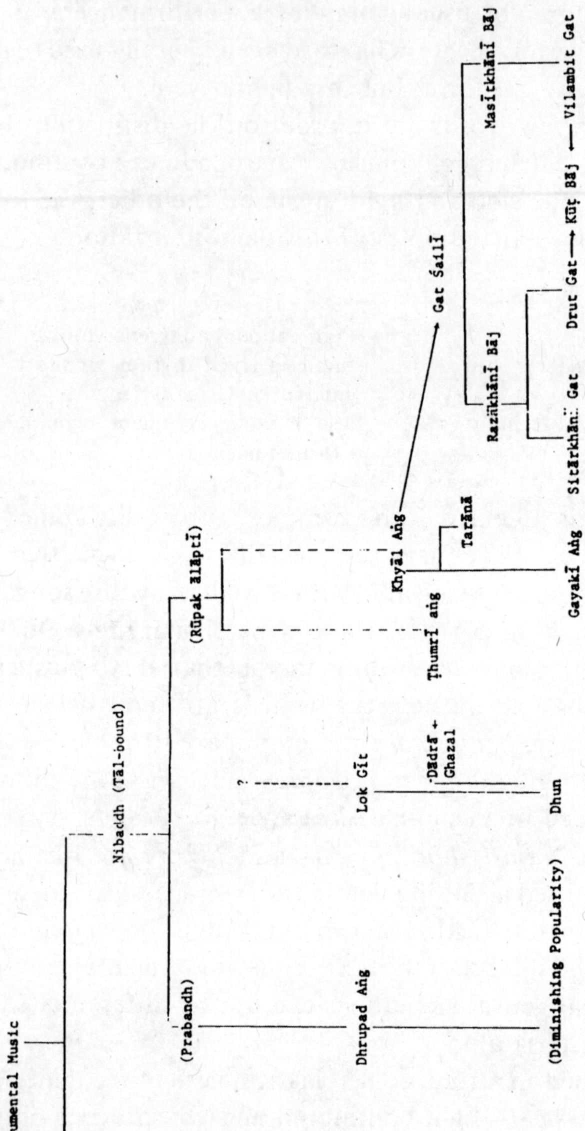

Figure 4: The Thesis Corpus in Historical Perspective and Contemporary Context

use a folk *dhun* as its source of tonal materials. A knowledgeable musician hearing this same *ṭhumrī* played on the sitar would be correct in calling the piece either a *ṭhumrī* or a *dhun*.

The *sitārkhānī gat*, popular among exponents of the *Razākhānī bāj* in the nineteenth century, is often performed today in a semi-classical manner. It is played exclusively in *addhā tāl*. Because of this association, *addhā* is now commonly known as *sitārkhānī tāl*.

The chart in Figure 4 summarizes the historical derivation of the repertory of the sitar as exemplified in present-day practices, and shows the relationship of the thesis corpus, the *vilambit* and *drut gat*-s (see 6.3.), to other genres presently in vogue.

NOTES TO CHAPTER II

1. An alternate theory concerning Amir Khusrau is that the *sitār* was invented by Nyamat Khan's younger brother, named Amir Khusrau Khan, in the early eighteenth century. It is possible that the credit due to Amir Khusrau Khan was mistakenly given to the thirteenth-century poet, Amir Khusrau. (Roach 1971 : 16)
2. The *kachuā* form is still seen on present day *surbahār*-s.
3. Gulam Raza Khan is also referred to as Ali Raza Khan.
4. *Addhe tāl* was probably a variant of *tīn-tāl*, as in *addhā tāl* today.
5. The terms *ḍhāh, dun,* and *kivāṛ* are no longer extant.
6. Here, *mizrāb* refers to the practice of varying the *gat* by changing the stroking patterns (*mizrāb bol*-s) while maintaining a similar melodic line as in the original *gat*.
7. Both Lalmani Misra and Ravi Shankar told me that until 1930, the *vilambit lay* was equivalent to the *madhya lay* of modern times.
8. *Dhun* is a Hindī word having several meanings. Two common meanings are 'impulse,' in the sense of perseverence, and 'tune,' in a general sense. Harold Powers has suggested that the musical term *dhun* is etymologically related to the Sanskrit word for sound, *dhvani* (*dhvani dhvan dhun*).

CHAPTER III

SOURCES OF TECHNIQUE

It was seen in the last chapter that both the *sitār* and its repertory have undergone a long process of development. It is interesting to note, however, that the present-day repertory has resulted from an evolutionary process only since the inception of the *gat śailī* (c. 1750), at the earliest, and at the latest, since the beginning of the twentieth century. The reason is that, except for the *gat* of the *gat śailī*, the techniques, archetypal forms, and stylized formal elements played on the *sitār* until the twentieth century were all borrowed from other instruments. In addition, there was a strong influence exerted by *khyāl aṅg* vocal music which has affected the treatment of ornamental techniques on the *sitār*. The present-day *sitār* technique is considered to be a synthesis of techniques and technical forms derived from the *bīn, rabāb, pakhāvaj* (and *tablā*), and voice (especially *khyāl aṅg* singing).

3.1. Contributions of the *Hastavyāpāra*

It is known that the North Indian *bīn* was a prime source of technique for the *sitār*. Also, the *bīn* has been shown to be related to the *eka-tantrī vīṇā* described in the *Saṅgīta Ratnākara* as an unfretted stick zither with gourd resonators at either end. The *kinnarī vīṇā*, a fretted stick zither with gourd resonators, appears to be the intermediate form linking the *bīn*, or *rūdrā vīṇā*, to the unfretted *eka-tantrī* vīṇā (Misra 1973:64). Śāraṅgadeva has given a detailed description of the techniques employed on the *eka-tantrī vīṇā* (see Appendix B). Some of these techniques resemble certain *sitār* techniques, either in their execution or in their musical product, so it is possible that some of the present day *sitār* techniques have an ancestral heritage extending back to techniques used on the *eka-tantrī vīṇā* seven hundred years ago. Śāraṅgadeva applied the collective term *hastavyāpāra* (Sk. 'hand movements') to the repertory of techniques incorporated on the *eka-tantrī vīṇā*. The *hastavyāpāra* was comprised of two left-hand techniques, nine right-hand techniques, and thirteen combined techniques.

The musical products of the left-hand techniques *sphurita* and *khasīta* of the *hastavyāpāra* appear to have been preserved in most of the melodic instruments of India, even though the manner of production varies according to the requirements of the instrument. *Sphurita* (Sk. 'shaken'), performed by shaking the wooden slide [*kamrikā*] in contact with the wire of the *eka-tantrī vīṇā*, produced a tremolo effect. A similar melodic ornament is produced by the *sitār* technique *kampan* (from Sk. *kampita*, 'oscillated'), performed by shaking the wire across the fret. In *khasīta* (Sk. 'rubbed'), the wire of the *vīṇā* was repeatedly and gently rubbed by the *kamrikā*. On *sitār*, the physical maneuver of rubbing the wire is called *ghasīṭ* (H. 'dragged'); however, the technique, *mīṇd* (Sk. 'rubbed'), on *sitār*, produces a musical realization that is more nearly like that which can be inferred from the description of *khasīta*. *Mīṇḍ* is performed on *sitār* by pulling the wire across the fret. This action produces the same melodic effect as rubbing the wire of a fretless instrument (e.g. *vichitrā vīṇā, gottūvādyam, sāraṅgī*, etc.).

Many of the right-hand techniques of the *hastavyāpāra* resemble *sitār* techniques. *Ghāta* (Sk. 'strike') and *saṅlekha* (Sk. 'write properly') were inward strokes of the index finger, the former technique also adding the support of the middle finger. These correspond to the '*da*' stroke on the *sitār* (see 4.1.1). *Pāta* (Sk. 'beat') was an outward stroke by the index finger. This corresponds to the '*rā*' stroke of the *sitār* techniques (see 4.1.1). Of the remaining six right-hand techniques in the *hastavyāpāra*, their physical production does not exist on the *sitār*; however, two techniques, *bhramara* (Sk. 'wander') and *nakhakartarī* (Sk. 'cutting by nails'), produce four rapid articulations. It can be inferred that this survives in the '*dir dir*' stroke on the *sitār* (see 4.1.1).

Of the combined techniques, *bindu, ardhakartarī*, and *skhalita* are of interest. *Bindu* (Sk. 'drop') was performed by first striking with the right-hand middle finger, and then pressing the wire with the left-hand index finger. This is somewhat akin to the technique known as *sparś* (H. 'touch') on the *sitār* (see 4.1.2.1). *Ardhakartarī* (Sk. 'half of *kartarī*') and *skhalita* (Sk. 'fallen') could be inferred to be a prototype from which *jhālā* evolved (see 5.2.2). All three of these formal techniques produce a repeatedly articulated tone intermittently interrrupted by the tones of a melodic line.

3.2. Contributions of the *Bīn* and *Rabāb*

The Seni *bīnkār* and *rabābiyā* lineages restricted access to the technical secrets of performance on their respective instruments to male family members (*gharānedār*-s). This practice ultimately was responsible for the popularization of instruments such as the *sitār*, *surbahār* and *sarod,* as *gharānedār* musicians taught these instruments to those students who bore no direct family ties to the *gharānā*. In the process, the repertory of these instruments grew more sophisticated as certain playing techniques were transferred to them from the traditional instruments of these *gharānā*-s.

Different sources provide varying accounts as to which techniques come from where.However, from what is known about the acoustical properties of the *bīn* and *rabāb*, and in accordance with what is generally agreed upon by practicing musicians, it is possible to ascertain the origins of some particular playing practices on the *sitār* to a degree of certainty.

It is common knowledge that the *rabāb* was incapable of sustaining a tone for any length of time. The instrument did lend itself to loud, percussive styles of playing, though, and it is generally believed that stroking techniques were well developed and differentiated in the *rabāb* repertory to compensate for the relatively restricted lyrical capabilities of the instrument. The *bīn*, conversely, was and has remained a chamber instrument possessing a soft tone of limited dynamic range but capable of producing the extended *portamenti* and intricately embellished melodic passages associated with vocal styles of Indian music. Both instruments were associated with the vocal dhrupad tradition, but each had some special elements in its repertory that were specific to instrumental music.

The contributions to the repertory of the *sitār* that are generally ascribed to the influence of the *rabāb* and *bīn* are in the nature of both stylized formal elements (i.e., procedural improvisation techniques that may also serve some structural purpose) and specific techniques (i.e., particular finger or hand movements). Of the former, the *ālāp, joṛ* and *jhālā* are known to be direct transfers from the *bīn* repertory, while *tār paran* and *katar jhār*[1] are adaptations from the *rabāb* repertory. Of the latter, the left-hand techniques *mīṇḍ, sparś, krintan* and *gamak* are transfers from the *bīn*, while *ghasīṭ* is the lone transfer from the *rabāb* (see 4.1.2.1 and 4.1.2.2).

All the formal elements and techniques donated by the *bīn* are still in common use today. The *ālāp* is considered to be the supreme test of a musician's creative talents. The predominant technique in *ālāp* is *mīṇḍ* which is performed by pulling the wire across the fret. It may be considered as the most valuable technique acquired by the *sitār* because it makes possible the extended *portamenti* that are the foundation of melodic progression in *Hindustānī* music. *Sparś* and *krintan* (H. 'cut'), two ornamental techniques acquired from the *bīn*, both articulate tones without striking the wire by the plectrum. *Sparś* accomplishes the articulation by driving the wire against the fret with a hammering action of the middle finger, while *krintan* employs a plucking action of the same finger. *Gamak* (H. 'a shake'), a specific type of shaking ornament popular in *dhrupad aṅg* music, is another *bīn* technique that has been transferred to the *sitār*.

In the *bīnkār* format of performance, the *joṛ* would follow the *ālāp*. The *joṛ* incorporates all of the above described ornamental techniques, but is characterized by melodic phrases grouped around a rhythmic pulse. The tempo of the *joṛ* is increased in stages, and then the section is climaxed by a *jhālā*. The performance aspects of *jhālā* will be discussed in Chapter V; however, it should be mentioned here that the practice of striking the *cikārī* wires by the little finger during the *jhālā* is a technique acquired from the *bīn*.

Tār paran (H. 'a paran played on a wire') is a compositional device utilized by instrumentalists to facilitate the spontaneous improvisation of rhythmically complex melodic passages that are exactly fit to the *tāl* cycle. The method behind *tār paran* is to superimpose *mizrāb bol*-s (striking patterns of the plectrum, see 4.2.1) on the rhythmic structure of precomposed *pakhāvaj bol*-s known as *paran*-s (see Ex. 3-4). Thus, a rhythmic pattern is produced that will automatically coincide with the *tāl* cycle.[2] *Tār paran*-s apparently orignated within the *rabābiyā gharānā*. According to Ravi Shankar, *rabāb* players added to the simulation of the *pakhāvaj*-derived *paran*-s by striking the plectrum against the skin-covered sound bowl of the instrument, producing loud, drum-like percussive tones that punctuated the *tār paran*. These same techniques can still be heard played on the modern sarod. *Katar jhār* was a specific variety of *tār paran* based on those *pakhāvaj paran*-s that contained long passages of the *bol* '*kata kata*'. (Shankar, personal communication: June 10, 1984).

Aside from these formal elements, the technique known as *sū̃t* (H. 'scoop up') on the *rabāb* has become the *ghasīṭ* on the *sitār*. *Ghasīṭ* is a fast slide, producing a *glissando* of at least a fourth in range, performed by pressing and sliding the left-hand index or middle finger along the wire.

The technical terms *laṛī*, *laṛ lapeṭ* and *laṛ guthāv* arose as metaphoric descriptions of various types of fast melodic passages played on the *bīn*. Three generalizations may be made about these terms: (1) they all use a predominance of the *bol* 'dir'; (2) although the musical elements represented by these terms may still appear in contemporary performances, the terms themselves are considered archaic and are no longer in common

Figure 5: **The *Bīn* Accompanied by the *Pakhāvaj***

practice; and (3) they are subject to different interpretations by different musicians (as readily admitted by practitioners).[3] Because these techniques appear to be outgrowths of rapid, back and forth stroking patterns, their origin would appear to lie in some aspect of the *rabāb* repertory. The issue, though, is confused. Vandhyopadhyaya (who presumably received his information from Ala-ud-din Khan) waffles to and fro, first stating that *laṛī, guthāv, laṛ guthāv, laṛ lapeṭ* and *katar* were derived from the *rabāb* repertory (1957: 117) and later stating that *laṛi, laṛ guthāv* and *guthāv* arose within the *bīn* repertory while *laṛ lapeṭ* (as well as *tār paran* and *katar*) originated in the *rabāb* repertory (1957: 131). Powers, apparently drawing his information from Vandhyopadhyaya, states:

> The sitar has also taken the centrally important improvisatory techniques of *ālāp* from the *bīn*. Other techniques or procedures it owes to the *rabāb*: the particular way of building *joḍ* around a final tone called *laḍī*, and the permutation technique called *guthāv*.
>
> (1980: v. 9, p. 130)

Ravi Shankar dismisses Vandhyopadhyaya's descriptions of *laṛī, guthāv* and the rest as erroneous misstatements. According to him, *laṛī* and *laṛ guthāv* co-existed in both the *bīn* and *rabāb* repertories, possibly being interpreted differently by the two *gharānā*-s; however, it was the *bīnkār* version of these techniques that survived. According to Shankaṛ, the *laṛī* was further developed and refined by *sarodiyā*-s trained by *bīnkār*-s. *Laṛ guthāv* and *laṛ lapeṭ* were adopted by *surbahāriyā*-s and then transferred to the *sitār*. Furthermore, *guthāv* is nothing more than a reduction of the term *laṛ guthāv* (personal communication: June 12, 1984).

Laṛī (H. 'garland', 'chain') is usually described as a melodic passage consisting of one prominent pitch being continuously articulated with the *bol*, 'dir'. The pattern may be broken (or established) with a single articulation of a different tone (Ex. 3-1). In *laṛ lapeṭ* (from H. *lapeṭnā* 'to wrap'), the original *laṛī* is surrounded with melodic fragments consisting of single or multiple neighboring tones above and below the original pitch level of the *laṛī* (Ex. 3-2). *Laṛ guthāv* (from H. *guthnā* 'to interlock') is formed by joining several *laṛ lapeṭ*-s at different pitch levels (Ex. 3-3) (Misra, personal communication: March 13, 1977).[4] In present-day usage, all of these technical forms are subsumed under the general heading, *toṛā* (H. 'breaks') (see 5.2.2).

3.3 Contributions of percussion instruments

The influence of the *pakhāvaj* has already been referred to in the discussion of *tār paran* (see 3.2). Many musicians also believe that *jhālā*

Ex. 3-1 Laṛī

Ex. 3-2 Laṛ Lapeṭ

Ex. 3-3 Laṛ Guthāv

Ex. 3-4 Tār Param

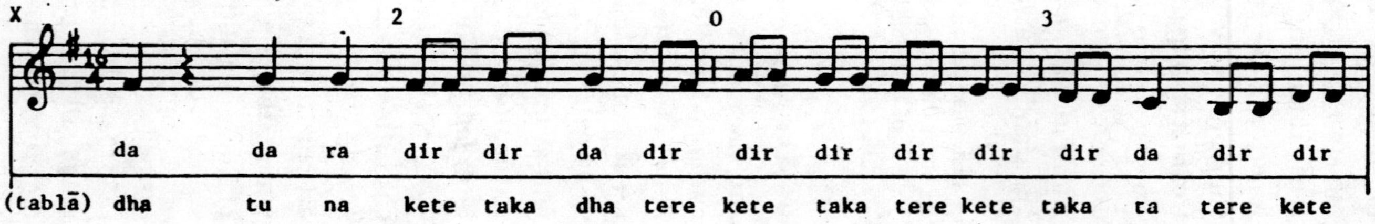

originated with the imitation of a specific class of *pakhāvaj bol*-s known as *tapiyā*. *Tapiyā*-s consisted of stroking patterns such as *ge na na na ge na na na ge na na na ge na na na* or *ge na na ge na na ge na ge na na ge na na ge na*. These are easily translated into the *mizrāb* stroking patterns of *da c c c da c c c da c c c da c c c* and *da c c da c c da c da c c da c c da c* (Shankar, personal communication: June, 1977). *Jhālā* will be discussed in detail in Chapter V. With the popularization of the *tablā*, *sitār* players began to apply the same practice of incorporating *bol*-s of the drum into their right-hand technique as the earlier *bīn* players had done with the *pakhāvaj*. The practice was not limited only to *paran*-s, however, and today it is a common practice for students to learn *tablā* simultaneously with *sitār* so they can incorporate the rhythmics of the drum into their *sitār* playing.

3.4. Contributions of Vocal Music

The *khyāl śailī* of vocal music has greatly influenced instrumental music in North India. It has been mentioned in the previous chapter that the *Masītkhānī gat* had been styled in the character of a *baṛā khyāl*. The *drut gat* of today is often based on a *choṭā khyāl*. Much of the ornamentation used in instrumental music has come from the *khyāl śailī* along with many types of *tān*-s (H. 'to extend'), the *sapāṭ tān* (literally 'straight extension') being the most distinct (see 4.3.). The style of ornamentation in *khyāl* can be described as being more sharply accentuated, with faster glides between tones, than the more clearly defined ornamentation used in *dhrupad*. Ravi Shankar has compared the former to filigree work and the latter to stone blockwork (personal communication: June 6, 1977). *Murkī* (H. 'a turn'), and *khaṭkā* (H. 'struck tone') are two ornaments that have been incorporated into *sitār* technique (see 4.1.2). Finally, it appears that the general progression in performing *gat vistār* has been developed on the model of the *khyāl śailī*.

From the foregoing discussion, it is apparent that *sitār* technique is a synthesis of material from diverse sources reaching back to possibly the thirteenth century, most definitely to the sixteenth century. Because it is a synthesis, and because the donor sources often borrowed from among themselves, it is almost impossible to sort out specific examples from the present repertory of techniques, styles, and forms to present any one of them as a 'pure' example of a particular source. Thus, material in the following chapters will describe contemporary practice in terms of itself and its relationship to the surrounding aural environment.

Notes to Chapter III

1. *Katar jhār* is also known as *katar*, or *jhār*.

2. In the *dhrupad* style, the *pakhāvaj* player normally performs intricate rhythmic improvisation while the vocalist or instrumentalist simultaneously improvises. Because of this, there are very few aids to define the *tāl*-s for the performer of the *rāg*. Thus, the necessity for memorizing pre-set rhythmic patterns arises.

3. Nazir Ali Jairazbhoy claims that a prominent member of the *Senī gharānā* had given conflicting interpretations of these terms on different occasions; thus, we may say that they are subject to different interpretations even by the same musician! (personal communication: August 16, 1977)

4. Recorded examples of two interpretations of these terms are given on a cassette tape deposited in the Hawaii Archives of Ethnic Music and Dance. (see Appendix C). It is interesting to note that both interpretations are consistent with the literal meanings of the words.

CHAPTER IV

CONTEMPORARY SITĀR TECHNIQUE: BASIC LEVEL, FIRST—, AND SECOND-LEVEL COMBINATIONS

Sitār technique lends itself to analysis at progressively complex levels. This chapter deals first with the basic-level techniques of each hand (independent of the other) and proceeds to combined techniques at two levels of complexity: (1) first-level combinations in which basic-level techniques of each hand are combined within themselves (independent of the other), and (2) second-level combinations in which basic-level techniques and/or first-level combinations of both hands are combined interdependently with each other. The second-level combinations comprise the *abhyās śṛṅkhalā* (H. 'practice routine').

Before proceeding to the kinetics of technique, it is desirable to discuss the static (or nearly static) elements of *sitār* playing because they are prerequisite to the successful performance of kinetic techniques. If one does not sit properly, or hold the instrument properly, the imbalance will be evident in the music produced owing to the resultant tension of poor posture. It is rather difficult for people brought up in Western-style houses with chairs to achieve the correct posture for playing the *sitār*. One must sit on the floor with the left leg bent acutely at the knee, keeping the knee in contact with the floor and the foot crossed under the right thigh so that it protrudes from under the right leg with the outer ankle resting on the floor, and the sole of the foot up. The right leg rests on top of the left calf and is bent slightly at the knee so that the outer ankle rests on the floor slightly to the left front of the knee.

The *sitār* is held in the correct playing position by the left foot, right thigh, and right forearm (see Fig. 6). The *tumbā* is fit into the curve of the sole of the foot, keeping the ventral plane of the instrument perpendicular to the floor, and the neck at approximately a forty-five degree angle. The left side of the *gulū* rests against the right thigh, and the inner surface of the right forearm rests on the right side of the *tumbā*. When held properly, the right arm provides sufficient weight to steady the instrument in this

Figure 6: **Playing Posture**

position; thus, the *sitār* is held without need for any exertion—a fine thing because playing the instrument requires a tremendous expenditure of energy!

4.1. **Basic-level Techniques**

The basic-level techniques of each hand will be classified and described independent of the other with the understanding that a right-hand stroke is required to initiate the vibration of the wire.

4.1.1 ***Right hand***

The right hand is correctly positioned by extending the thumb to the side, anchoring it on the right side of the neck just below the last fret, and extending the fingers across the playing wires, keeping them rounded and held firmly together. The *mizrāb* is worn on the index finger, held in place by callouses that develop with practice (see Fig. 8).

There are six basic right-hand strokes: two single strokes, and four composites comprised of durational variants of the single strokes. In common practice, each is referred to by a phonemic vocalization, *mizrāb bol*[1] (H. 'stroke syllable'). The term '*mizrāb bol*' is often abbreviated to either of the component words. The strokes, with their corresponding *bol*-s, method of performance, and notational symbols, are as follows (for a compact listing of the same, see Key to Special Symbols, Fig. 15):

(a) *Dā:* is an inward stroke by the index finger performed by folding the fingers, thus increasing their curvature, until the *mizrāb* strikes the desired wire. The action is not actually a plucking of the wire, but rather a pushing of the *mizrāb* against the wire until its force overcomes the force of the wire's tension. Tonal color varies according to the angle at which the *mizrāb* meets the wire. The potential variety of tonal color is enhanced by the wide bridge, creating a distinct overtone series, and thus, timbre, for each angle of stroke. The bol, *dā*, will be notated as '*da*'.

(b) *Rā:* is any outward stroke, but usually refers to the reverse of *dā*, that is an outward stroke by the right index finger. *Rā* may also be performed by the little finger, in which case the nail of the finger strikes either the *cikārī* or *taraf* wires. The *rā* stroke will be notated as '*ra*' except when it is performed on the *cikārī* or *taraf* wires, in which instances it will be notated as 'c' or 't', respectively.

(c) *Dir*[2]*:* is a composite stroke formed by combining the *dā* and *rā* strokes at double or more their original speed. *Dir* usually denotes a double articulation of a tone. Each of the articulations should be equal in duration, intensity, and tonal color. The *dir* bol will be notated as '*dir*'.

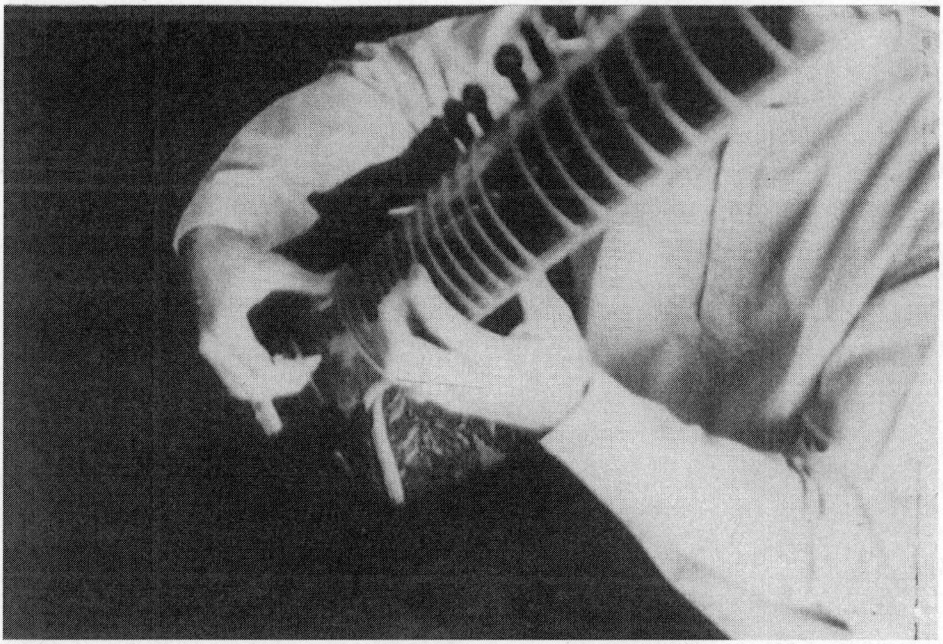

Figure 8: Left- and Right-hand Positions

(d) *Dār:* is a combination of *dā* with the *ra* portion of the bol, *dir*. The durational ratio of its components is usually either 2:1 or 3:1. *Dār* will be notated as '*dar*'.

(e) *Dirā:* is the '*dī*' portion of *dir* combined with a *rā* stroke. The durational ratio of its components is usually 1:2. *Dirā* will be notated as '*dira*'.

(f) *Radā:* is the retrograde form of *dār*. It is formed by joining the *ra* portion of the *dir* bol to a *dā* stroke. Its durational ratio is usually 1:2, *Radā* will be notated as '*rda*'.

This system of terminology for the right-hand *mizrāb bol*-s is uniform among *sitār*-ists. All extended *mizrāb-bol* patterns are formed by combining the above basic *bol*-s.

4.1.2 ***Left hand***

The techniques of the left hand are difficult to classify because the traditional terminology is, for the most part, borrowed from that of vocal ornaments. This borrowing of terms has led to ambiguities because the effect of a particular vocal ornament may be produced on the *sitār* by a number of different physical methods. To further complicate the situation, musicians of different schools differ among themselves in regards to terminology. Compounded by the Indian taxonomic practice of naming a class within a system by the term of one of its component parts, confusion appears inevitable. For the sake of consistency of this study, the techniques will be classified according to physical production. Traditional terminology will be assigned according to the following criteria: (1) majority opinion among available sources, (2) correspondence of the literal meaning of the term with the physical action of the technique, and (3) level of specificity in analysis (especially when referring to composite forms).

Left-hand techniques may be classed in two categories: (1) movements parallel to the wire, and (2) movements parallel to the frets and perpendicular to the wire (referred to in this study as perpendicular movements). In all techniques, the left hand is placed with the thumb on the dorsal portion of the neck, the hand and fingers arching around the left side and ventral portion of the neck. Although some performers use three, or even four, fingers to perform certain techniques, the traditional manner is to touch the wire by only the index and middle fingers.

4.1.2.1 parallel movement techniques

In parallel movement techniques, the index finger frets all the notes of ascending passages except the last, and all notes of descending passages except the first. The middle finger frets the exceptions. *Krintan, sparś*, and *gharṣaṇ* are left-hand techniques of this category that produce more than one tone per *mizrāb bol.*

(a) *Krintan* is performed by placing the middle and index fingers on the desired frets and then, immediately after striking the wire with the *mizrāb*, the left middle finger, with a slight plucking action, articulates the tone fretted by the index finger. This technique will be notated by a dot placed above the note articulated by it .

(b) *Sparś*, not to be confused with *sparś svar* (H. 'grace tone'), is the opposite of *krintan*. In *sparś*, the wire is first fretted by the left index finger, then struck by the *mizrāb*, and then struck by the left middle finger, articulating a second, higher pitched tone. The movement of the middle finger is a hammering action, with the finger maintaining contact with the wire after the hammer stroke for the desired duration of the articulation. This technique will also be notated by a dot. In the transcription, the two techniques may be easily differentiated by melodic motion. In *krintan*, the note preceding the note under the dot will be higher in pitch; in *sparś*, it wll be lower .

(c) *Gharṣaṇ* (H. 'slide') is performed by sliding either the index or middle finger on the wire from one fret to another while maintaining constant pressure. *Ghasīṭ* is a specific variety of *gharṣaṇ*. In *ghasīṭ*, the interval spanned in the slide is greater than a fourth, and only the outer pitch limits of the slide are articulated. *Gharṣaṇ* (and *ghasīṭ*) will be notated by placing a vertical line over the latter pitch of the slide. A *gharṣaṇ*, or *ghasīṭ*, may be *arohī* (H. 'ascending')  or *avarohī* (H. 'descending') .

4.1.2.2 perpendicular movement techniques

In what I call perpendicular movement techniques, melodic movement is accomplished by first striking with the *mizrāb*, and then pulling the wire across the fret. This action will be indicated by a horizontal line above the note(s) being produced by pulling the wire. On the *sitār*, this technique helps to sustain the sound of an articulated tone and thus creates a sound continuum between pitches. Ornaments produced by the deflection of the wire across a fret are grouped according to the following criteria: (1) speed of deflection, (2) pitch-interval spanned by the deflection, (3) relative duration of the outer pitch limits of the deflection, (4) the melodic character of the musical product of the technique, and (5) the musical context of the ornament.

Mīṇḍ, kaṇ, murkī, khaṭkā, kampan, āndolan, and *gamak* are common terms used to classify ornaments produced by pulling the wire. Mīṇḍ (Ex. 4-1) is a slow glide connecting two or more pitches. The distinguishing criterion of *mīṇḍ* is that each tone is equally expressed within the continuum of sound. (Throughout this study the word 'tone' infers an accepted scale-degree within a *ṭhāṭ* [or a *rāg*]). *Kaṇ*[3] (Sk. 'particle') is a grace note (Ex. 4-2). The duration of the *kaṇ svar* will be less than that of the tone being decorated. A *kaṇ svar* may be either the upper- or lower-neighbor tone of the decorated pitch.

Ex. 4-1 *Mīṇḍ* Ex. 4-2 *Kaṇ*

A *murkī* (H. 'turn') is a turn around a principal tone (Ex. 4-3). A *murkī* is comprised of a number of elided *kaṇ svar*-s. *Khaṭkā* (H. 'collision') is similar to *kaṇ*; however, whereas *kaṇ* maintains the clear expression of the decorative tone, *khaṭkā* does not, thus becoming a gliding attack on the principal tone (Ex. 4-4). The relative speed of performance of the ornament is greater in *khaṭkā* than in *kaṇ*.

Ex. 4-3 *Murkī* Ex. 4-4 *Khaṭkā*

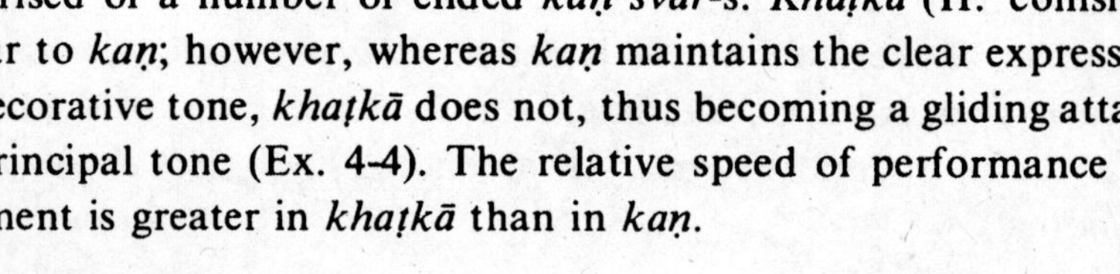

Kampan (H. 'tremolo') and *āndolan* (H. 'undulation') both denote oscillations, the difference being that in *kampan*, the frequency of oscillation is faster than that of *āndolan* (Ex. 4-5, 4-6). Also, *āndolan* normally has a greater amplitude of vibration, even extending to a neighboring pitch, while *kampan* produces a very slight alteration of pitch.

Ex. 4-5 *Kampan* Ex. 4-6 *Āndolan*

The term *gamak*, in ancient times, encompassed all ornamental techniques. This particular meaning of the word is still adhered to; however, in North Indian music, it has also acquired a specialized usage denoting a specific shaking of tone. In this other usage, the shake is: (1) heavy and fast, (2) may start from a higher (Ex. 4-7a) or lower tone (Ex. 4-7b) than the prominent tone, or the prominent tone itself, and (3) may accentuate either of the outer limits of oscillation (Ex. 4-7c and 4-7d), or create an ambiguity by accentuating the inner span of the oscillation (Ex. 4-7e). The latter variant is more commonly performed in vocal music and on unfretted instruments than on *sitār*. A post-positioned *kaṇ svar* and various other ornaments are often called *gamak* for want of any other term (Ex. 4-7f).

Ex. 4-7 (a–f) *Gamak*

4.2 First-level Combinations

At this level of analysis, the hands are still perceived as independent of one another. Larger forms are constructed by combining basic techniques of only one hand; thus, a first-level combined technique of the left hand will require only a single right-hand stroke, and one of the right hand will require only one tone produced by fretting the wire by either the left index or middle finger.

4.2.1 *Right hand*

There are two processes that underlie the formation of extended *mizāb-bol* patterns, one being conceptual, the other reiterative. The former is based on the concept of creating new patterns by the permutation and combination of simpler forms; the latter is based on the transmission of a stock of traditional *bol* patterns from teacher to student which serve as pre-fabricated sections from which extended forms are constructed. It is probable that the second process is an evolutionary offshoot of the first, in that development in Indian music has been conceived of as permutation and combination since the time of Bharata (c. 300 A.D.?). A probable occurrence is that, through time, a corpus of *bol* patterns was formed by the acceptance of certain *bol*-s as artistically superior to the limitless numbers of patterns that could be generated by permutation and combination.

An example of extended *mizrāb-bol* patterns generated through the process of permutation and combination is seen in Figure 9a. The example shows how the two sub-sections '*da ra*' and '*da ra da*' are used to generate larger forms. The resultant set of *mizrāb bol*-s is ubiquitous among *sitār* players, and, with the addition of a principled substitution factor, it provides a seemingly inexhaustible source of extended *mizrāb bol*-s. The principle of substitution is relatively simple—'*ra*' never follows '*r*', and '*da*' never follows '*di*'. Figure 9b shows the substitution of '*dir*' for the '*ra*' of the three-*bol* sub-unit '*da ra da*' in the unit patterns of eight elements. Figure 9c shows the substitution of '*dir*' for the terminal '*da*' of '*da ra da*' in the same. This process may be carried on *ad infinitum*.

The transmission from *guru* to *śiṣya* of widely known *bol* patterns is an essential element in the musical education of a student of *sitār*. The list of *bol*-s in Figure 10 is given by Misra as representative of the types of *bol*-s that well-versed musicians use in their playing (1973: 145). This list shows a wide variety of commonly encountered *mizrāb* patterns that combine a number of the basic *bol*-s given in section 4.1.1.

	Division	Elements/unit (*bol*)
a) *Bol*		
da ra	2	2
da ra da	3	3
da ra da ra	2+2	4
da ra da ra da	2+3	5
da ra da da ra	3+2	5
da ra da ra da ra	2+2+2	6
da ra da da ra da	3+3	6
da ra da da ra da ra	3+2+2	7
da ra da ra da da ra	2+3+2	7
da ra da ra da ra da	2+2+3	7
da ra da ra da ra da ra	2+2+2+2	8
da ra da da ra da da ra	3+3+2	8
da ra da da ra da ra da	3+2+3	8
da ra da ra da da ra da	2+3+3	8
da ra da da ra da da ra da	3+3+3	9
da ra da ra da ra da ra da	2+2+2+3	9
da ra da ra da ra da da ra	2+2+3+2	9
da ra da ra da da ra da ra	2+3+2+2	9
da ra da da ra da ra da ra	3+2+2+2	9
etc.		
b) Substituting '*dir*' for '*ra*' of '*da ra da*'		
da dir da da dir da da ra	3+3+2	8
da dir da da ra da dir da	3+2+3	8
da ra da dir da da dir da	2+3+3	8
c) Substituting '*dir*' for terminal '*da*' of '*da ra da*'		
da ra dir da ra dir da ra	3+3+2	8
da ra dir da ra da ra dir	3+2+3	8
da ra da ra dir da ra dir	2+3+3	8

Figure 9: Permutation and Combination of *Bol*-s

Bol — Rhythmic Structure

da dir da ra
da ra dir da
dir da da ra
da ra da dir
dir dir da ra
da ra dir dir
da dir dir dir
da rda rda
da -rda ra
da dira rda
da dir dir dir da rda rda
da ra dir dir da rda rda
da dir da ra -dir da ra
da rda rdir da dir da ra
da dir da da dir dir da ra
da dir dir da -rdirda ra
da dira rdir da dir da ra
dir da ra dir da ra dir dir
da dir da dir da ra
da rda rda rda rda ra

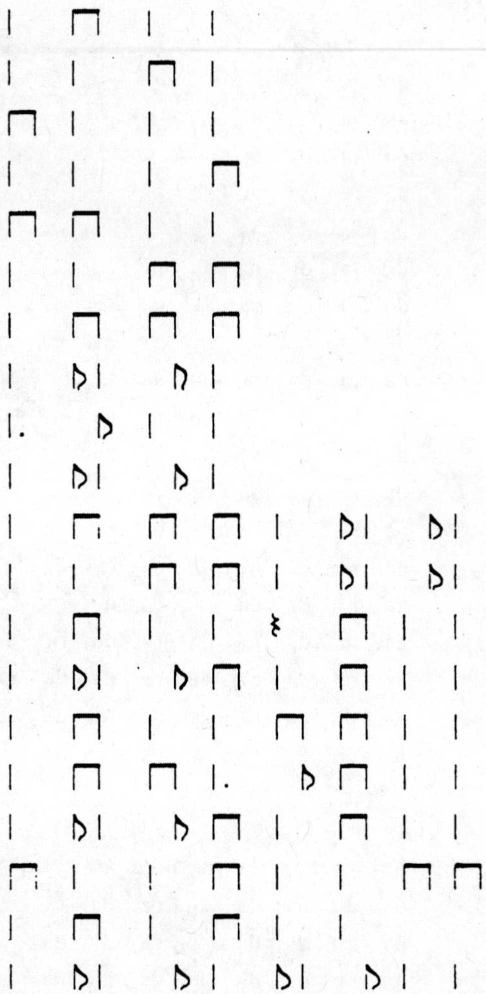

Figure 10: Common *Mizrāb Bol*-s

4.2.2 ***Left hand***

The majority of composite left-hand techniques are not designated by specific terms. The usual practice is to designate extended combinations of parallel movements as *krintan*, and those of perpendicular movements as *mīṇḍ* or *gamak*. Again, this practice exemplifies the Indian idea of terming a broad form by one of its component parts.

In this study, *krintan*$_1$ will refer to any composite form that incorporates any combination of the techniques *krintan*, *sparś*, and *gharṣaṇ* performed on no more than three scale-degrees (Ex. 4-8). There are two varieties of *krintan*$_1$ that are occasionally designated by separate terms. The pattern '*krintan (sparś krintan)*$_{(n)}$'[4] is known as *zamzamā* (H. onomatapoetic) (Ex. 4-9). *Giṭkiṛī* is a combination of three pitches performed either as *krintan-gharṣaṇ* or *gharṣaṇ-sparś* (Ex. 4-10).

Ex. 4-8 *Krintan*$_1$ Ex. 4-9 *Zamzamā* Ex. 4-10 *Giṭkiṛī*

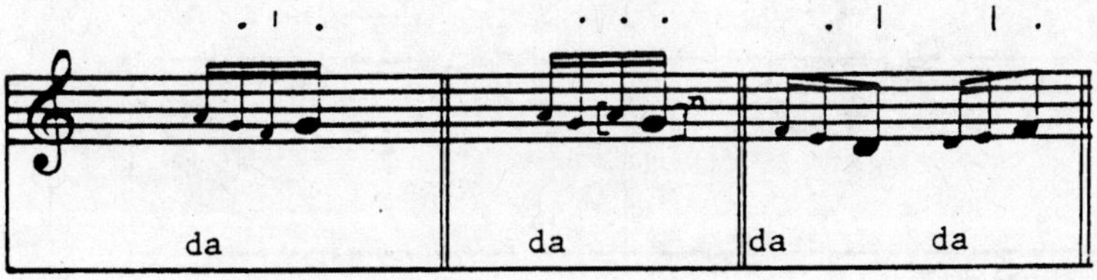

In addition to those described above, there are a number of other composite techniques that are common in *sitār* playing, but are not designated by a specific term. Two examples are: (1) repeated *gharṣaṇ*-s terminated by *sparś* (Ex. 4-11a), and (2) its retrograde form, *krintan* followed by repeated *gharṣaṇ*-s (Ex. 4-11b).

Ex. 4-11 a) *Gharṣaṇ*^{n} —*sparś* b) *Krintan—gharṣaṇ*^{n}

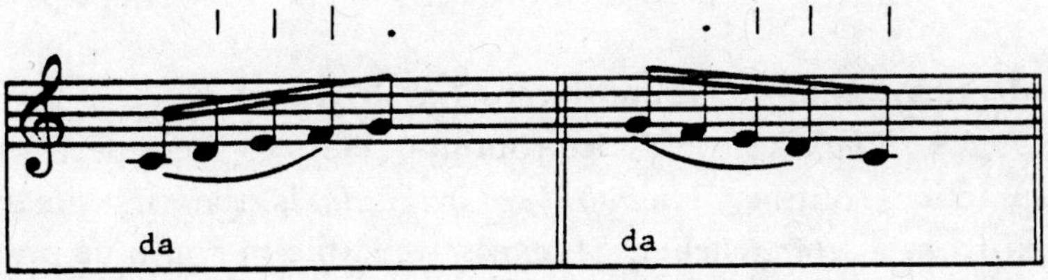

Five composite techniques combining parallel and perpendicular movements all produce the effect of extended *mīṇḍ*-s. They are: (1) *ghasīṭ* plus *mīṇḍ* (2) *gharṣaṇ*$^{(n)}$ plus *mīṇḍ* (3) *sparś* plus *mīṇḍ*, (4) *gharṣaṇ*$^{(n)}$ plus *sparś* plus *mīṇḍ*, and (5) *krintan* plus *gharṣaṇ* plus *mīṇḍ*. The first four techniques produce ascending melodic contours, the fifth descending (Ex. 4-12a-e).

Ex. 4-12 a) Ghasīṭ—mīṇḍ b) *Gharṣaṇ*$^{(n)}$ *—mīṇḍ* c) *Sparś—mīṇḍ*

d) *Gharṣaṇ—sparś—mīṇḍ* e) *Krintan—gharṣaṇ—mīṇḍ*

As mentioned above, perpendicular techniques, when combined, are usually referred to as *mīṇḍ* or *gamak* (in the sense of any ornament), however, there are no systematic rules governing this terminology. At a lower level of specificity of analysis in this study, any composite technique consisting of *mīṇḍ* plus any other perpendicular movement technique(s) will be referred to as *mīṇḍ*$_1$; and any combination of *kaṇ, khaṭkā, kampan*, and *āndolan* which serves to embellish one tone will be referred to as *gamak*$_1$. In other words, *mīṇḍ*$_1$ is any type of a glide, and *gamak*$_1$ is any type of shake. At a higher level of specificity of analysis, a composite form will be described in terms of its component parts.

4.3 *Abhyās Śṛṅkhalā*—Second-level Combinations

Abhyās śṛṅkhalā (H. 'practice routine') refers to the repertory of the daily practice routine. The *abhyās śṛṅkhalā* is the first instruction received from a *sitār* teacher. Students are liable to continue practicing exercises for months before they learn even the simplest musical form, the *sargam*. The reason for this, as mentioned in Chapter I, is that the practice exercises are the foundation of the musical forms that advanced students learn and professional musicians perform. Writing of his training period under Ustad Ala' ud-din Khan, Ravi Shankar states:

> Usually I would wake up about four o'clock in the morning and have a quick wash, not the regular bath, and drink a cup of tea. I took my sitār and practiced the basic scales until six o'clock or so.
>
> (1968:73)

When I asked him in June, 1977 (some forty years later) if he still begins the day with the basic exercises, he replied in the affirmative: "Of course, I have to—otherwise it's not possible to play."

Most of the *abhyās śṛṅkhalā* consists of melodic patterns that serve to provide exercise of the corpus of left-hand techniques. Each pattern is played over and over on successive scale degrees in the manner of tonal sequences, i.e. intervallic structure is governed by that of the *ṭhāṭ* (H. 'scale') in which it is played as the pattern is transposed throughout the course of the exercise. The right-hand exercises consist of memorized *mizrāb bol*-s that are repeated on successive scale degrees in both ascending and descending modes (cf. Fig. 10).

It is usual to begin a practice session with exercises called *sapāṭ*. A very good *sapāṭ* exercise devised by Ravi Shankar is given in Example 4-13. This exercise not only assures left-hand mastery over the range of the *bāj tār*, but also strengthens right-hand *bol* patterns by permutating a twelve-element unit comprised of sub-sections of fives and sevens. As is shown in Example 4-13, the *sapāṭ* exercise is designed to make the hand facile in extended ascending and descending passages.

Exercises performed as sequences are known as *alaṅkār*-s (H. 'ornament') or *palṭā*-s (H. 'divide'). Misra speaks of two types of *alaṅkār*-s: (1) those in which only '*da*' and '*ra*' strokes are performed, and (2) those in which '*dir*' and other *bol*-s, in addition to '*da*' and '*ra*', are performed, and both strokes of '*dir*' articulate the same tone. The first category *alaṅkār*-s forms the basis of extended melodic passages known as '*tān*-s', and the second forms the foundation of *toṛā*-s (1973:145).

A special type of *alaṅkār* is known as *mūrcchanā* (Sk. 'octave species'). In *mūrcchanā*, the melodic unit-pattern of the sequence must have a range of one octave. The simplest *mūrcchanā* exercise is formed by playing octave species in the ascending and descending mode on the scale degrees 'g' (*bāj tār*—second fret) through 'e^{1}' (*bāj tār*—tenth fret). A more complex *mūrcchanā* exercise is shown in Example 4-14. This *mūrcchanā* is made rhythmically complex by placing the grouping 5-5-6 against the

Ex. 4-13 Sapāṭ

da	da	da	da	da	da	da	da	da	da	da	da	da	da	da	da	da	da	da	da	da	da	da	da
ra	ra	ra	ra	ra	ra	ra	ra	ra	ra	ra	ra	ra	ra	ra	ra	ra	ra	ra	ra	ra	ra	ra	ra
da	ra	da	ra	da	ra	da	ra	da	ra	da	ra	da	ra	da	ra	da	ra	da	ra	da	ra	da	ra
da	ra	da	ra	da	da	ra	da	da	ra	da	ra	da	ra	da	ra	da	da	ra	da	da	ra	da	ra
da	ra	da	da	ra	da	ra	da	ra	da	ra	da	da	ra	da	da	ra	da	ra	da	ra	da	ra	da
da	ra	da	ra	da	da	ra	da	ra	da	da	ra	da	da	ra	da	ra	da	ra	da	da	ra	da	ra
da	ra	da	da	ra	da	ra	da	ra	da	da	ra	da	ra	da	ra	da	ra	da	da	ra	da	ra	da
da	ra	da	ra	da	da	ra	da	da	ra	da	ra	da	ra	da	da	ra	da	ra	da	ra	da	ra	da
da	ra	da	da	ra	da	ra	da	ra	da	ra	da	da	ra	da	ra	da	da	ra	da	da	ra	da	ra
da	ra	da	da	ra	da	da	ra	da	da	ra	da	da	ra	da	da	ra	da	da	ra	da	da	ra	da

underlying 4-4-4-4 metrical pattern. The example shows only the first octave species of the exercise. The exercise is completed by playing the same pattern on the octave species starting on the tones a, b, c^1, d^1, e^1, f^1, and g^1, and then back through the series to g.

Ex. 4-14 *Mūrcchanā*

A typical *alaṅkār* is shown in Example 4-15. The melodic unit is comprised of an ascending skip followed by two descending steps. Notice that in the descending mode, this form is inverted. An alternate way to perform the *alaṅkār* is to maintain the same form in the descending mode as in the ascending mode. This *alaṅkār* is useful for developing the fingering technique of the left hand (see 4.1.2) as well as providing a common melodic motif found in *cakrā tān*-s (H. 'circular melodic passages').

Ex. 4-15 *Alaṅkār*

Ex. 4-16 *Toṛā Alaṅkār*

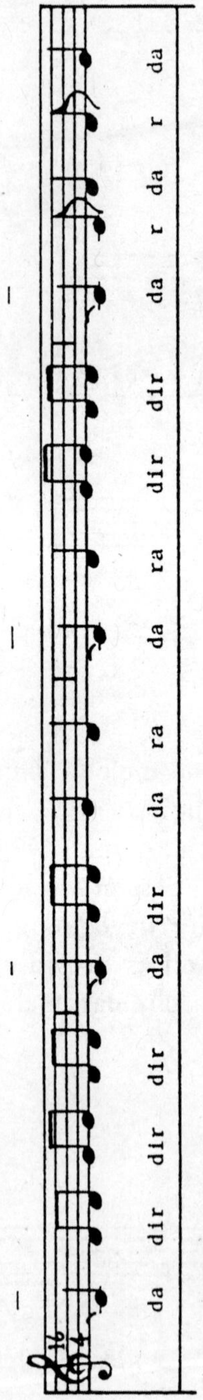

Ex. 4-17 *Toṛā Alaṅkār*

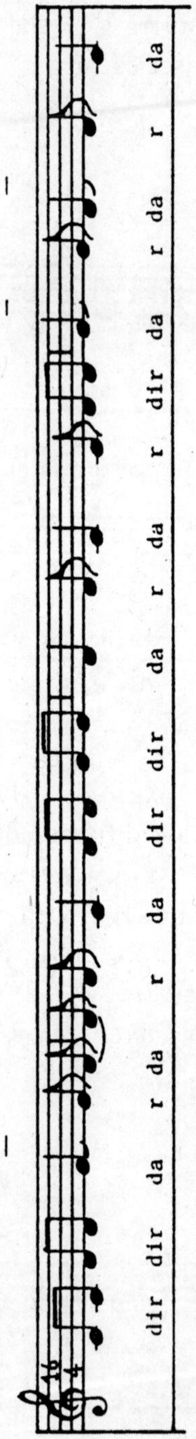

Ex. 4-18 *Toṛā Alaṅkār* (with *zamzamā*)

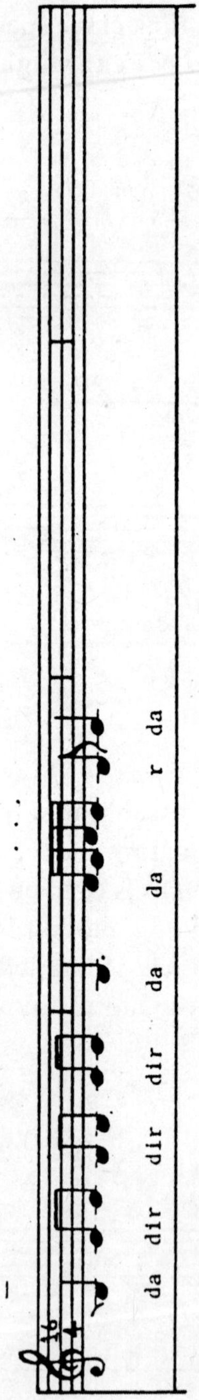

Ex. 4-19 *Toṛā Alaṅkār*

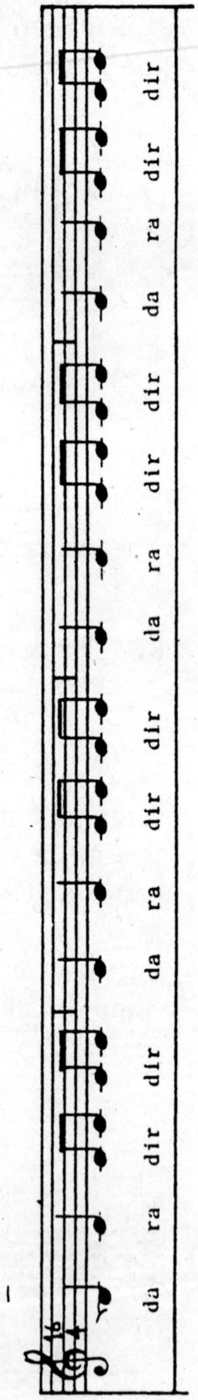

Ex. 4-20 *Alaṅkar (mīṇḍ)*

Ex. 4-21 *Alaṅkar (murkī)*

Ex. 4-22a *Alaṅkar (gamak)*)

Ex. 4-22b Alaṅkar (gamak)

The *alaṅkār*-s seen in Examples 4-16, 4-17, 4-18, and 4-19 are exemplary of Misra's second category, i.e., those forming the basis of the stylized formal elements known as *toṛā.* The primary purpose of these *alaṅkār*-s is to provide a base for extended repetition of *mizrāb bol*-s that are incorporated when playing *toṛā*-s. As mentioned above, *toṛā*-s are improvised passages that must incorporate the *bol 'dir'* in their *mizrāb* patterns. Examples 4-16 and 4-17 are structured on many sub-units of *bol* patterns while Example 4-18 and 4-19 are more compact structures. Examples 4-18 is very common in music performance, as is Example 4-19, which is often played during the *jhālā* because it may be performed at an extremely fast tempo. Example 4-18 provides the added benefit of exercising the *zamzamā* technique of the left hand. Each of the exercises is completed by repeating the pattern on successive scale degrees in the ascending and descending modes.

Alaṅkār-s that provide exercise for *mīṇḍ, murkī,* and *gamak* are seen in Examples 4-20, 4-21, and 4-22 (a) and (b). In all of these *alaṅkār*-s, the maintenance of correct intonation while pulling the wire is the stressed factor. Techniques incorporating pulling are *sine qua non* in *sitār* playing. These *alaṅkār*-s, and numerous others of similar quality, appear profusely in performance practice. The same format of performance applies to these *alaṅkār*-s as was described for the preceding *alaṅkār*-s.

NOTES TO CHAPTER IV

1. *Mizrāb bol* also refers to extended passages of stylized patterns that are constructed for many, if not all, of the basic *bol*-s (see 4.2.1.).

2. Note that although *'dir'* is a double stroke (the composite of *di* and *ra*), because the *ra* occurs as a final consonant, it drops the '*a*' according to standard Hindi pronunciation, thus appearing as a monosyllabic bol in the transliteration. In actual pronunciation, '*r*' is produced with a flap of the tongue against the back of the upper teeth, producing a sufficient separation from the preceding '*di*' to allow the *bol* to be heard as bi-syllabic.

3. *Kaṇ*, or *kaṇ svar*, is used interchangeably with the term *sparś svar* (H. 'touch tone') in common practice; however, to avoid confusion with the technique *'sparś'*, the latter term will be avoided in this study.

4. The super-script 'n' designates an optional number of repetitions, while '(n)' designates that an optional number of repetitions is optional.

CHAPTER V

THE *TĀLĪM ŚṚNKHALĀ*—THIRD-LEVEL COMBINATIONS

Tālīm (H. 'education') is the rigorous regimen of training that the *guru* bestows upon his disciples. The primary objective of the *tālīm* is to prepare a student to perform *rāg*-s; however, teaching *rāg*-s is an activity to which comparatively less time is devoted in the *tālīm* than teaching how to properly develop a *rāg* in performance. Thus, in the traditional *tālīm*, a student will devote months, or even years, to learning a single *rāg*, in order to build the solid foundation of techniques essential to *rāg vistār* (H. 'expansion'). After perfecting the methods of doing *vistār*, it is a relatively easy task to improvise freely in any *rāg*, once having learned the melodic structure of the *rāg*. All of the items comprising present day repertory (see 2.3.3) are taught in a thorough *tālīm*; however, it is the *gat śailī*, the *vilambit gat* in particular, that receives the most emphasis during the entire duration of a student's *tālīm*.

5.1 *Gat* Patterns

The term *'gat'* is subject to a number of interpretations at different levels of specificity. *Gat* may denote a particular style of music in which *gatkārī* (proficiency in *nibaddh saṅgīt*) is the distinguishing characteristic (as in *gat śailī). Gat* may also refer to a particular movement in the performance of a *rāg* which is comprised of both precomposed and improvised portions (as in *gat vistār*). At yet a more specific level, *gat* refers to the pre-composed melody (archetypal form) that serves as the point of departure and return for improvisations during *gat vistār* (as in *Masītkhānī gat*, *kūṭ bāj gat*, etc.). In this study, these three levels of interpretation will be referred to as *gat śailī*, *gat vistār*, and *gat*, respectively.

Although there are many different types of *gat*-s, the following five features are common to all *gat*-s, regardless of their specific classification:

(a) A *gat* must be composed in one *rāg* and one *tāl*.

(b) A *gat* must have a *sam* (Sk. 'together'). *Sam* (indicted by 'X') is a particular point of rhythmical emphasis that coincides with the *sam* (starting point) of the *tāl* cycle. Many *gat*-s incorporate a compositional device known as *mukhṛā* (H. 'opening') to further emphasize the *sam*. *Mukhṛā* is a melodic phrase that produces both a melodic and rhythmic cadence effect on *sam*.

(c) *Gat*-s, in general, are multisectional. All *gat*-s contain a *sthāyī* (Sk. 'unchanging'), alternately referred to as 'first line'. The *sthāyī* usually dwells in the *madhya saptak* (H. 'middle octave') which, on the *sitār*, normally extends from c^1 to c^2. A *gat* may or may not have a second line complementary to the *sthāyī*. The optional line, known as *manjhā* (from H. madhya—'middle'), usually extends to a lower register than the *sthāyī*. The majority of *gat*-s contain an *antarā* (Sk. 'within'). The *antarā* normally consists of two lines. The first is ascending and emphasizes the upper-octave tonic; the second, descending, returns to the *sthāyī*.

(d) The rhythmic component of a *gat* is defined by the *mizrāb bol*. In the teaching situation, the *mizrāb bol* functions as a pseudo-text to which the melody of the *gat* is sung.

(e) *Gat*-s, in general, permit a degree of variation of their melodic and rhythmic components. A particular *gat* may be made more simple or complex by a teacher to suit a student's capabilities.

The most standardized *gat* form in the contemporary repertory is the *vilambit gat* played in *tīn-tāl*. *Tīn-tāl* is a rhythmic cycle comprised of sixteen *mātrā*-s [the basic durational units in a *tāl*] divided 4-4-4-4 (X, 2, 0, 3). This *gat* form has evolved from the *Masītkhānī gat* (see 2.3.2). The *drut gat*-s and *kūṭ bāj gat*-s are so diversified that it is impossible to give a complete catalogue of their structural patterns. However, an attempt will be made to deal with underlying concepts that formulate their construction (see 5.1.2 and 5.1.3).

5.1.1 *Vilambit gat* (*tīn-tāl*)

As a compositional form, the *vilambit gat* provides far greater potential for expressing the gestalt of a *rāg* than any other *gat* type. The reason is that the slow tempo (e.g. 40-90 *mātrā*-s per minute) provides more temporal space within which melodic motives may be arranged, and allows for an abundance of the techniques described as perpendicular in the previous chapter. The intricate tonal relationships of a *rāg* are more clearly manifested by techniques such as *mīṇḍ*, *kaṇ* and *murkī*, than by *krintan*, *sparś*, and *gharṣaṇ*.

The *vilambit gat*, as a rule, follows the same structural form as its prototype, the *Masītkhānī gat*. The structure is created on the foundation of a standardized *mizrāb bol*:

X				2				0				3			
1	2	3	4	5	6	7	8	9	10	11	12	13	14	15	16
da	da	ra	dir	da	dir	da	ra	da	da	ra	dir	da	dir	da	ra

This bol pattern is made distinctive by constructing the melody in asymmetric groupings, the most important of these being the *mukhṛā*, a group five *mātrā*-s long, starting on *mātrā* 12 (hereafter abbreviated to m 12, etc.) of the rhythmic cycle. Thus, the *gat* is composed in groupings of 5-3-5-3 while the *tāl* is in groupings of 4-4-4-4. The following infra-structure results:

												3			
											12	13	14	15	16
											dir	da	dir	da	ra
X				2				0							
1	2	3	4	5	6	7	8	9	10	11					
da	da	ra	dir	da	dir	da	ra	da	da	ra					

In this structure, the *gat* is in synchronization with the *tāl* on the first (*sam*) and ninth (*khālī* [H. 'empty']) *mātrā*-s—the two most structurally important beats in the rhythmic cycle. This infra-structure is maintained in all of the lines that comprise the *gat*.

An entire *vilambit gat* in *rāg Yaman Kalyān* is transcribed in Example 5-1a, b, c (see 6.2 and Fig. 15 for explanations of notational symbols). This *gat* is comprised of three sections: *sthāyī, manjhā,* and *antarā*. The *sthāyī* and *manjhā* are each one *āvartan* long, while the *antarā* is two. Each of these sections starts on m 12 and is independent of the others in that each may be repeated an optional number of times and/or be followed by improvisation(s) before proceeding to the next. The initial order of entry would normally be *sthāyī, manjhā,* and *antarā*. After all lines have occurred once, the order may vary.

The asymmetrical construction of the melodic lines is easily seen in this *gat*. A common feature in *vilambit gat*-s of this structure is the alternation of melodically active five-*mātrā* groups with melodically passive three-*mātrā* groups. While, in general, both the tonal and rhythmic components of the melody conform to this pattern, it will suffice here

Rāg Yaman Kalyāṇ
Ex. 5-1a *Sthāyī*

Ex. 5-1b *Manjhā*

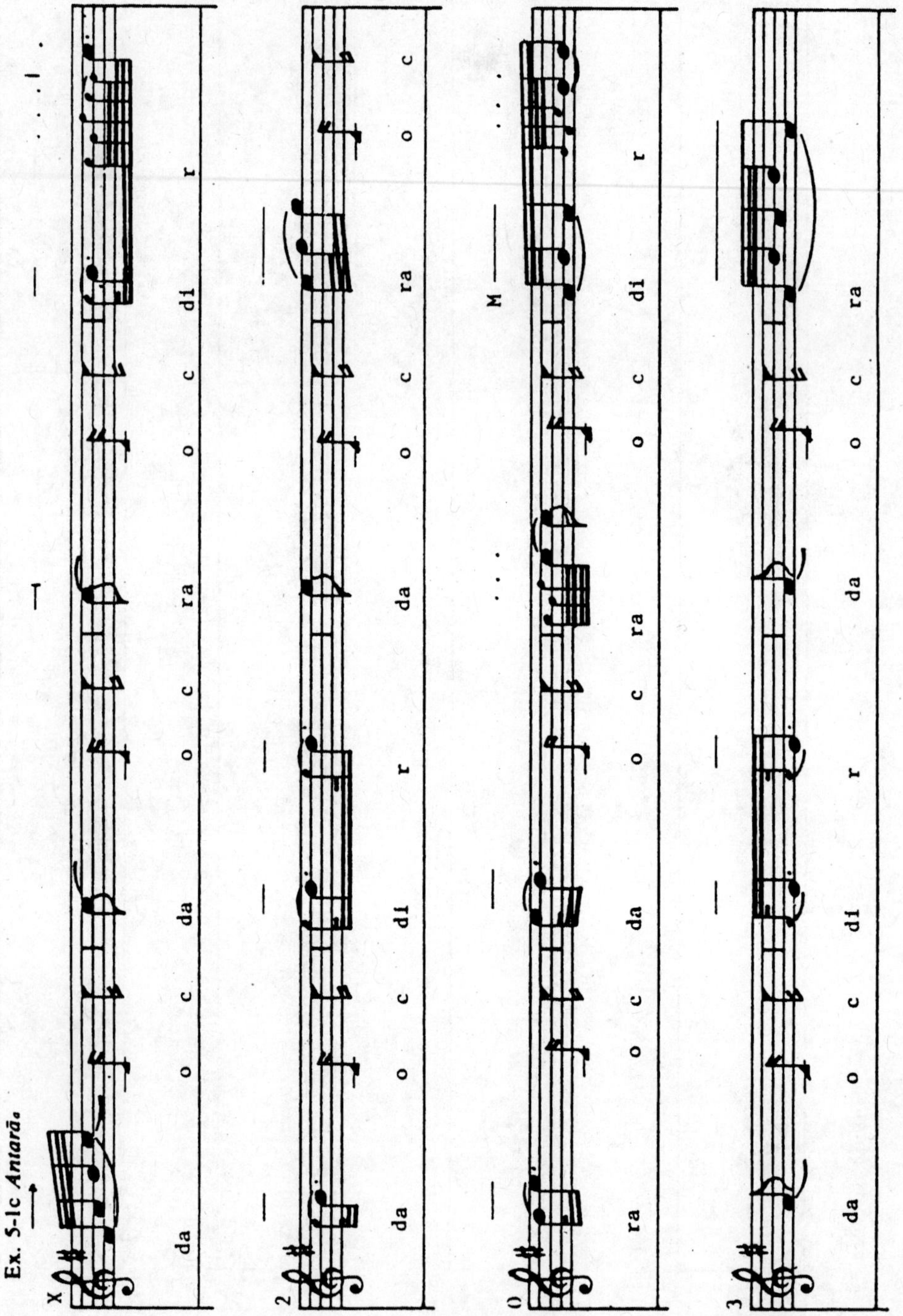
Ex. 5-1c *Antarā*
X
da o c da o c ra o c dī r
2
da o c dī r da o c ra o c
0
ra o c da o c ra o c dī r
3
da o c dī r da o c ra

Ex. 5-1c *Antarā*$_b$

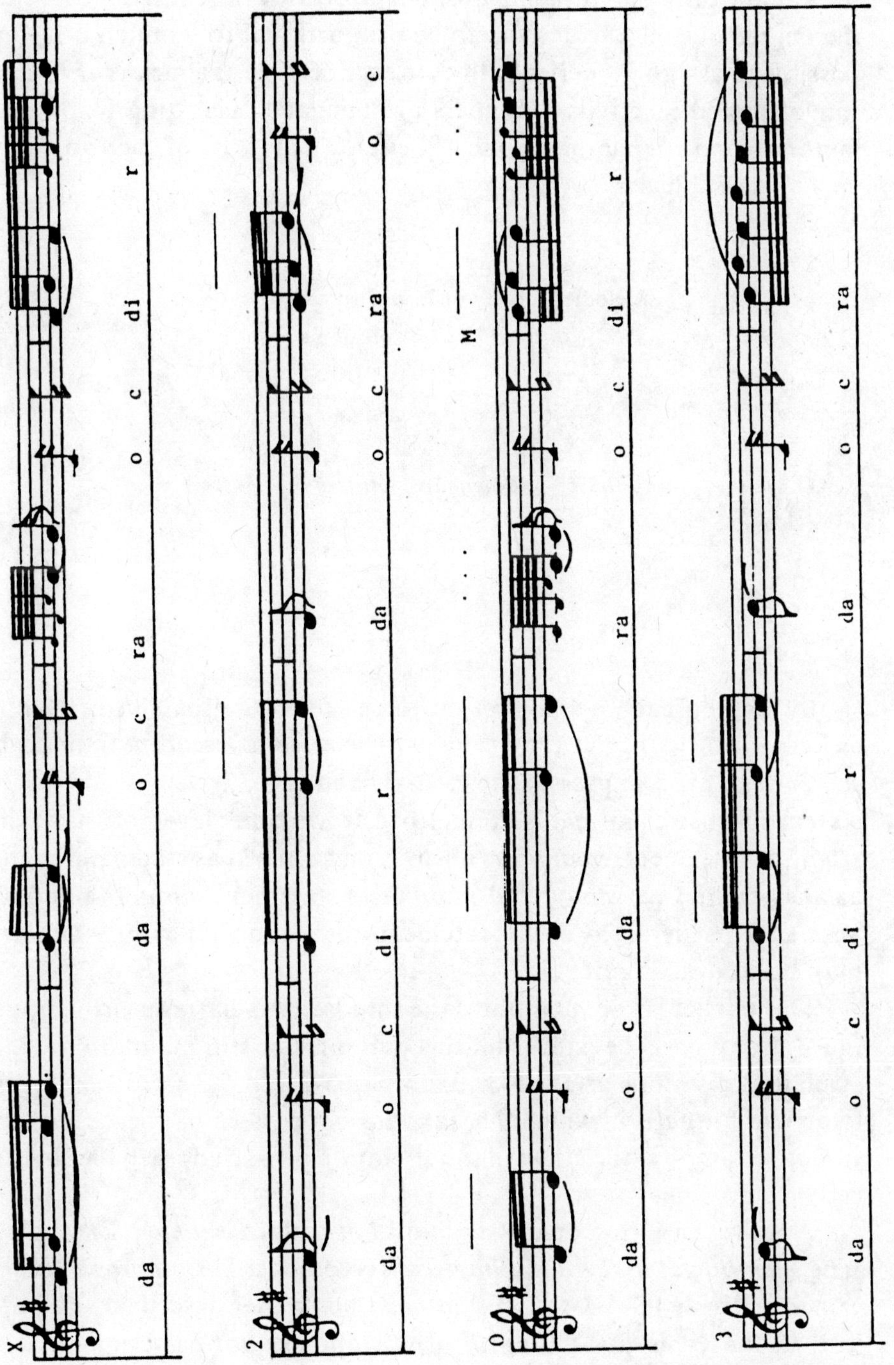

to examine only the former in order to illustrate this feature. By accepting the degree of melodic activity to be proportional to its pitch range, it is possible to assign numerical values to each section as a means of comparison of melodic activity (numbers are assigned according to prime = 0, minor second = 1, major second = 2, etc.). The results of such an analysis appear in Table 1.

Table 1
Melodic Activity of Infra-structural Divisions
of the *Vilambit Gat* of Ex. 5-1

Mātrā-s	Range				*Average Range/ group*
	Sthāyī	*Manjhā*	*Antarā*a	*Antarā*b	
12-16	8	10	7	5	7.5
1-3	0	5	6	6	4.25
4-8	9	13	8	5	8.75
9-11	5	5	5	5	5

By joining each active section to the following passive section, the melodic character of the *gat* obtains an antecedent-consequent format, where the statement is expressed in m 12-3, and the answer in m 4-11. The statement-answer format is exemplified at two other levels of analysis: (1) *sthāyī* as statement, *manjhā* as answer, and *antarā*a as statement, *antarā*b as answer, and (2) *sthāyī* and *manjhā* as statement, *antarā* (a and b) as answer. This hierarchy of the statement-answer format of the *vilambit gat* may be seen in Figure 11.

This particular *gat* maintains the standard *bol* pattern throughout all lines. Many *gat*-s deviate from this pattern, but still maintain the infra-structural divisions as 5-3-5-3. Examples 5-2 and 5-3 show *mukhṛā*-s of two vilambit *gat*-s in which the standard *bol* pattern has become altered. In both examples, the effect of the alteration is to strengthen the rhythmic cadence on *sam*.

Another variation on the standard *bol* pattern is seen in Example 5-4. The *vilambit gat* in *rāg Bilāskhānī Toḍī* is composed in *jhūmrā tāl* (fourteen *mātrā*-s; divided 3-4-3-4). This *gat* may be further described as a *kūṭ bāj gat*, in that it is not in *tīn-tāl*. The standard *bol* pattern geared to a sixteen-*mātrā tāl* is compressed by substituting '*r da r*' for the '*dir da ra*' which occurs on *mātrā*-s 6-8 and 14-16. These substitutions create a *bol* pattern fourteen *mātrā*-s long, divided 3-4-3-4. *Mukhṛā* starts on m 11.

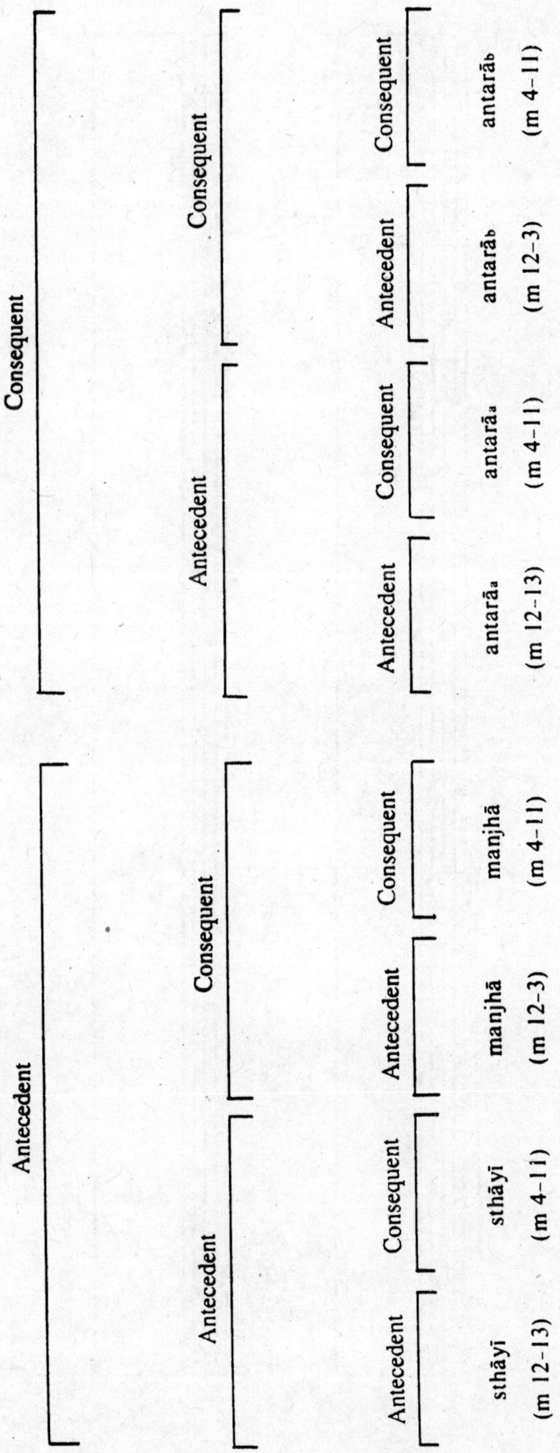

Figure 11: Antecedent-Consequent Hierarchy in *Vilambit Gat*

Ex. 5-2 Bol Variation of *Mukhṛa—Rāg Yaman*

Ex. 5-3 Bol Variation of *Mukhṛa—Rāg Desh*

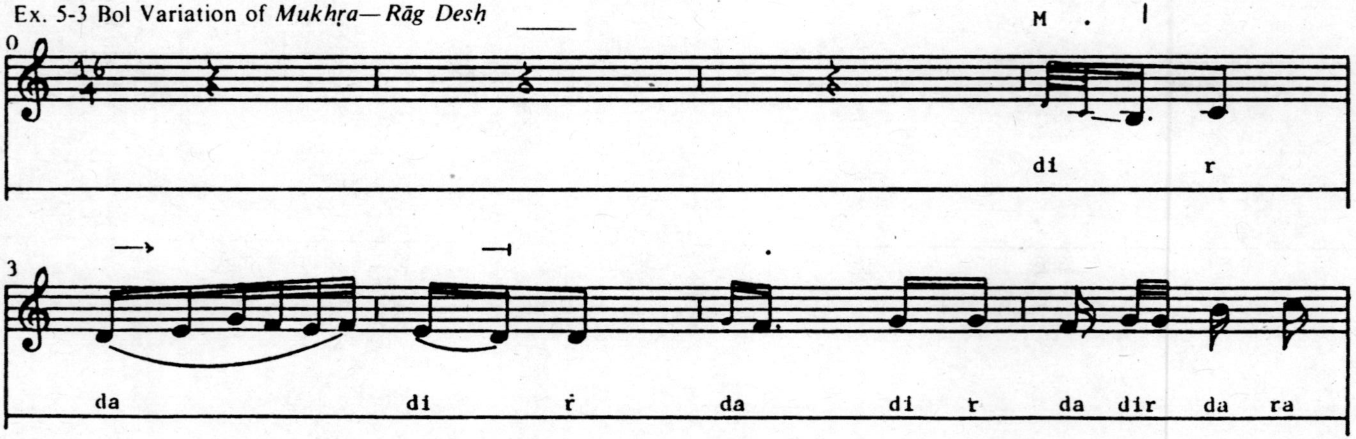

Ex. 5-4 Bol Variation of *Vilambit Gat*—*Rāg Bilāskhānī Toḍī* in *Jhūmrā Tāl*, *Rāg Yaman* in *Tīn tāl*

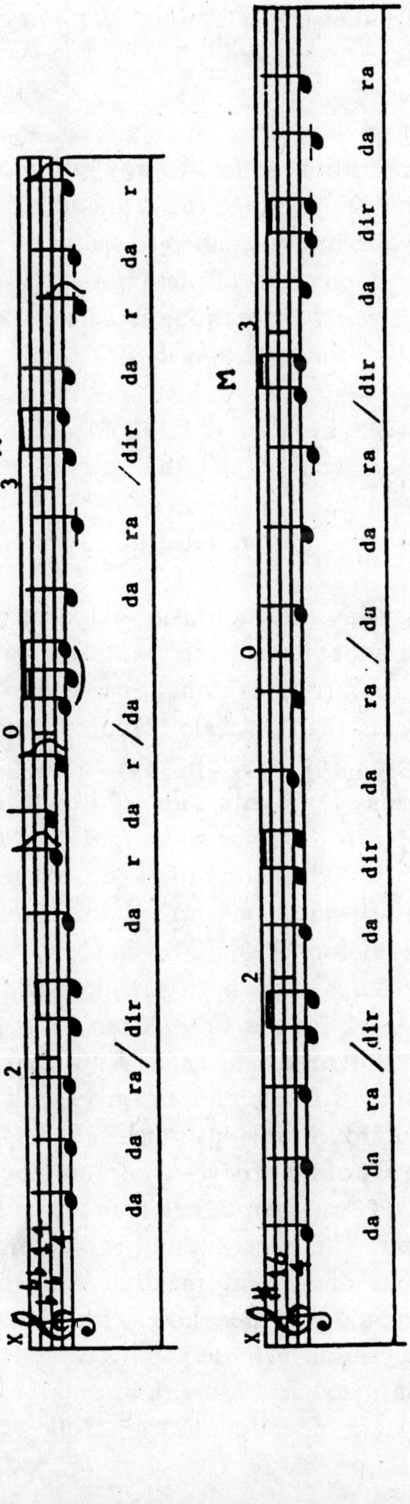

The same *bol* pattern is maintained in the *manjhā* and *antarā* (not notated) and the *gat* is similar in all other respects to the *vilambit gat* in *tīn-tāl.*

5.1.2 ***Drut gat (tīn-tāl)***

The term *drut gat* (H. 'fast composition') refers to any *gat* in a fast tempo (e.g. 150-400 *mātrā*-s per minute). Although the *drut gat* has as its prototype the *Razākhānī gat*, the genre has diversified to such an extent that it is no longer possible to group the corpus of them into a standard form. The original *gat*-s of the *Razākhānī bāj* are thought to have started from the seventh *mātrā*, incorporating the following *bol*:

1	2	3	4	5	6	7	8	9	10	11	12	13	14	15	16
						dir	dir	da	rda	-r	da	da	dir	da	ra
da	—	—	ra	da	ra										

(Shankar, personal communication: June, 1977)

This *bol* is found in many *drut gat*-s today, but compositional forms have incorporated other tactics of structure that have led to a wide diversity of archetypal forms comprising the genre. Compositional procedures may include: (1) starting the *gat* from any *mātrā* in the cycle, (2) composing the *sthāyī* in two *āvartan*-s (H. 'revolution' [of a cycle]), thus creating two *sam*-s in the *sthāyī*, each of which may serve as a cadence point in the cycle[1], and (3) composing the *sthāyī* in the form of a *tihāī* (H. 'three times'), a cadence formula in which a rhythmic motif is constructed in such a way as to allow the end of third statement of the motif to either elide with or terminate immediately before the *sam* or *mukhṛa*.

The *Razākhānī gat* in Example 5-5 a, b, c has been transnotated from the *Sitār Darpaṇ*, an instructional book for the *sitār* (Khan 1972: 210-211). The composition is credited to Bhikan Khan, a *sitār*-ist of the early twentieth century. The *mizrāb bol* of the *sthāyī* of the *gat* agrees with that expressed by Shankar as being standard in previous times. The *bol*-s of the *manjhā* and *antarā* differ from that of the *sthāyī*—a common occurrence in *drut gat*-s. Also, while the *sthāyī* and *manjhā* begin on the seventh *mātrā*, the *antarā* begins on the *sam*. This presents no problem in the performance situation, where periods of melodic inactivity are freely incorporated. In this gat, the *antarā* could be either elided with the *sthāyī* at *sam*, or could be started after a cycle of melodic inactivity.

Though *drut gat*-s are not standardized according to internal rhythmic structure, form (at least to the extent of sectionalization) follows the

Ex. 5-5 *Razākhānī Gat—Rāg Toḍī*

Ex. 5-5c *Antarā*

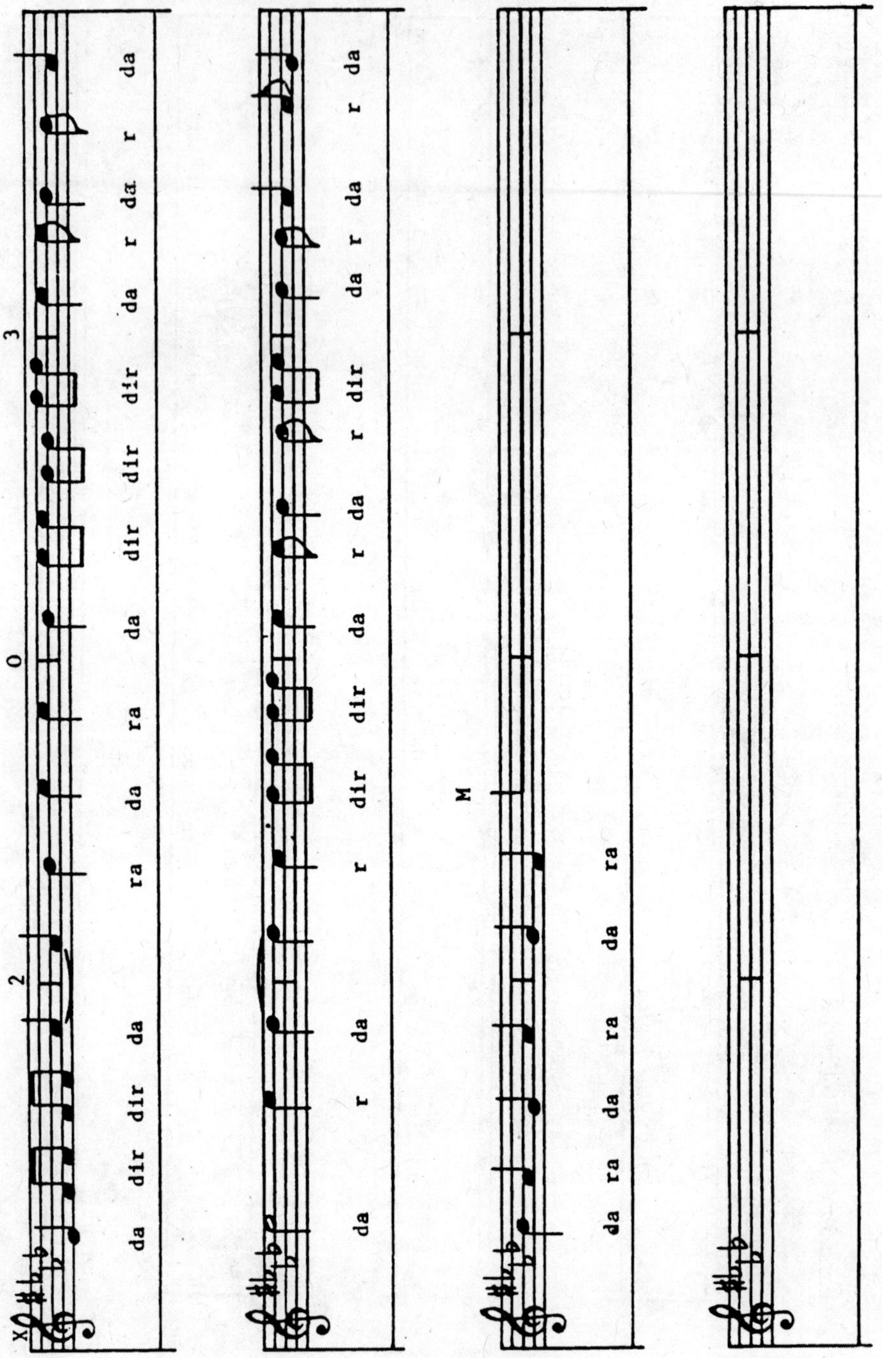

same principles as those governing the *vilambit gat*. While occasionally one may encounter a *drut gat* lacking *manjhā* or *antarā*, the principle of contrasting sections is, for the most part, adhered to.

A *drut gat* in *rāg Kāmod*, starting from m 16 of *tīn-tāl* is seen Example 5-6 a, b, c. The *gat* is comprised of a *sthāyī*, *manjhā*, and *antarā*, each starting on the sixteenth *mātrā* of the *tāl*. This particular *gat* is rather unusual in that the *mukhṛā* is only one *mātrā* in length. The one-*mātrā* *mukhṛā* is created by dividing the last group of four *mātrā*-s as 3-1 with the use of the *bol*-s '*dar*' and '*dir*', the *bol* '*dir*' serving as *mukhṛā*.

The *drut gat* in *rāg Yaman* (Ex. 5-7a, b) begins on the *sam* of the *tāl*, contains a *sthāyī* two *āvartan*-s long, and incorporates a *tihāī* in the second line of the *antarā* which serves as a return to the *sthāyī*. The repeated unit of the *tihāī* is defined by the *mizrāb bol* five *mātrā*-s long—'*dira r dir da ra*'. The groupings of the beats according to the *bol* pattern are as follows:

(a) *sthāyī* 3-3-3-2-3 and 3-3-5-5

(b) *antarā* 5-5-3-3 and (1)-5-5-5

It is evident that consistency of internal rhythmic structure within the sections of a *drut gat* is not considered to be mandatory. Both this *gat* and the preceding example were composed by Lalmani Misra.

5.1.3 *Kūṭ-bāj gat*-s

The term '*kūṭ bāj*' is applied to those *gat*-s that are composed in *tāl*-s other than *tīn-tāl*, regardless of the *lay*. These *gat*-s follow the same structural principle of sectionalization as were discussed above. A common feature of *kūṭ-bāj gat*-s is that their *mizrāb-bol* patterns are usually governed by the divisions of the *tāl* in which they are composed (Misra, personal communication: March 13, 1978). Occasionally, as in the *Masītkhānī bāj* the *bol* will be out of synchronization with the *tāl* cycle at certain points of stress. A number of bol patterns composed for *kūṭ-bāj gat*-s are seen in Figure 12. Excepting the *bol* for *ek-tāl*, all are styled to the division of the *tāl*. The *bol* for *jhap-tāl* is evidently a modification of the *mizrāb bol* of *Masītkhānī gat* (cf. Ex. 5-4).

A *kūṭ-bāj gat* in *rāg Śyām Kalyāṇ* is seen in Example 5-8 a, b. The *gat* is composed in *āṛā cautāl* (fourteen *mātrā*-s; divided 6-4-4) in a medium tempo (e.g. 80-160 mātrā-s per minute). The *sthāyī* has the same *mizrāb bol* as is seen in the example of *āṛā cautāl* in Figure 12. Although this *bol* is varied in the remaining lines, the division of each line into six- and eight-*mātrā* portions is maintained.

Ex. 5-6 *Drut Gat* in *Tīn-tāl—Rāg Kāmod*

a) Sthāyī

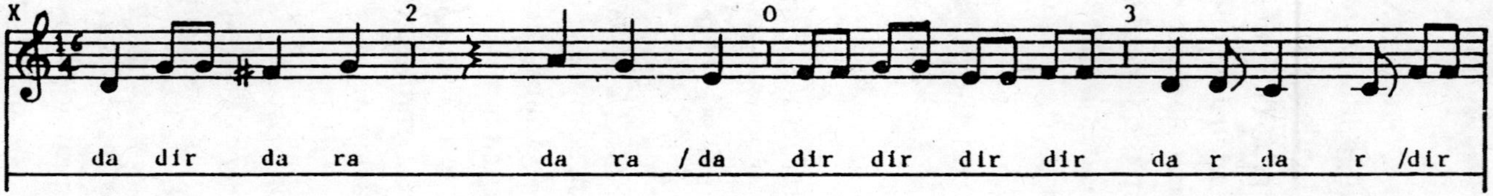

b) *Manjhā*

c) *Antarā*

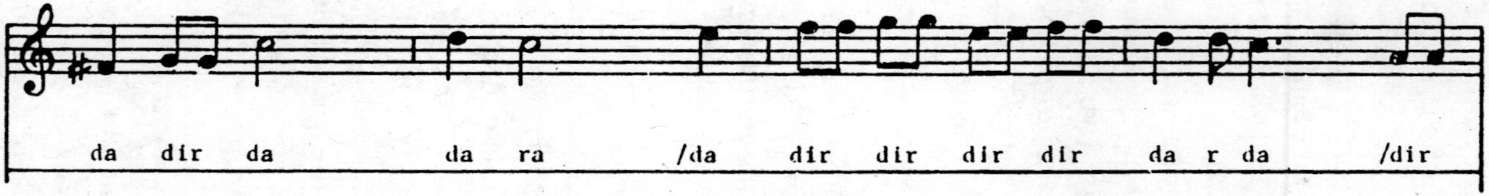

Ex. 5-7 *Drut Gat* in *Tintāl*—*Rāg Yaman*

a) *Sthāyī*

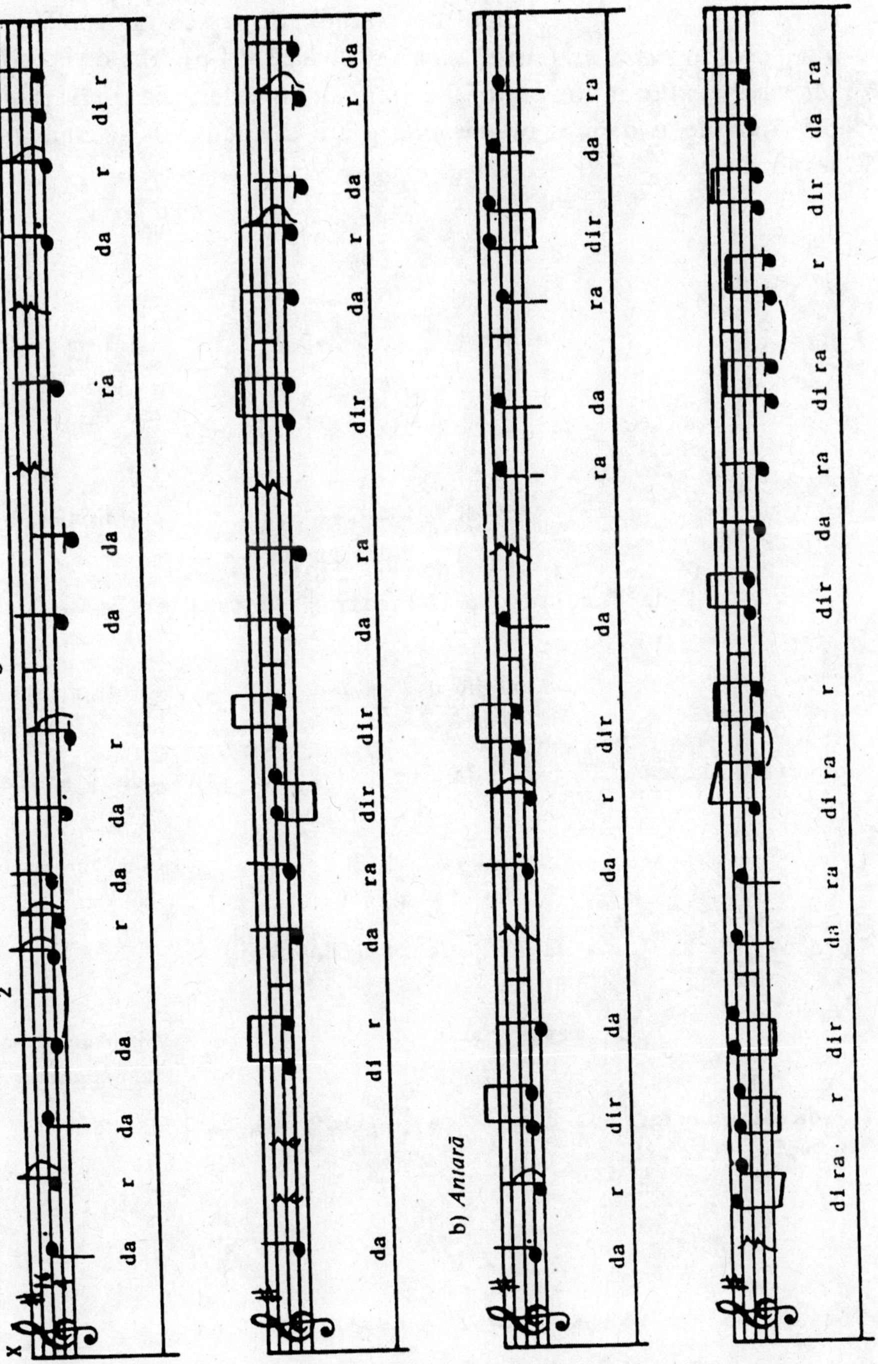

The *kūṭ-bāj gat* in Example 5-9 a, b, c displays greater variation in the *mizrāb bol* of each line than the example discussed above. The *gat* is composed in *rudra tāl* (eleven *mātrā*-s; divided 4-4-3). The division of the *tāl* is adhered to in the *bol* of the *manjhā*; however, the *sthāyī* is divided 6-5 and the two lines of the *antarā* are divided 3-3-3-2 and 2-3-3-3, respectively.

jhap-tāl 2-3-2-3 (Misra 1973:31)

```
X       2           0 M      3
 da ra | da da ra | dir da | rda -da -r
```

ek-tāl 4-4-2-2 (Misra 1973:31)

```
X    0        2       0        3       4
da - | da dir | da ra | da dir | da ra | da ra
```

āṛā cautāl 6-4-4 (Misra 1973:31)

```
X       2       0       3        0         4        0
 da dir | da ra | da ra | da dir | dir dir | da rda | -r da
```

rūpak tāl 3-2-2 (Shankar, personal communication)

```
0          1       2
 da da ra | da ra | da ra
```

F pañcam savārī tāl 4-4-4-3 (Shankar, personal communication)

```
X              2              0              3
 da dir da ra | da dir da ra | da dir da ra | da rda -r
```

Figure 12: *Mizrāb Bol*-s of *Kut-Bāj Gat*-s

Ex. 5-8 *Kūṭ-Bāj Gat* in *Āṛā Cautāl— Rāg Śyām Kalyāṇ*

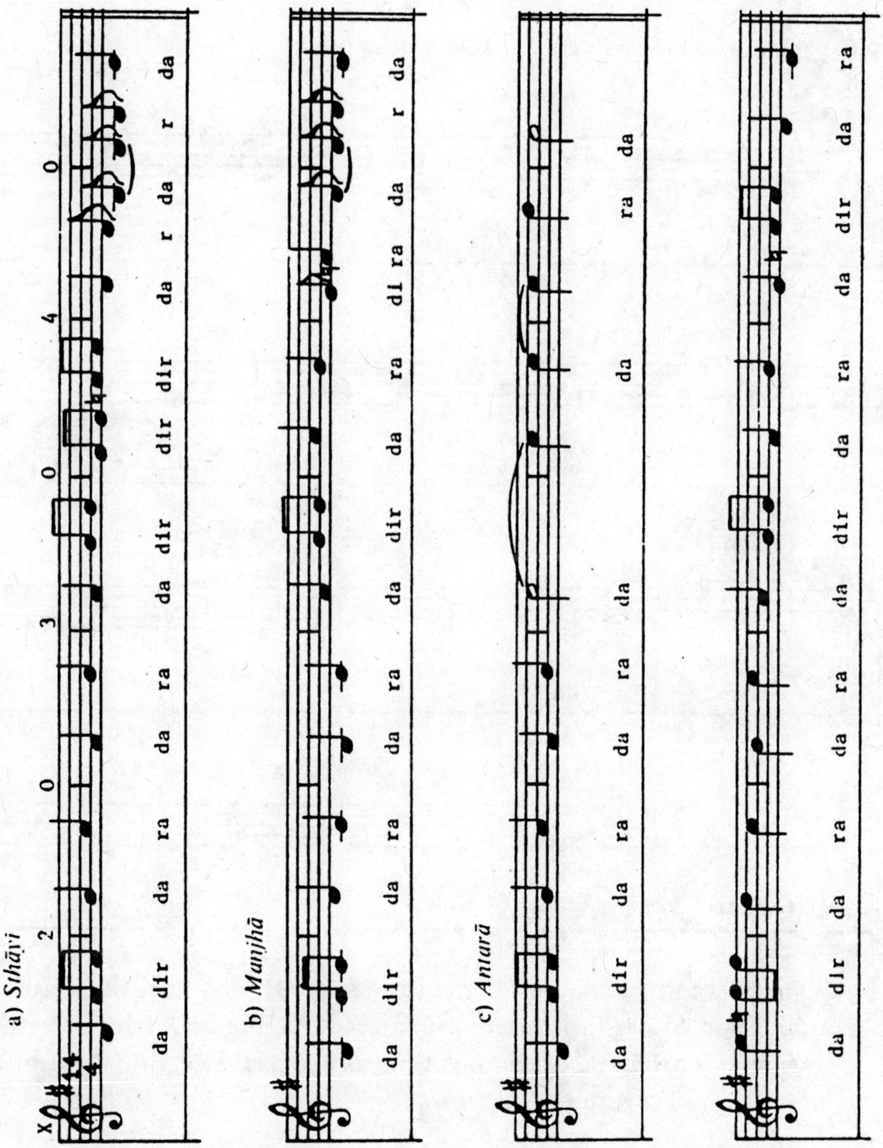

Ex. 5-9 *Kūṭ-Bāj Gat* in *Rudra Tāl*– *Rāg Hansadhvani*

The preceding examples of *drut* and *kūṭ-bāj gat*-s have illustrated the combination of pre-fabricated *bol* patterns having an intrinsic rhythmic duration as a principle of composition, as well as the sectionalization of a composition according to *tessitura*.

5.2 Gat Vistār

Gat vistār refers to the expansion, or development, of the *gat*. In the performance situation, the method of *gat vistār* is primarily improvisational. There are two general improvisational processes active during *gat vistār*: (1) variation of the pre-composed *gat*, and (2) alternation of the precomposed *gat*, or fragments of it, with stylized formal elements such as *tān*-s, *toṛā*-s and *tihāī*-s. *Gat vistār* in the performance situation will be dealt with in detail in Chapter VII.

In the *tālīm*, a far greater emphasis is put on the latter of the abovementioned processes than the former. It has been my own experience that the technique of varying the *gat* is learned through an osmosis process. During the teaching process, the *guru* will rarely play the *gat* the same way twice after the student has mastered the standardized form of it. Rather, on each return to the *gat*, he will create some variation to please both himself and the student. Once the variation is performed, it either passes into oblivion or is stored in the subconscious of one or both of the participants, hopefully to resurface during some performance or teaching situation in the future.

A great deal of time is devoted to the creation and memorization of *tān*-s, *toṛā*-s, and *tihāī*-s in the *tālīm*. According to Ravi Shankar, the logic behind teaching improvisation through memorization is analogous to programming a computer.

> It is the teacher's responsibility to fill the student with "fixed" improvisations. It is like programming a computer—once the student is fed all the data, he stores it in his memory cells through rigorous practice, and then in a performance situation, the correct data needed to "solve a problem" [such as ending a tān with a tihāī that elides with sam] will emerge effortlessly.
>
> (Personal communication: June, 1977)

5.2.1 *Vistār in vilambit gat*

During the last thirty years, a systematic method of development of the *vilambit gat* has evolved from the format that had been prevalent during the nineteenth and early twentieth centuries. The principle underlying the process is that each tone of the *rāg*, and each *layakārī* (H. 'division of the *mātrā*') in the *tāl*, receives amplification by becoming the focus, in successive stages, of improvisational passages. The process is known as *śṛṅkhalā*, or *silsillā* (H. 'progression'), and is synonomous with that I have termed the substratum repertory. Although the *śṛṅkhalā* serves as a convenient frame for *gat vistār* in both the teaching and performing situations, it is not considered to be a canon to which a performer must adhere.

The following examples are representative of the *śṛṅkhalā* of the *gat vistār* according to Ravi Shankar. Each illustrates a particular stage in the progression of the *vistār*. It should be noted that although this method of *vistār* is very widespread among *sitār*-ists, there may be certain schools that have a different opinion of the manner in which *gat vistār* should be performed. All the examples are in *rāg Yaman Kalyāṇ*. Each example starts on the first beat of the *tāl* and ends just before the *mukhṛā* of the gat (see Ex. 5-1). A return to the *mukhṛā*, or variation of the same, would be the normal procedure after the performance of each example.

After playing the *sthāyī* and *manjhā*, the characteristics of each tone in the rāg are explored in *baṛhat* tān-s. In a *baṛhat* (H. 'increase') *tān*, a particular tone of the *rāg* is emphasized in a passage comprised of melodic fragments performed in *ālāp* style (incorporating a preponderance of *mīṇḍ*). Example 5-10 is a *baṛhat* tān on *niṣād* (H. 'seventh scale-degree'). The most obvious feature of a *baṛhat tān* is that the number of tones articulated by left-hand techniques far exceeds the number by right-hand strokes. The right-hand strokes in this example are, for the most part, on the beat. In the teaching session with Ravi Shankar, a number of *baṛhat tān*-s of a similar nature were taught for each successive scale degree in the ascent up to and including tone b^1, after which the *antarā* was taught (see Ex. 5-1c). Thus, the *sthāyī, manjhā, baṛhat* tān-s, and *antarā* comprise a full exploration of the melodic relationships of the tones of the *rāg*. After completing this section of the *gat vistār*, Ravi Shankar proceeded to teach a number of sets of *tān*-s, each set representing a particular rhythmic division of the *mātrā*.

The *vilambit tān* shown in Example 5-11 is very similar in rhythmic structure to a *baṛhat tān*. However, ornamentation is more varied, and the melodic line has better defined contours than was seen in the *baṛhat tān*, in which a principal tone acted as an anchor to melodic activity. *Mīṇḍ*$_1$ (m 1), and *krintan*$_1$ (m 8) as well as *kaṇ* (m 2, 3) and *gamak*$_1$ (m 5) are all incorporated in this example. In that the right-hand strokes are generally one per *mātrā*, this *tān* could also be called a *thā guṇ tān*. *Thā guṇ* (H. 'equal [number of] times') refers to the division of the *mātrā* by one, resulting in one rhythmic pulse per *mātrā*, and on the beat.

Examples 5-12 through 5-18 are representative of the process of the progressive division of the *mātrā* in performing *gat vistār*. Each example represents a different *layakāri*, and the order of the examples indicates the progression of the *layakārī*-s in the *tālīm śṛṅkhalā*. It is interesting to note that the criterion for assigning a *layakārī* to a melodic passage is the number of articulations performed by the right hand. Thus, while five of the first eight *mātrā*-s of Example 5-12 contain more than two notes, the right-hand articulations create the impression that each *mātrā* is comprised of two prominent tones, one on the downbeat and one on the upbeat. Such *tān*-s are known as *du guṇ* (H. 'two times') *tān*-s. *Du guṇ* refers to the division of the *mātrā* into two equal parts. The techniques of *kaṇ* (m 1, 2), *krintan*$_1$ (m 4), and *gamak*$_1$ (m 7) serve to embellish the

Ex. 5-10 Baṛhat Tān

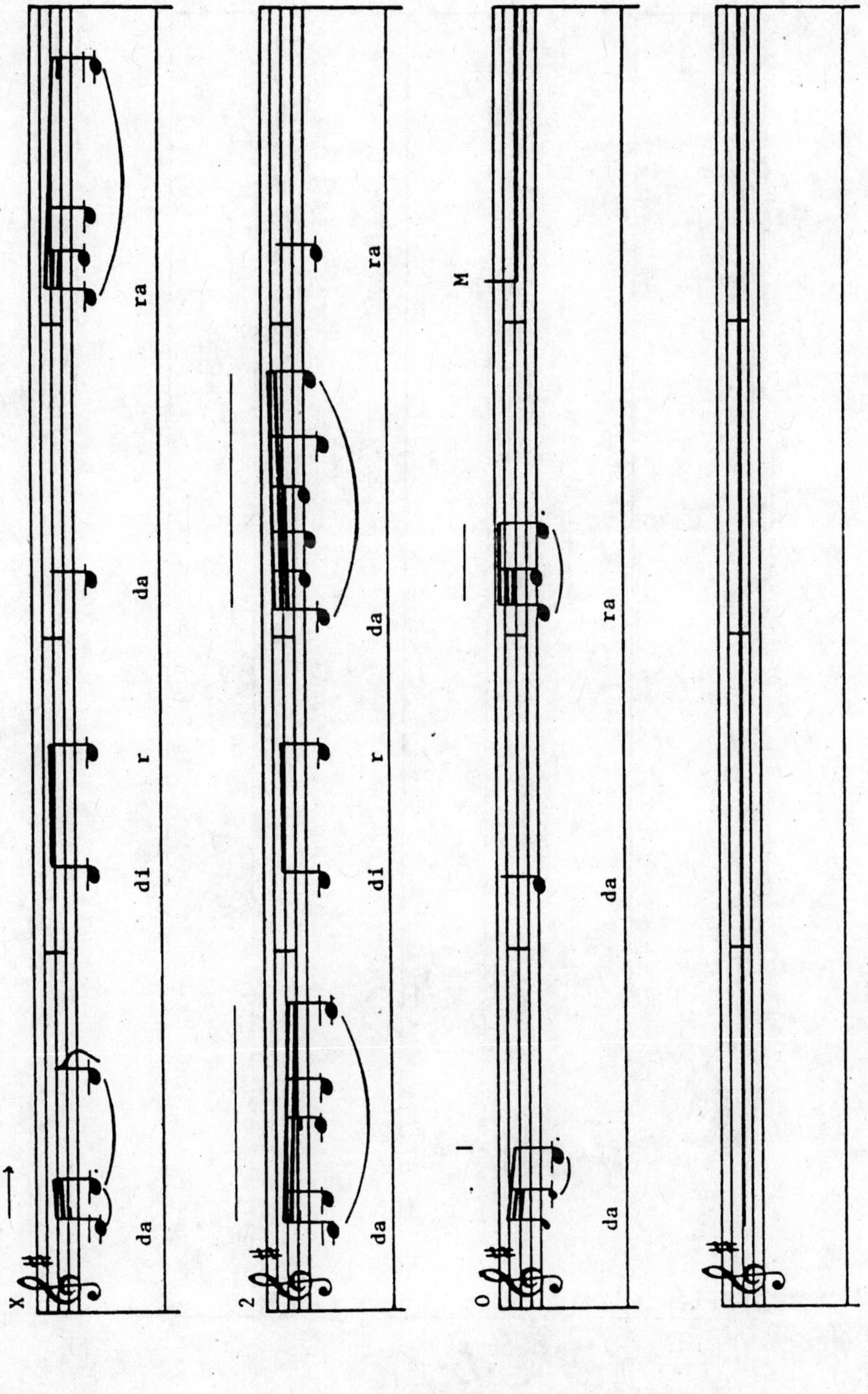

Ex. 5-11 *Vilambit Tān*

principal tones. The composite of the techniques *krintan, gharṣaṇ*, and *mīṇḍ* is seen in m 9 of Example 5-12.

Example 5-13 is a *ti guṇ* (H. 'three times') *tān*. *Ti guṇ* refers to the division of the *mātrā* into three equal parts. This *tān* exemplifies transposition in improvisation as a compositional device. The *tān* is comprised of three melodic motifs (m 1-2, 5-6, and 9, respectively), the first two of which are transposed once each, and the third, twice. The first motif, with its transposition, defines a statement that is answered by the second motif and its transpositions. This concluding event is known as a *tihāī*, which functions here as a cadence to the *mukhṛā*.

Example 5-14 is a *cau guṇ* (H. 'four times') *tān*. *Cau guṇ* refers to the division of the beat into four equal parts. The *tān* is comprised of a *sapāṭ* passage (i.e., a straight line in the ascent and descent) and a *tihāī*. The particular method of forming the *tihāī* incorporated in this example has been devised by Ravi Shankar. The method may be elucidated by analysis of the example. The *tihāī* begins on the second quarter of the fifth *mātrā*. The melodic motif of the *tihāī* is one and three quarters of a *mātrā* long and is transposed twice, a half-*mātrā* rest (articulated by *cikārī* strokes) intervening before each transposition. The last transposition ends on the second quarter of m 11 and is followed by a half-*mātrā* rest before the return to the *mukhṛā*. By the inclusion of the rests into the melodic motif, it becomes evident that this *tihāī* is comprised of three sections, each two and one quarter (9/4) *mātrā*-s in length. The method of construction requires working backwards from the *mukhṛā*. The process may be summarized in the following steps:

(a) Define the motivic length of the *tihāī* relative to the *layakārī*. (In Ex. 5-14, nine quarters *mātrā*-s.)

(b) Compose a melodic motif not exceeding the above length. (In Ex. 5-14, motif = seven quarters *mātrā*-s.)

(c) Formulate the motivic unit by adding the required number of rests to the melodic motif necessary to expand the motif to the motivic length. (In Ex. 5-14, rests = two quarters *mātrā*.)

(d) Count backwards three motivic lengths from the last division of the eleventh *mātrā* in order to find the correct starting place for the *tihāī*.

(e) Perform the motivic unit three times, creating a *tihāī*. Although this process is quite simple, it results in *tihāī*-s of great rhythmic complexity.

The *pāñc guṇ* (H. 'five times') *tān* in Example 5-15 is based on the division of the *mātrā* into five equal parts. The *tān* is comprised of three motifs: the first motif repeats twice at transpositions of a third; the second

Ex. 5-12 *Du guṇ Tān*

Ex. 5-13 Ti guṇ Tān

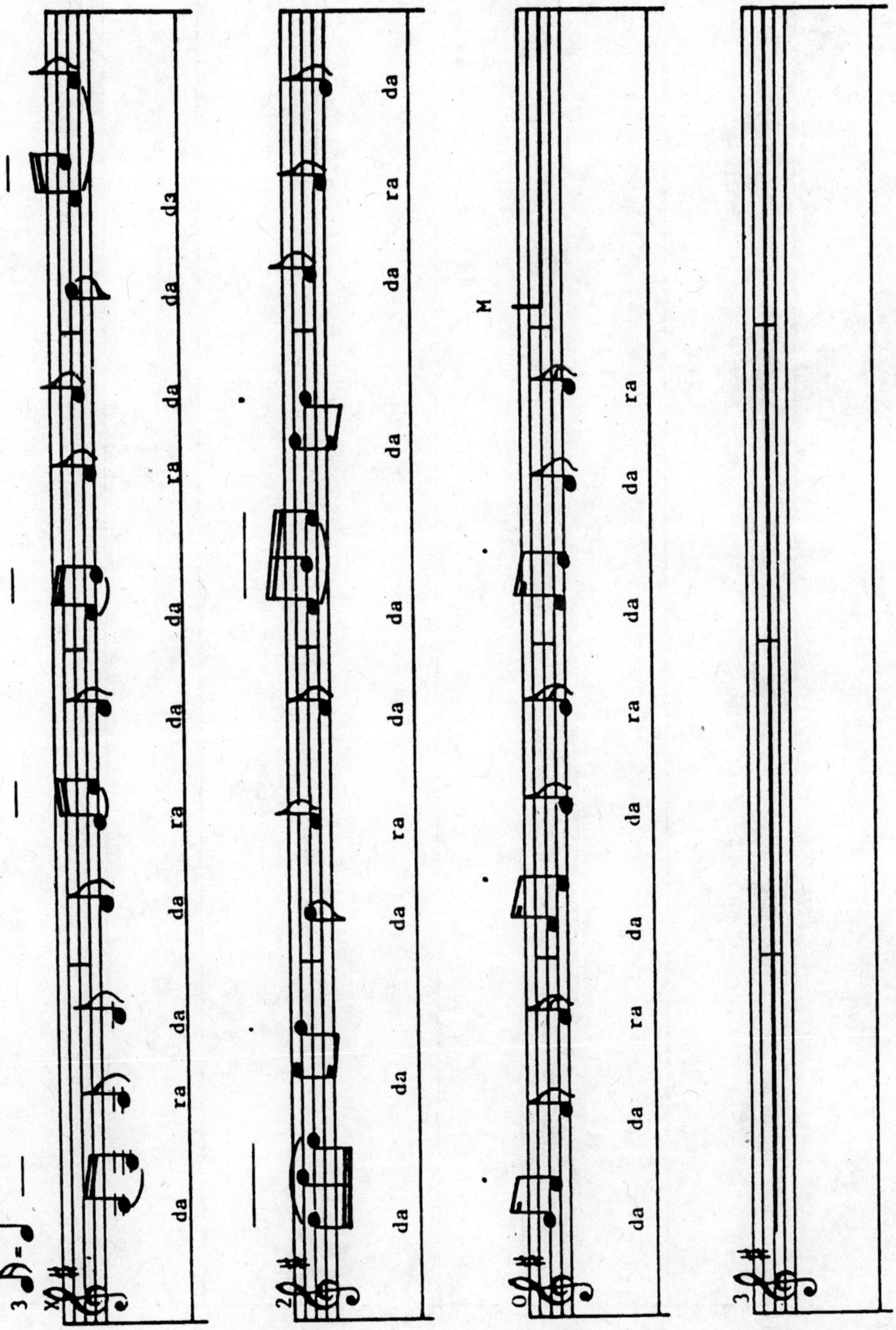

Ex. 5-14 *Cau guṇ Tān*

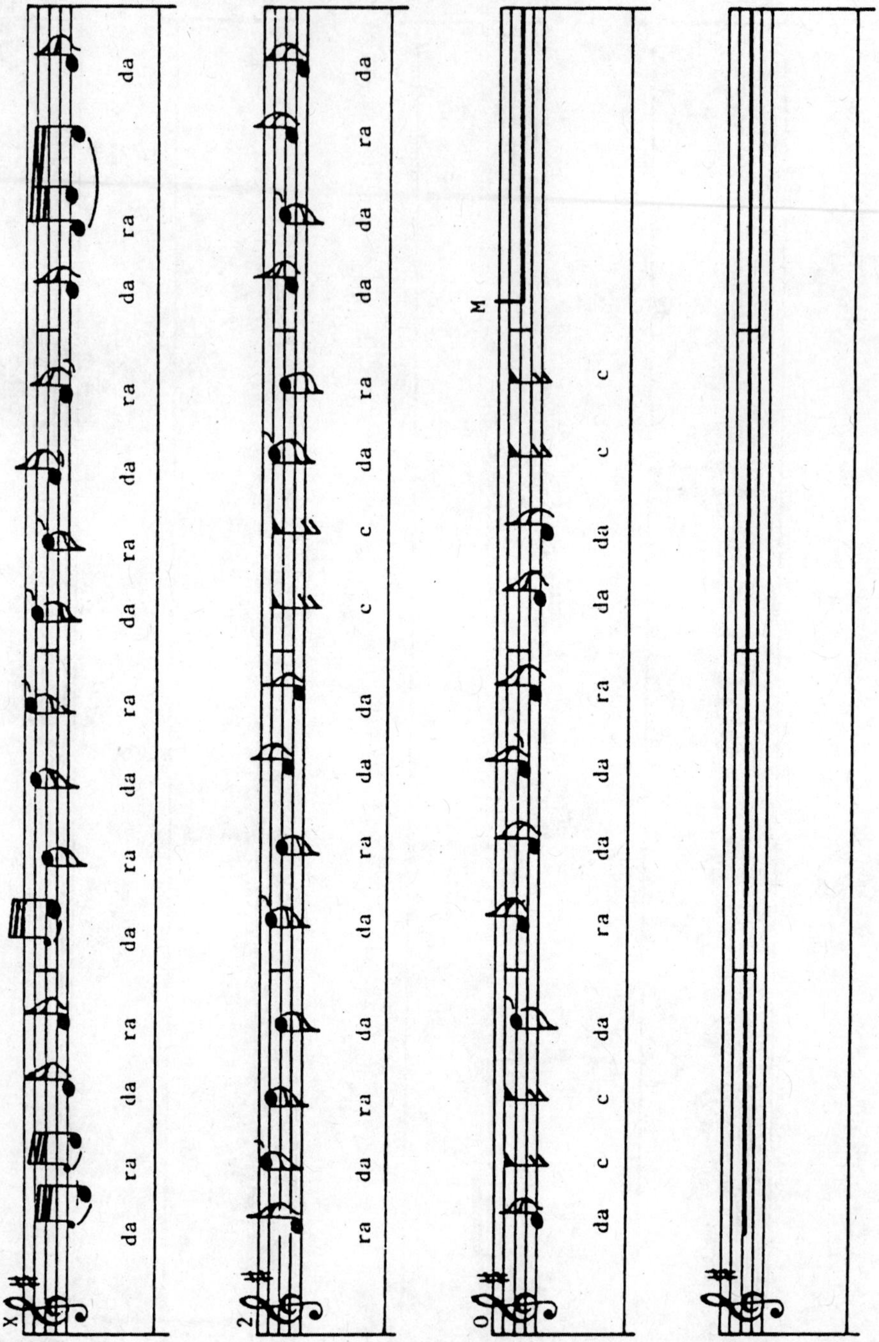

consists of a descending *sapāṭ*, passage; the third repeats twice to form a *tihāī*. The motivic unit of the *tihāī* is one *mātrā* long. A subtle variation of articulation occurs at the second fifth of a *mātrā* in the first *mātrā* of the first motif with the technique, *krintan*. A '*rā*' stroke on the cikari strings could be interpolated at this point to maintain the proper kinesthetic balance in the right hand *mizrāb* pattern.

Example 5-16 is a *chaḥ guṇ* (H. 'six times') *tān*. *Chaḥ guṇ* means the division of the *mātrā* into six equal parts. Both of the *mizrāb bol*-s commonly used in *chaḥ guṇ tān*-s are illustrated in the example. The more common of these is the grouping 3-3 seen in the *bol* '*da ra da da ra da*'. The other, 2-2-2, is '*da ra da ra da ra*'. In this example, '*da ra da ra da ra*' is expanded by doubling each of the groups, resulting in twelve units divided 4-4-4; and modified by deleting the '*ra*' strokes occurring on the second, sixth, and tenth subdivisions of the two-*mātrā* phrase (m 1 and 2). The articulation is performed at these places by *krintan*.

Examples 5-17 and 5-18 are representative of the last two stages in the *śṛṇkhalā* of the *gat vistār* in the *vilambit gat*, that is, *tān*-s in *sāt guṇ* (H.'seven times') and *āṭh guṇ* (H. 'eight times') *layakārī*-s, respectively. Example 5-17 is based on a division of the beat into seven equal units. In this example, the predominant grouping of the seven is 4-3, although a syncopation created by grouping fourteen units across two *mātrā*-s as 3-3-4-4 occurs (m 7 and 8). Two techniques common in *āṭh guṇ tān*-s are seen in Example 5-18: (1) the double (or more) articulation of a tone with *gamak* (m 1), and (2) the incorporation of *mīṇḍ* in *tān*-s (m 1 and 2). A summary of the *sṛṅkhalā* of the *gat vistār* is depicted in Figure 13. As shown in the figure, the *gat vistār* may be considered as bi-sectional—the first section oriented towards a full exposition of the melodic characteristics of the *rāg*, the second towards the development of *layakārī*-s (i.e., rhythmic intricacies). The tendency of musicians to relax the rules governing melodic progression in the *rāg* in order to facilitate the performance of rhythmically complex, or very fast, *tān*-s would appear to support this observation.

5.2.2 *Vistār in drut gat*

Vistār in the *drut gat* is usually not as systematic nor as diversified as in the *vilambit gat*. The usual practice is to play the *sthāyī* and *manjhā* of the *gat*, and then perform short *tān*-s (i.e., less than one *āvartan* in length) which either end on *sam*, or, if the *gat* is composed with a *mukhṛā*, on *mukhṛā* (see 6.3 [*drut gat*] *āvartan* 7). The *tān*-s are, for the most part, in *du guṇ layakārī* (which, in the *lay* of the *drut gat*, approximates the

Ex. 5-15 *Pañc guṇ Tān*

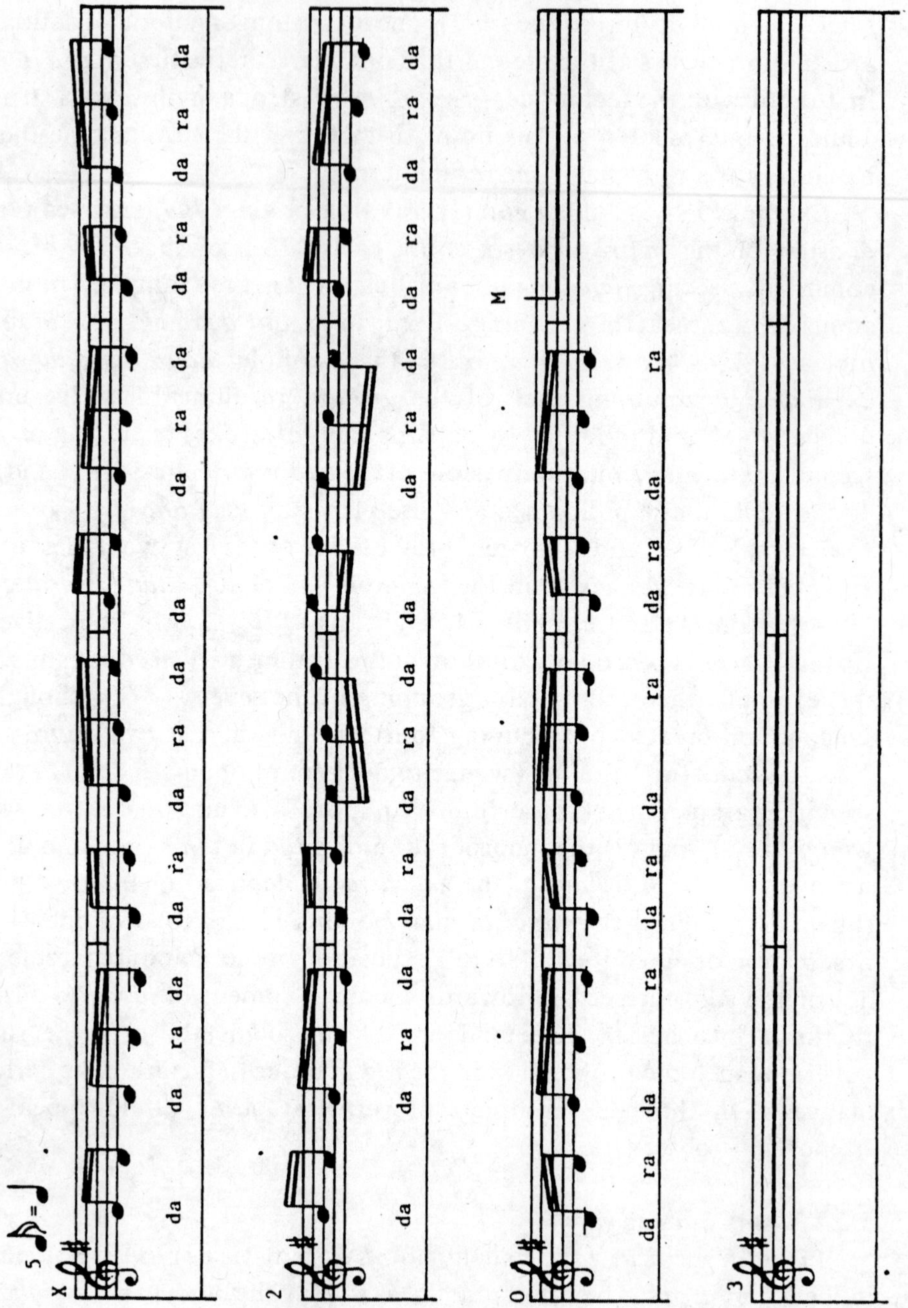

Ex. 5-16 *Chaḥ guṇ Tān*

Ex. 5-17 *Sāī guṇ Tān*

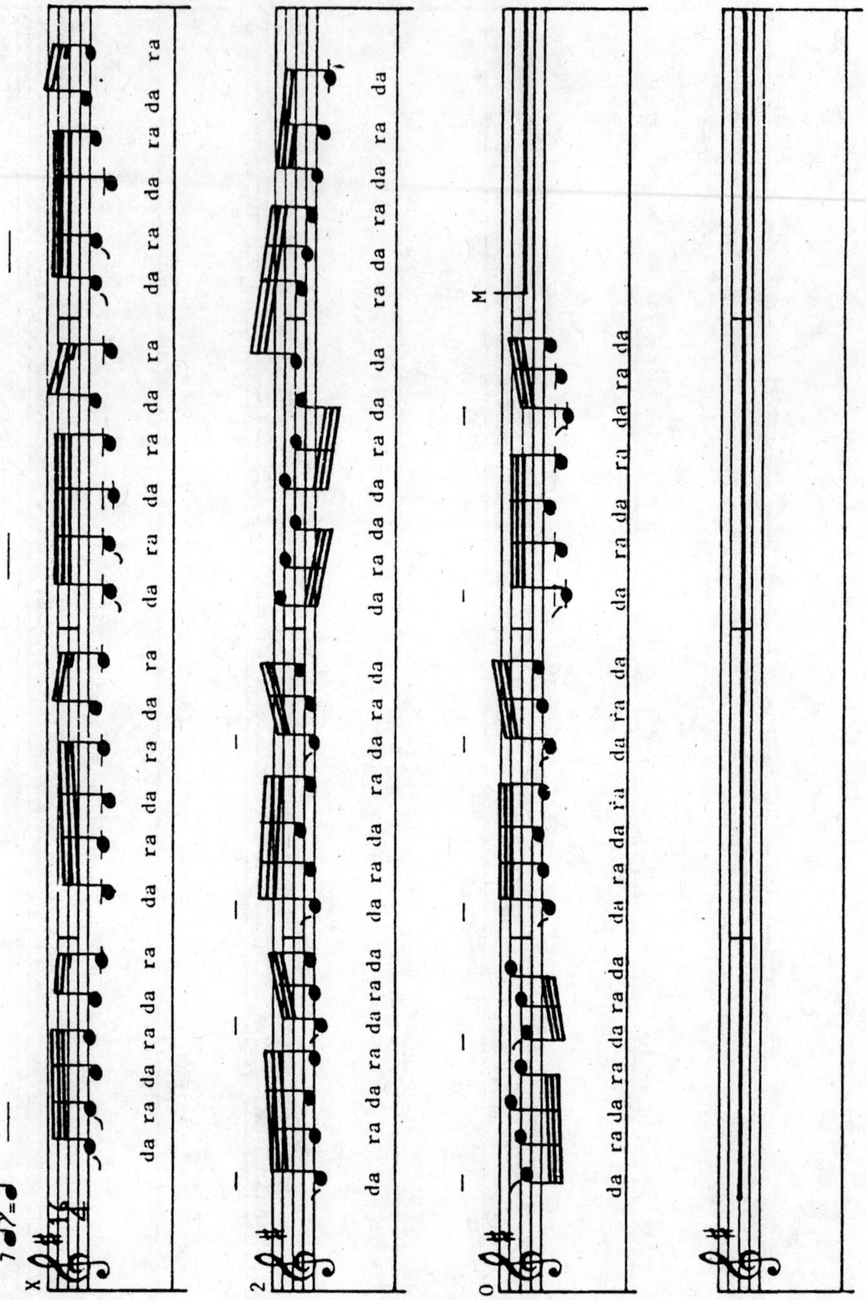

Ex. 5-18 *Āṛi guṇ Tān*

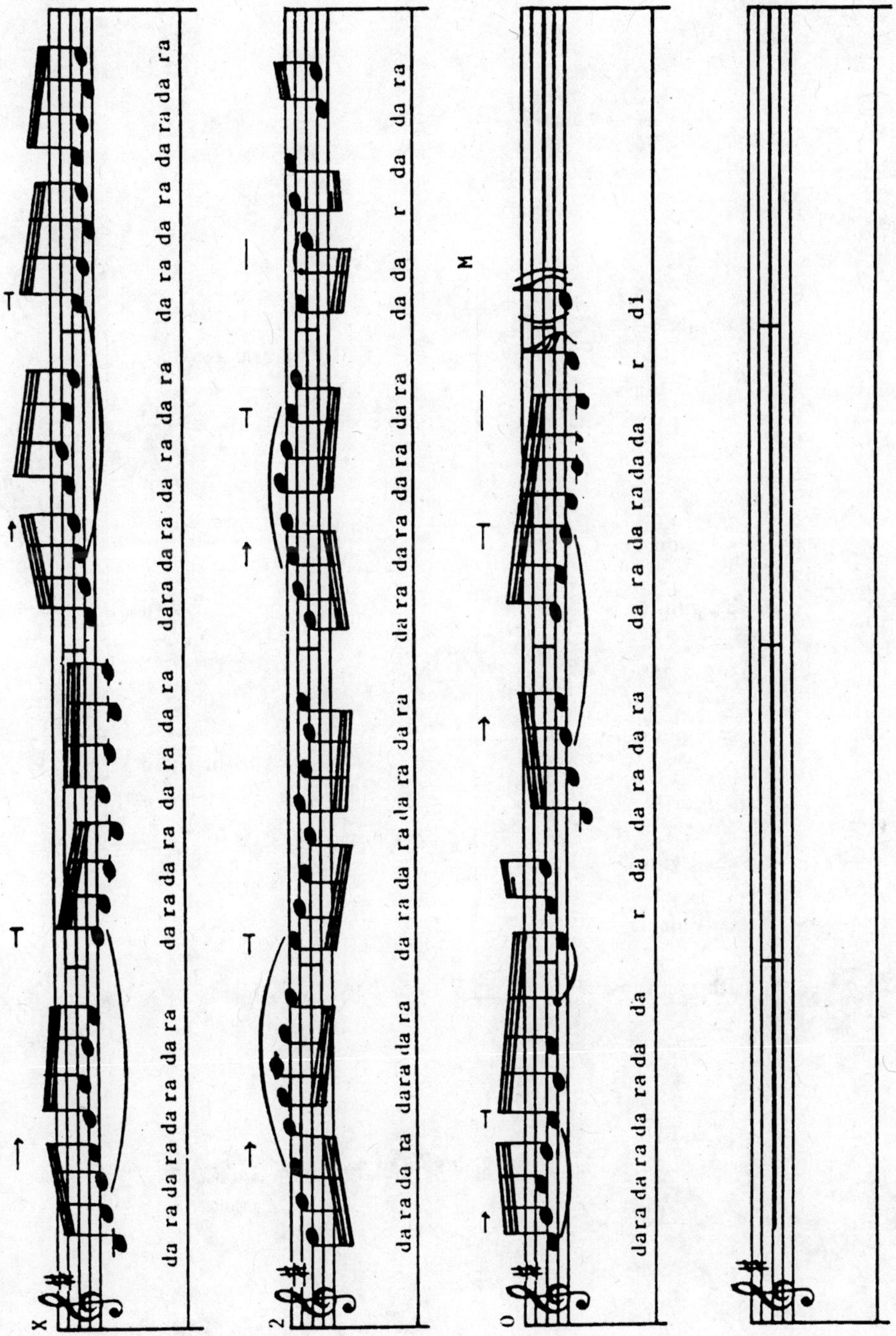

sthāyī manjhā baṛhat tān-s antarā	Rāg-oriented
vilambit tān-s du guṇ tān-s ti guṇ tān-s cau guṇ tān-s pāñc guṇ tān-s chaḥ guṇ tān-s sāt guṇ tān-s āṭh guṇ tān-s	Layakārī-oriented

Figure 13: Śṛṅkhalā of *Vilambit Gat Vistār*

density referent produced by the *āṭh guṇ tān* in a *vilambit lay*). Following these short *tān*-s, the *antarā* may be played, after which varieties of *tān*-s are developed, usually in *du guṇ layakārī* although, as the tempo is increased, *āṛī* (H. 'slanted') and *thā guṇ layakārī*-s may arise (see 6.3. [*drut gat*] *āvartan*-s 53-56). *Āṛī layakārī* refers to the cross rhythms three against two and four against three. The *tān*-s may be ended with a *tihāī* (see 6.3 [*drut gat*] *āvartan*-s 15-19), or may themselves elide with the *sam* or *mukhṛā* of the *gat*. As the *gat vistār* progresses, *tān*-s are likely to become longer and also acquire a greater melodic range.

Two stylized formal elements, *toṛā* and *jhālā*, which had previously (i.e., prior to 1930) been performed in the *Masītkhānī gat* are now performed in the *drut gat*. Some artists still play *toṛā*-s in the *vilambit gat*; however, the tendency is to restrict their use to *gat*-s in *madhya* and *drut lay*-s.

Examples 5-19 and 5-20 are representative of the types of *bol* combinations incorporated in *toṛā*-s. As mentioned before, both strokes of the '*dir*' *bol* usually articulate the same pitch (when occurring in a *toṛā*). The *bol* incorporated in the first two lines of Example 5-19 is ubiquitous among *sitār*-ists. It is one of the first extended *bol*-s taught to students because the double articulations make left-hand technique simple in that there are fewer movements necessary to provide a melodic line. Example 5-20 incorporates more complex *bol*-s and also a difficult insertion of *krintan* between the '*ra*' and '*r*' strokes of the composite *bol* pattern '*dira r da*'. Whereas the *toṛā* in Example 5-19 incorporates repeating lines, Example 5-20 is through composed.

Jhālā is believed to have originated as an imitation on *bīn* of certain drum strokes performed on the *pakhāvaj* (see 3.3). *Jhālā* is now used primarily as a concluding section in a *drut gat*. It may also be performed as a conclusion to the *ālāp* and *joṛ* of the solo movement in a *sitār* performance. As a formal element, *jhālā* refers to the activity of alternating strokes on the *bāj* wire with strokes on the *cikārī* wires at very high speeds (e.g. 400-500 *mātrā*-s per minute). When only '*da*' strokes are played on the *bāj* wire, the *jhālā* is referred to as *śuddh* (H. 'pure') *jhālā*. When other *bol-s* in addition to '*da*' are played on the *bāj* wire, the *jhālā* is known as *ṭhoṅk* (H. 'hammering') *jhālā*. Some common *bol* pattern of both types of *jhālā* are listed in Figure 14.

5.2.3 *Vistār in kūṭ-bāj gat*-s

The *vistār of kūṭ bāj gat*-s is dependent upon the *lay* in which they are meant to be performed. Those that are to be performed in a *vilambit lay*

Ex. 5-19 *Toṛā*

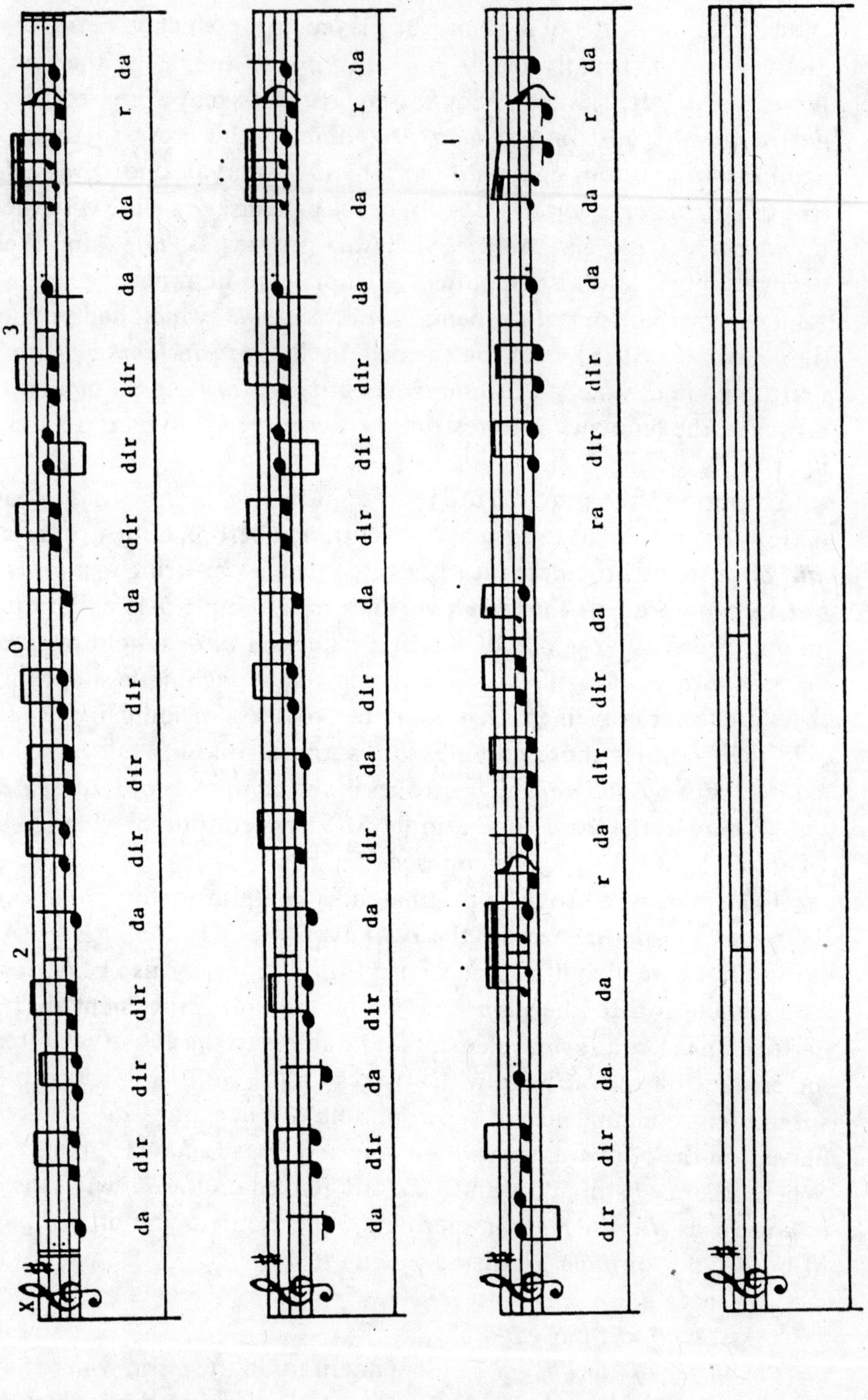
X
2
0
3
da dir dir dir da dir dir da dir dir dir da da r da
da dir da dir da dir da dir da dir dir da da r da
dir dir da da r da dir dir da ra dir dir da da r da

Ex. 5-20 *Toṛā*

X 2 0 3
da dir da di ra r da da ra da ra dir dir da r da r da
da dir da di ra r da da dir da di ra r da da di ra r da
da dir da ra da ra da ra da ra dir dir da da r da

Śuddh Jhālā

	X				2				0				3			
a)	da	c	c	c	da	c	c	c	da	c	c	c	da	c	c	c
b)	c	da	c	c	c	da	c	c	c	da	c	c	c	da	c	c
c)	c	c	da	c	c	c	da	c	c	c	da	c	c	c	da	c
d)	c	c	c	da	c	c	c	da	c	c	c	da	c	c	c	da
e)	da	c	c	da	c	c	da	c	da	c	c	da	c	c	da	c
f)	c	da	da	da	c	da	da	da	c	da	da	da	c	da	da	da
g)	c	da	da	c	da	da	c	da	da	c	da	da	c	da	da	da
h)	c	da	—	da	c	da	da	da	c	da	—	da	c	da	da	da
i)	da	c	c	da	c	da	da	c	da	c	c	da	c	da	da	c
j)	da	c	c	da	da	c	da	c	c	da	da	c	da	c	c	c

Ţhoṅk Jhālā

	X				2				0				3			
a)	ra	da	c	c	ra	da	c	c	ra	da	c	c	ra	da	c	c
b)	c	dir	da	c	c	dir	da	c	c	dir	da	c	c	dir	da	c
c)	da	dir	da	c	da	c	c	c	da	c	c	c	da	c	c	c
d)	da	ra	dir	dir	da	ra	dir	dir	da	ra	dir	dir	da	ra	dir	dir
	da	c	c	c	da	c	c	c	da	c	c	c	da	c	c	c
e)	dir	da	da	ra	da	c	c	c	dir	da	da	ra	da	c	c	c
f)	dir	da	c	dir	da	c	da	c	dir	da	c	dir	da	c	da	c
g)	c	dir	da	c	dir	da	c	dir	da	c	dir	da	c	dir	da	c
h)	ra	da	ra	da	ra	c	c	c	ra	c	c	c	ra	c	c	c
i)	c	da	ra	da	c	da	ra	da	c	da	ra	da	c	da	ra	da

Figure 14: *Jhālā Bol*-s (*tīn-tāl*)

will follow the *vistār* discussed in section 5.2.1, those in a *drut lay* will follow the *vistār* discussed in the preceding section. A *madhya lay gat* may follow either of the two procedures, or may combine certain elements from both, depending on the tempo.

Notes to Chapter V

1. *Gat*-s composed in this manner are often referred to as *do muhā* (H. 'two openings')

CHAPTER VI

TECHNIQUE IN PERFORMANCE PRACTICE

The concepts and practices underlying the progression of the *gat vistār* were discussed in the last chapter. In the present chapter, a detailed transcription of an actual performance will be presented; however, it is desirable to first examine some of the variables that may modify the actual course of a performance.

6.1 Musical Variables

As mentioned previously, the *sṛṅkhalā* of the *vistār* is not necessarily adhered to in performance practice. Although the relaxation of this particular order of progression is primarily the choice of the individual artist, there are certain constraints inherent in the music that also have an effect on the manner in which *gat vistār* is treated. These constraints may be categorized within the musical variables of *rāg*,*tāl*, and *lay*. The abundance of available literature dealing with these concepts obviates any necessity of discussing their definitive characteristics in the present study. However, an examination of those characteristics that exert a specific influence on *vistār* is relevant to the present discussion.

6.1.1 *Rāg*

There are certain characteristics active in defining a *rāg* that are also operative in directing the particular manner in which the *rāg prastār* is performed during *gat vistār*. Undoubtedly, the most influential of these is the *prakṛti* (Sk. 'elemental nature') of the *rāg*. According to Thakur, those *rāg*-s whose character is sprightly [cañcal] are those whose *tessitura* is predominantly in the upper region of the central octave and whose *svar*-s are not sounded with *mīṇḍ*, *āndolan*, or slow pacing. In contrast, those *rāg*-s considered to be serious in nature [*gambhir*] have their *tessitura* centered in the lower region of the central octave and dictate the usage of *mīṇḍ* and *āndolan* on specific tones, with slow pacing of melodic movement (vol. V, pt. 2:82). *Rāg*-s of a showy or self-willed character ought to be performed using only the central and upper octaves, in medium and fast tempos (vol. II, pt. 1:38-39). That such constraints would have a definite impact on the *gat vistār* is quite apparent. For instance a *rāg* considered to be sprightly in nature with a *tessitura* in the upper part of the central octave may allow only limited development in the lower octave or may even prohibit the use of that register altogether, in which case a *gat* composed in that *rāg* may not have the section known as *manjhā*, or may combine *manjhā* with the *antarā*, keeping the register above the middle-octave tonic.

Another feature inherent in *rāg* structure that directly affects *gat vistār* is the relative flexibility of melodic progression between the tones of a *rāg*. Some *rāg*-s are considered to be very broad, while others are limited, when examined from the viewpoint of potential melodic pathways that exist within the *rāg* structure. Those *rāg*-s relatively free of restrictions regarding melodic movement lend themselves to extended improvisation (e.g., one often hears the story that the famed *sitār*-ist, Imdad Khan, played *ālāp* in *rāg Toḍī* nonstop for eight days without once repeating a melodic phrase!) On the other hand, many *rāg*-s are quite limited, with a low potential for generating melodic motifs. In many instances this is because a *rāg* has many specific melodic motifs that must be strictly adhered to in order to maintain its integrity. Such *rāg*-s do not easily lend themselves to the detailed *śṛṅkhalā* observed in the *vistār* of a *vilambit gat*.

Specific ornamentation assigned to particular tones of a *rāg* is yet another factor influencing the way in which a *rāg* will be performed on *sitār*. For example, the third scale-degree of *rāg Darbārī Kāṇaḍā* is to be taken as 'very flat', and oscillated by diminishing degrees of amplitude. As a result, that scale-degree is more often articulated by the techniques of *mīṇḍ*, *kaṇ*, and *āndolan*, rather than articulating the tone on the fret. Another *rāg*, *Śuddh Kalyāṇ*, requires a *glissando* from the lower-octave fifth scale-degree to the middle-octave fifth scale-degree and back to the third scale-degree of the middle octave. On *sitār*, this can be performed only by combining *ghasīṭ* and *mīṇḍ* (Misra, personal communication, 1975).

6.1.2 *Tāl and lay*

A peculiar feature in Indian music is the association of particular rhythm cycles with certain styles of performance. Thus, *cau-tāl, sul-tāl, pañcam savārī tāl, tivrā tāl*, and *dhamār tāl* are associated with the *dhrupad aṅg* music that was predominant in the late medieval period (c. 1400-1800). Although it is rare to find *sitār*-ists playing in these *tāl*-s, one does occasionally hear *gat*-s in *dhamār* and *pañcam savārī*. According to Ravi Shankar, the correct rendition of *gat vistār* in such *tāl*-s requires the musician to avoid certain ornaments and *tān*-s that are peculiar to the *ṭhumrī* and the *khyāl śailī-s*, such as *khaṭkā* and *murkī* of the former, and *sapāṭ tān*-s of the latter (personal communication, 1977).

Tīn-tāl, tilvāṛā tāl, āṛā cau-tāl, jhūmrā tāl, rūpak tāl, jhap-tāl, ek-tāl, and others are associated with *khyāl aṅg* vocal music and the *gat śailī*. The association of the *Masītkhānī* and *Razākhānī bāj*-s with *tīn-tāl* has been discussed before (see 2.3.2) as well as the correlation of *bol* patterns with *tāl* divisions in the *kūṭ-bāj gat*-s (see 5.1.3). Beyond this, certain *tāl*-s are restricted to particular tempo ranges. Thus, only *vilambit gat*-s will be played in *jhūmrā* or *tilvāṛā tāl*-s, and only *madhya lay* or *drut gat*-s in *rūpak tāl*.

Beyond determining the particular gat form one will perform, tempo plays an important role in the unfolding of the *gat vistār*. In North Indian music, during the performance of *tāl*-regulated music, the tempo is increased gradually by stages. The particular subdivisions within the *gat vistār* proceed in correlation with the progression in tempo changes. Hence, *baṛhat tān*-s and *vilambit tān*-s will be played during a certain tempo range, then *du guṇ tān*-s, *ti guṇ tān*-s, and so forth, increasing the tempo as each new phase of the *vistār* begins.

6.2. Transcription Methodology

The immediate problem in transcribing any piece of music is determining those aspects that are essential to the discussion at hand, and devising methods to adequately represent them in a transcription. In the present study, the central concern has been how the playing techniques of the *sitār* are utilized in performing precomposed and improvised music, and how those techniques are involved in determining the structural and stylistic characteristics of the music. Accordingly, one of the foremost requirements of a transcription in this study is that it depicts the actual techniques that are producing the sound(s). Thus, for the *sitār*, I have chosen to have three separate lines of notation: (1) the traditional Western staff to accommodate the melodic line and drone tones, (2) the space above the staff to depict left-hand technique, and (3) the space below the staff to depict right-hand technique.

Another essential requirement in transcribing music set to a cyclic rhythm is that the layout of the transcription should easily translate into a recurring cycle. To facilitate this, I have followed the traditional premise that the *tāl* cycle is the regulatory factor in governing the phrasing of the melodic line, and thus, the layout of the manuscript paper is based on the *tāl* cycle, with the standard symbols for the points of stress and antistress at the appropriate places as dictated by traditional practice. Because compositions of varying lengths and tempos have been discussed in this study, it was desirable to make the layout of the manuscript page adaptable to the requirements of the tempo and number of *mātrā*-s in a *tāl*. The following method is adhered to throughout the study:

(a) For slow tempo [*vilambit lay*], an entire page (four staffs) is devoted to one *āvartan* of the *tāl*. Sam is indicated by an 'X' placed at the upper left of the first staff to mark the first *mātrā*. The *āvartan* number is indicated by the appropriate cardinal placed directly above the 'X'. Partial barlines indicate the durational limit of the *mātrā*-s. The division of the cycle by *khālī*-s (H. 'empty') and *tālī*-s (H. 'clap') into sections is indicated by complete barlines. *Khālī*-s (points of antistress within the *tāl*) are marked by a 'O' positioned above the *mātrā*-(s) at which they occur. *Tālī*-s (points of stress) are marked by the cardinals '2', '3', etc. ('1' is absorbed by the sam), which are positioned above the *mātrā*-(s) at which they occur. Thus, when transcribing isolated *gat*-s (see, e.g., Ex. 5-1) even though the gat may incorporate the *mukhṛā*, the sam will always appear to the upper left. Accordingly, if a *gat* begins with *mukhṛā* on the twelfth *mātrā* of *tīn-tāl*, its transcription should be read starting from that *mātrā* (third staff, last division), proceeding to the next staff, and then to the top left of the page and down again to the twelfth *mātrā*. This arrangement emphasizes the individuality and independent nature of the subsections of the *gat*, although admittedly, to the Western reader it may seem awkward to begin a musical phrase in the interior of a page and then jump to the top of the same page to continue the same line. To facilitate the location of *mukhṛā*, an 'M' is placed above the *mātrā* at which it begins. In the *vilambit gat* of the corpus, consecutive *āvartan*-s are read on successive pages.

(b) For medium and fast tempos [*madhya* and *drut lay*-s], each staff represents one *āvartan* of a *tāl*, hence, there are four *āvartan*-s per page. Here, the partial bar lines represent the division of the *tāl* into its subsections, full barlines indicate the end of one *āvartan*. The symbols for *sam, khālī*-(s), and *tālī*-(s) are placed across the top of the page at the appropriate places, and are effective for each of the lower staffs. As was the case above, for isolated *gat*-s in the music examples, sections of the *gat* (*sthāyi*, *manjhā*, *antarā*) that are one *āvartan* in length are placed within one *āvartan*, regardless of whether or not there is a *mukhṛā* leading to the *sam*. The notational symbols for left- and right-hand techniques have been presented in Chapter IV. In that their application is fairly straightforward, they need not be further discussed here. Some problems encountered in notating the melody do require comment. The inclusion of the drone tones on the same staff as the melody presented a predicament because often a tone of the melodic line continues sounding simultaneously with the drone wire, and to show each of the sounds in their entire rhythmic duration would create an overfilled *mātrā*. One solution would have been to use a separate staff, or line, to notate the drone tones; however, this was not desirable because: (1) it would take up an undue amount of space, and (2) strokes on the drone wires often become musically significant within the context of the melodic line (e.g., articulating the rests within a *tihāī*), in which case it is desirable to include them on the main staff. In order to resolve this problem, open ties are used to indicate that a melodic tone continues to sound after the articulation of a drone tone. In such cases, the melodic tones are assigned rhythmic values according to their duration prior to the articulation of the drone tones. Ambiguity of drone tones and melodic tones was avoided by the use of triangular noteheads for the former. In order to distinguish drone tones on the *cikārī* from those on the *joṛī* wire, particular positions on the staff were assigned to each. The *cikārī* tones (c^1, c^2) are represented by a triangular notehead on the third space of the staff, and the open *joṛī* wire (c), when functioning as a drone tone, is notated by a triangular notehead on the first ledger line below the staff. It should be noted that this tone is actually sounding an octave lower than notated. When the open *joṛī* wire is used to sound a tone in the melodic line, the actual pitch is notated by the standard notehead.

The notation of the melodic line posed a few problems regarding both its tonal and rhythmic components. Regarding the former, the most difficult aspect of Indian melody to notate is the persistent use of continuous sound connecting many different pitches. The slur sign (incorporated in this study) helps to indicate what is going on; but, the essence of the process—the sound between the pitches—is completely lost when one resorts to the use of Western notational symbols. A graphic display could come closer to representing the actual sound in this situation, but I am convinced that only a machine transcription can actually give a correct visual representation of this aural phenomenon. Because such a level of detail in transcription is not necessary for the level of analysis in this study, let it suffice to acknowledge that the system employed herein has its limitations and may not be suitable for more specific studies of the kinetics of melody in Indian music.

Ornamental tones and their connotations also provided some difficulty in transcribing the melody. In the Western connotation of the word, an ornament is something extra, of relatively less significance than that to which it is attached, and is separable (or, at least, may be considered separately) from that which it embellishes. Indian music is so replete with ornamentation that it is almost impossible, and certainly not desirable, to classify tones as ornamental or ornamented. The essence of the Indian concept of ornamentation lies in the manner in which the space between tones is traversed, not in the boundaries of that space. On the other hand, there are many instances in which tones of melodic passages are of differing significance, and to notate them all the same way distorts their actual relationship. I prefer to term those tones which are aurally less prominent as auxiliary tones, rather than ornamental tones and, in this study, I have notated them by small noteheads. The main purpose in using small noteheads is to enhance the detail of the visual representation of an aural phenomenon. They are not intended as a source of data to be extracted for analysis.

Regarding the rhythmic component of the melody, those passages played in such a way as to give the impression of being non-metrical while being set to *tāl* presented the greatest difficulty in transcribing. While every effort was made to maintain a high degree of accuracy in notating the rhythm throughout, the writer makes no pretensions of perfection in regards to this aspect of the transcription.

A summary of all the special symbols appearing in the music examples and the corpus is given in Figure 15.

The transcription of the corpus was accomplished with the aid of a half-speed dubbing that was made on a Teac A-7030 reel-to-reel tape recorder and transferred to a Sony TC-126 stereo cassette recording. Tempo readings were made of each *āvartan* of the *vilambit gat* with the help of a Heuer Tempowatch. The readings were made on the basis of the duration of the first six *mātrā*-s of each *āvartan*. Tempo values of alternate *āvartan*-s of the *drut gat* were made on the basis of the duration of the first twelve *mātrā*-s of the designated *āvartan*.

6.3. Corpus

The following is a transcription of the *vilambit* and *drut gat* vistār-s of a performance on *sitār* by Paṇḍit Ravi Shankar. He was accompanied on *tablā* by *Śrī* Kanai Dutt. The source for this performance is the Capitol International Series SP 10482 long playing 12" stereo disc. The transcrip-

Key to Special Symbols

Symbol	Example	Explanation
(1)		A small notehead indicates in auxiliary tone.
(2)		A slur indicates pitches connected by a sound continuum.
(3)	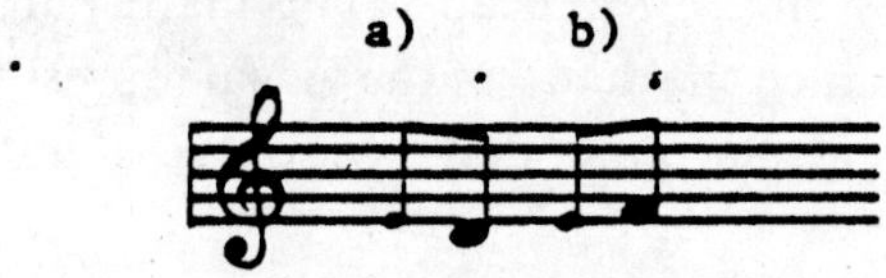	A dot above a note indicates: (a) *Krintan* (b) *sparś*
(4)		A vertical line above a note indicates a *gharṣaṇ* or *ghasīṭ*
(5)		A horizontal line above two or more notes (as in *mīṇḍ*) indicates that those tones (excepting the lowest-pitched tone) are produced by pulling the wire. When the technique is prolonged, the line is broken, the continuation indicated by an arrow, the termination by a vertical line.
(6)		A wavy line indicates a *kampan*.

Figure 15: Key to Special Symbols

	Symbol	Example	Explanation
(7)			A vertical line connected to the beginning of a horizontal line indicates a *gharṣaṇ* combined with *mīṇḍ*.
(8)			A short, open slur indicates a fast approach from or departure to a tone of indefinite pitch.
(9)		a) b) 	Triangular noteheads indicate drone tones occurring on the: (a) *joṛī* wire (b) *cikārī* wire
(10)			An open tie indicates that the tone continues to sound although drone strokes occur.
(11)			A diagonal wavy line indicates a cluster of tones articulated by the nail of the right little finger on the sympathetic resonating wires.
(12)	t	t	A 't' represents the stroke of the little finger on the sympathetic wires.
(13)	da	 da	An inward stroke by the right index finger.
(14)	ra	 ra	An outward stroke by the right index finger.

Figure 15: Key to Special Symbols (Continued)

Symbol	Example	Explanation

(15) di

A *'da'* stroke of relatively short duration.

(16) r

A *'ra'* stroke of relatively short duration.

(17) c

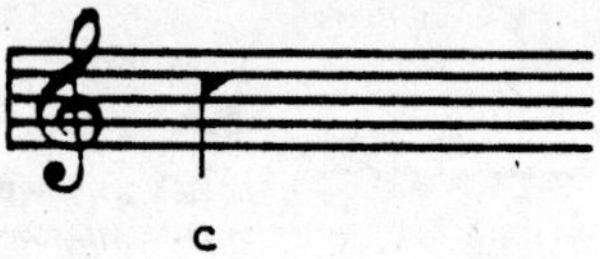

An outward stroke on the *cikārī* wires by the right index finger.

(18) o

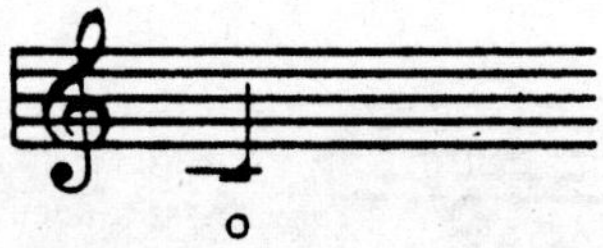

A *'da̦'* stroke on the *joṛī* wire serving as a drone tone.

(19) X

An 'X' indicates the *sam* of a *tāl.*

(20) 2,3, etc.

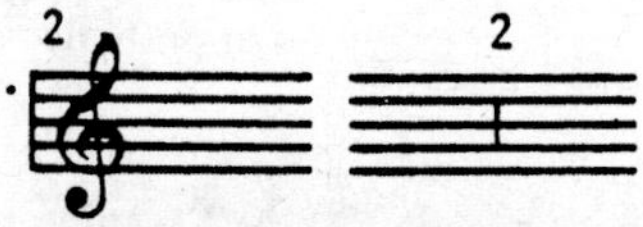

Numerals indicate *tālī*(-s) (points of stress) in a *tāl.*

(21) O

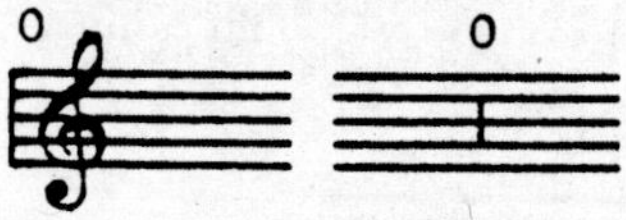

An 'O' indicates the *khālī*(-s) of a *tāl*

(22) M

An 'M' indicates *mukhṛā* of a *gat.*

(23) 

A partial bar line indicates durational limits of *mātrā*-s in slow tempo; indicates divisions of the *tāl* in medium and fast tempos.

Figure 15: Key to Special Symbols (Continued)

	Symbol	Example	Explanation
(24)			A full bar line indicates divisions of the tāl in a slow tempo; end of tāl cycle in a medium or fast tempo.

Figure 15: Key to Special Symbols

tion of this performance is included in this study with the permission of Ravi Shankar.

This particular performance was chosen for transcription and analysis for a variety of reasons: (1) the performance is by one of the best-known and most highly respected *sitār*-ists of India, (2) its duration was within a workable limit in relation to the task of transcription, (3) it is exemplary of the discussions presented in the previous chapters, yet also provides new material for further discussion, (4) the quality of the recording is very good, facilitating an accurate transcription, (5) the *rāg*, derived from a folk melody, is of recent origin, hence, free of any controversial features, and may be presented to those versed in the tradition without any fear of inviting argument over whether or not it is the "correct" version of the *rāg*, which, in this study, would detract from the central issue, and (6) it was stated by the artist that the performance represents an authentic rendition of a *vilambit* and *drut gat*.

Rāg Rasiyā
Vilambit and *Drut Gat Vistār*-s
Tin-tāl

Performers:
sitār: Ravi Shankar
tablā: Kanai Dutt
tanpurā-s: Gopi Mohan, Niren Roy

Source: Capitol International Series SP—10482, side 2

	Duration		
Vilambit Gat Vistār	16 : 33	Actual starting pitch	$g^{\#1}$ — 40 cents—transcribed as g^1
Drut Gat Vistār	3 : 40	Actual tonic pitch	$c^{\#1}$ — 42 cents—transcribed as c^1

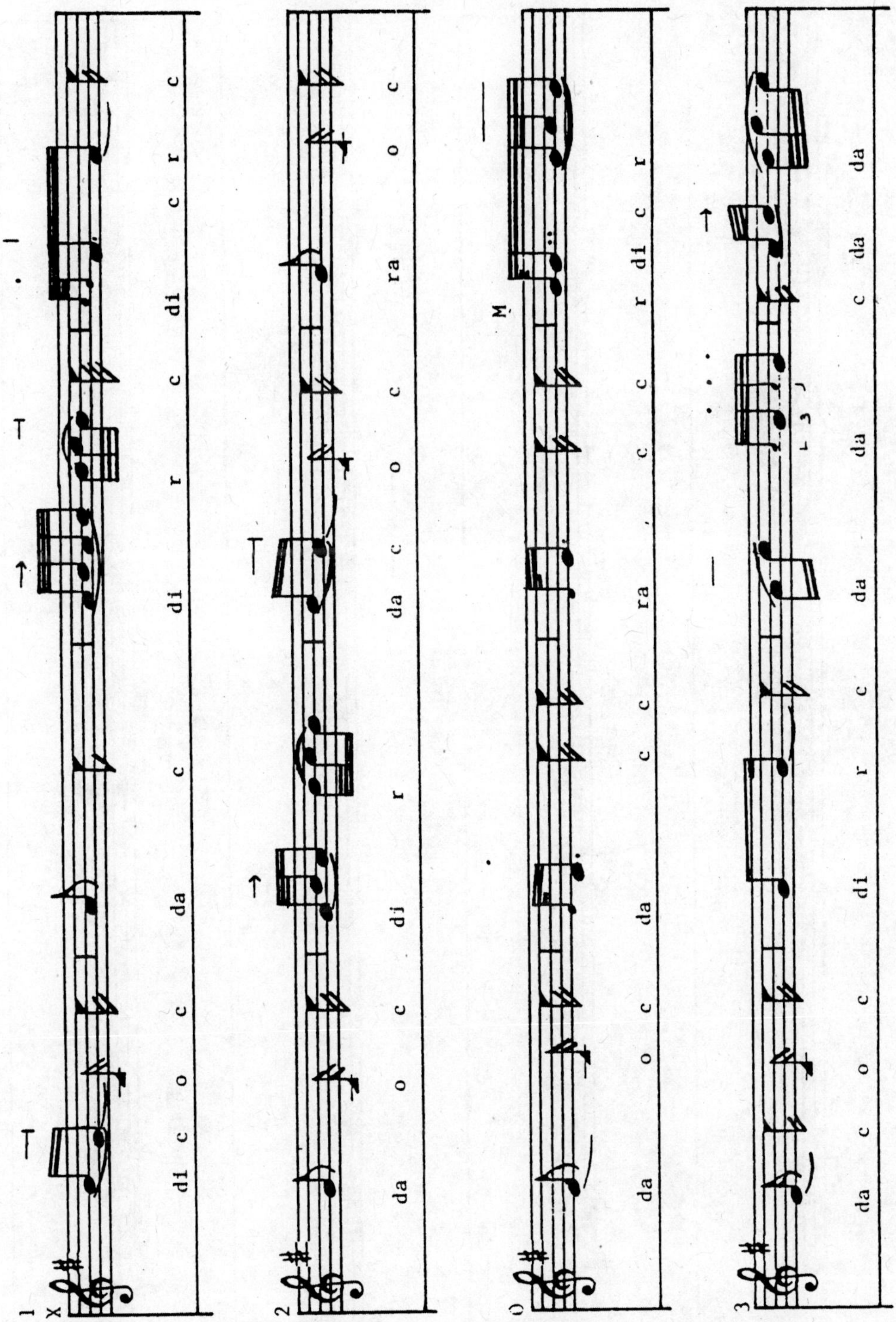
dī c o c da c dī r c dī c r c
da o c dī r da c o c ra c o c
da o c da c c ra c c r dī c r
da c o c dī r c da da c da da

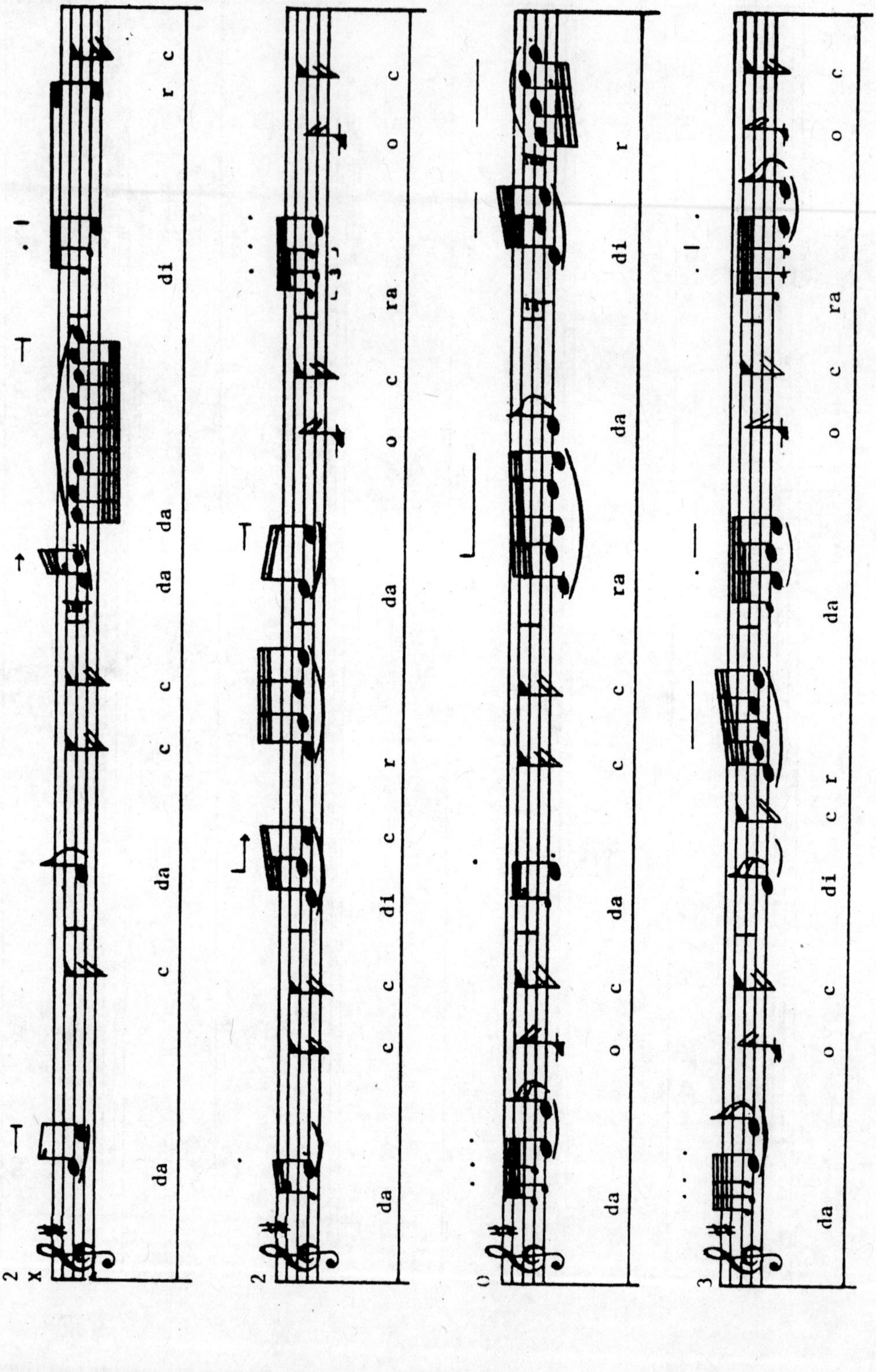
2
X
da c da c c da da di r c
2
da c c di c r da o c ra o c
0
da o c da c c ra da di r
3
da o c di c r da o c ra o c

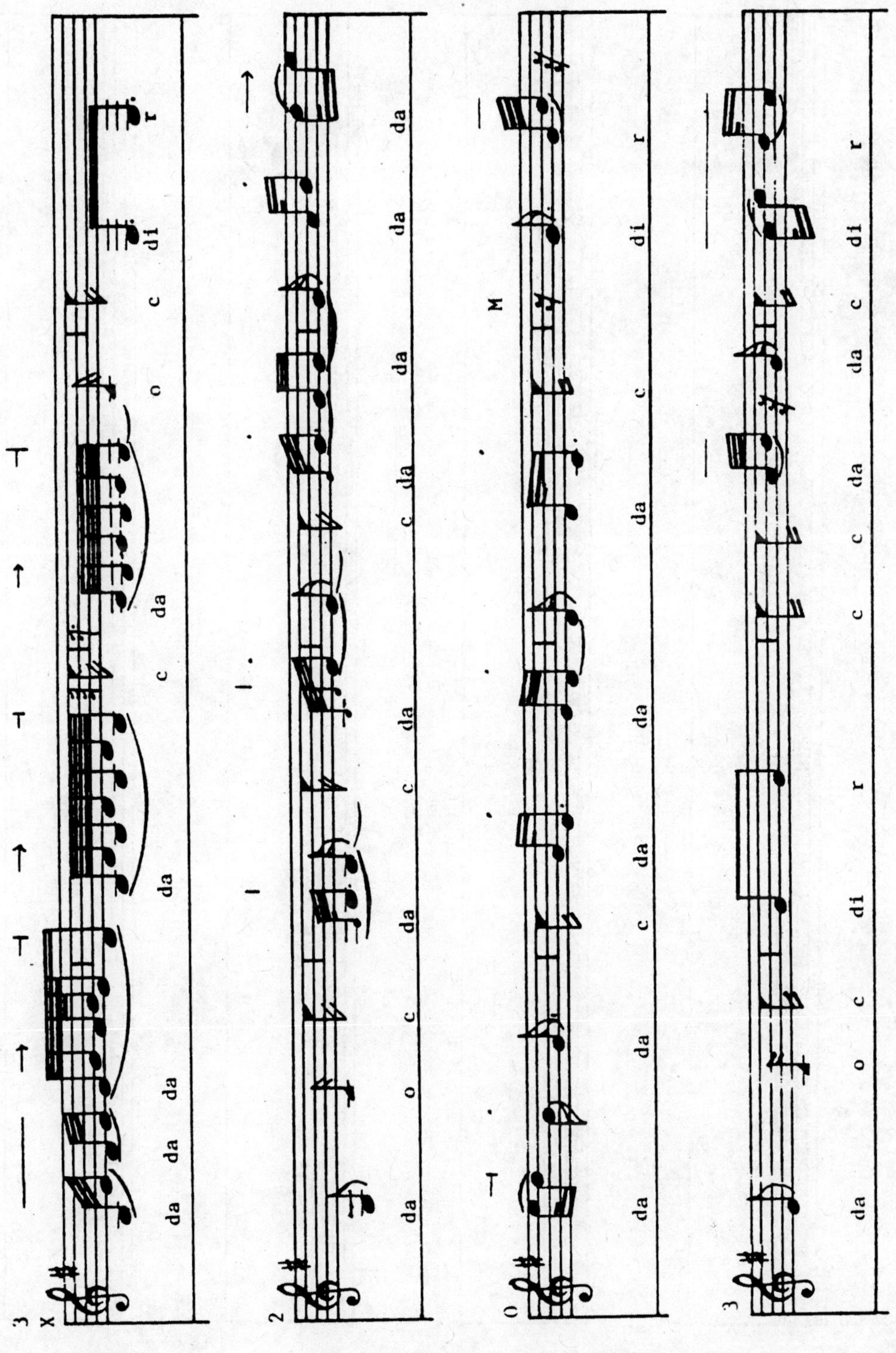

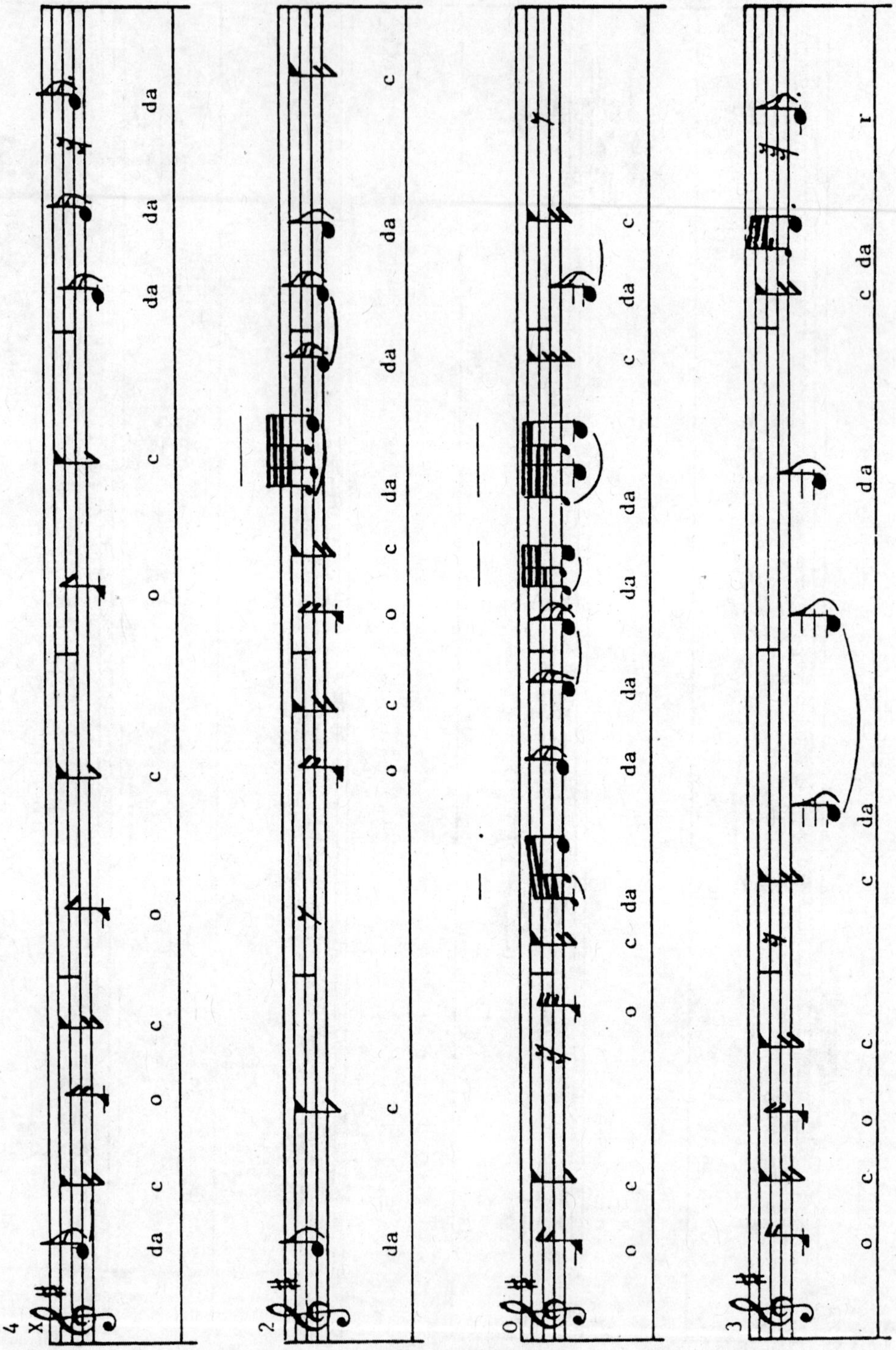
4 X
da c o c o c o c da da da
2
da c o c o c da da da c
0
o c o c da da da da da c da c
3
o c o c c da da c da r

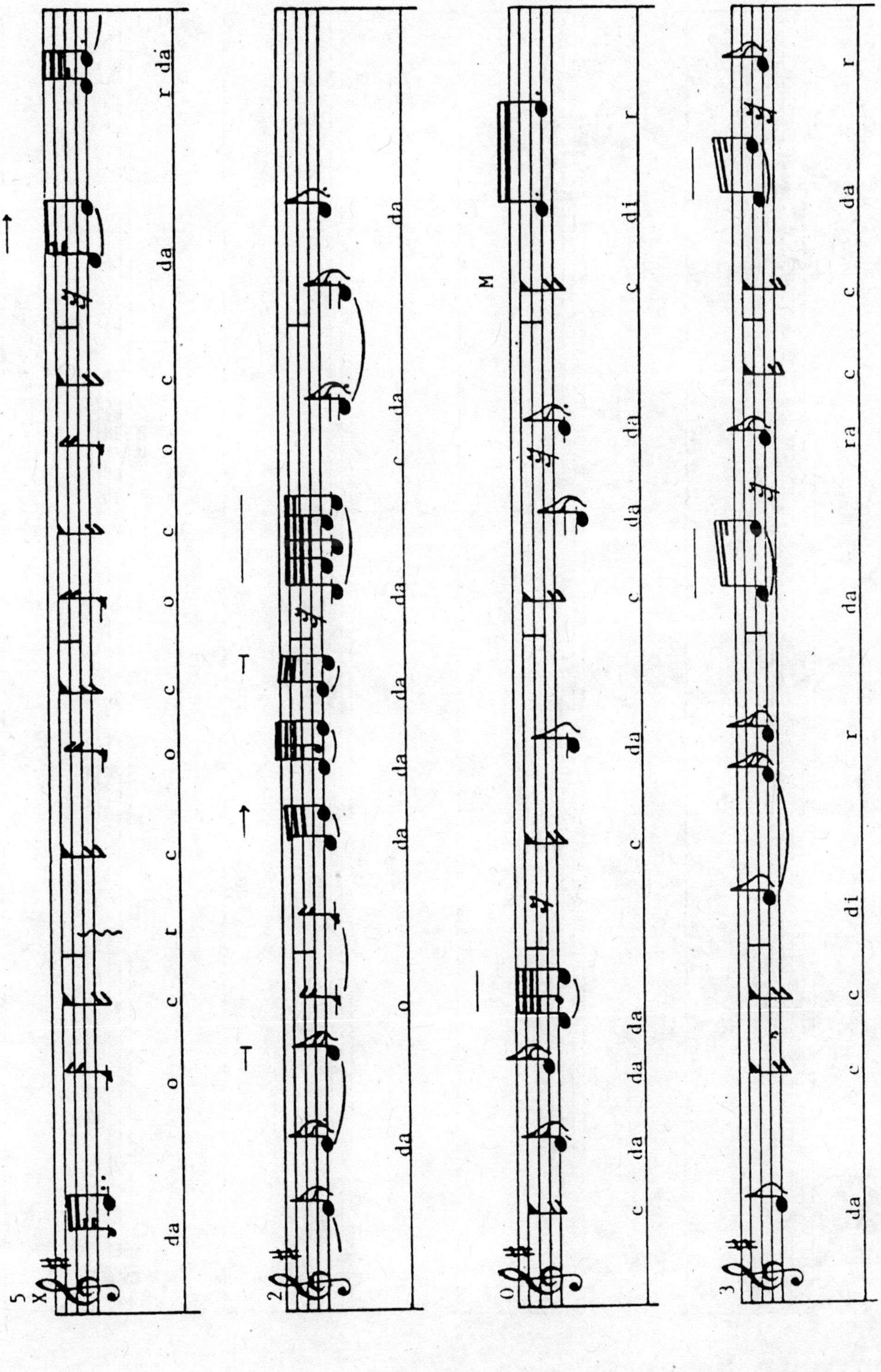
da o c t c o c o c o c da r da
da o da da da da c da da
c da da da c da da da c di r
da c c di r da ra c c da r

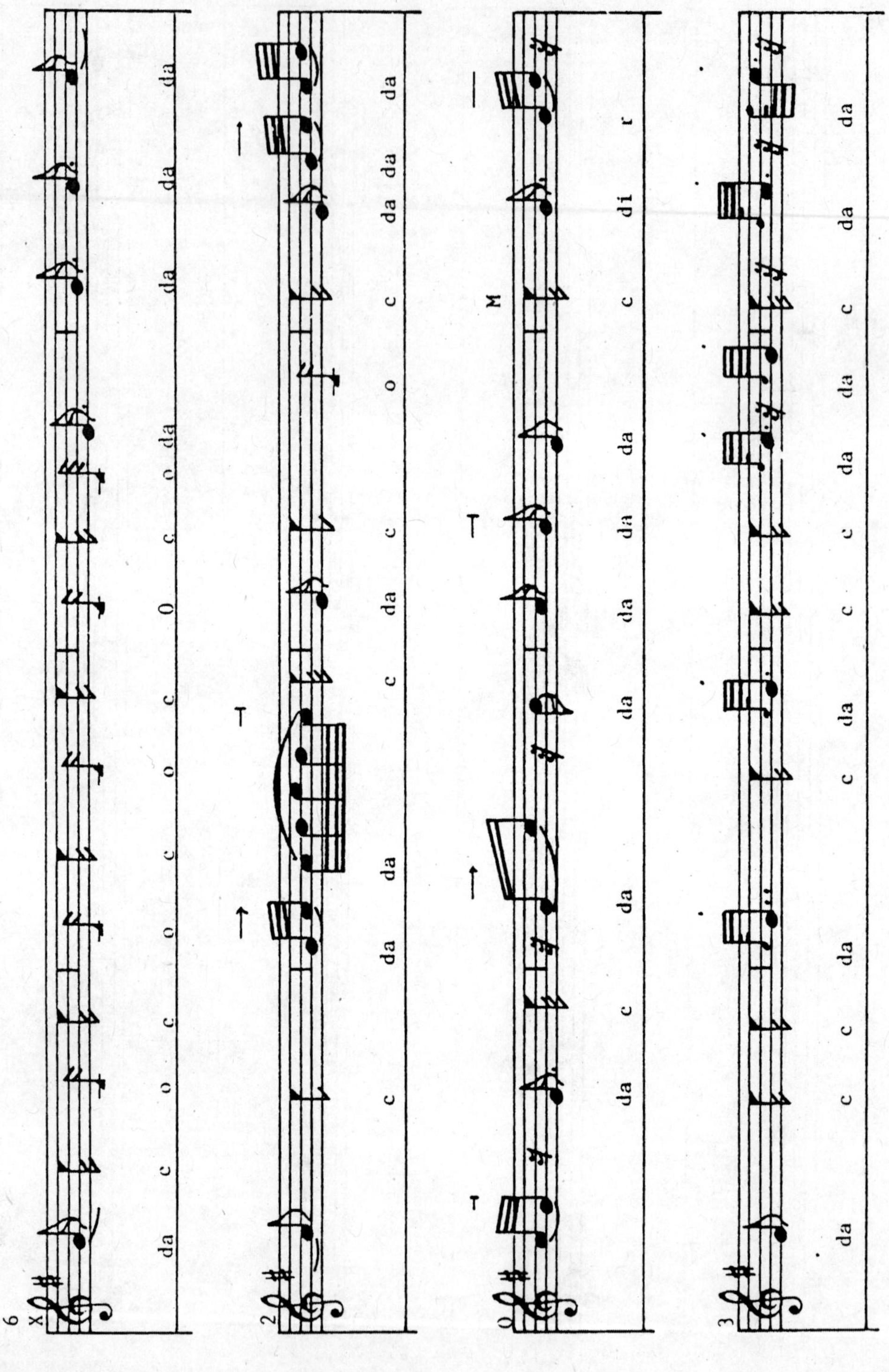

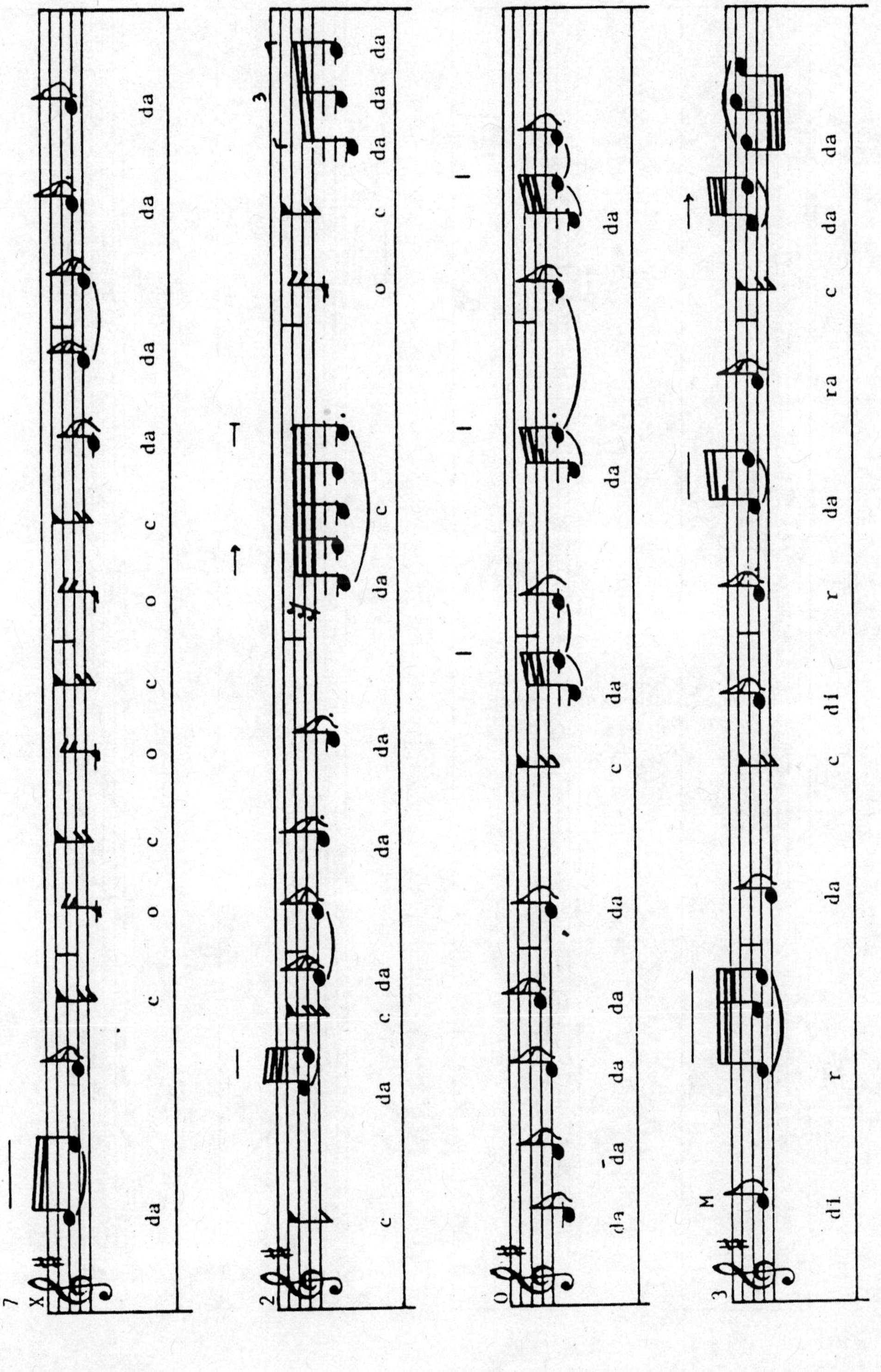
da c o c o c o c da da da da
c da c da da da da c o c da da da
da da da da da c da da da
dl r da c dl r da ra c da da

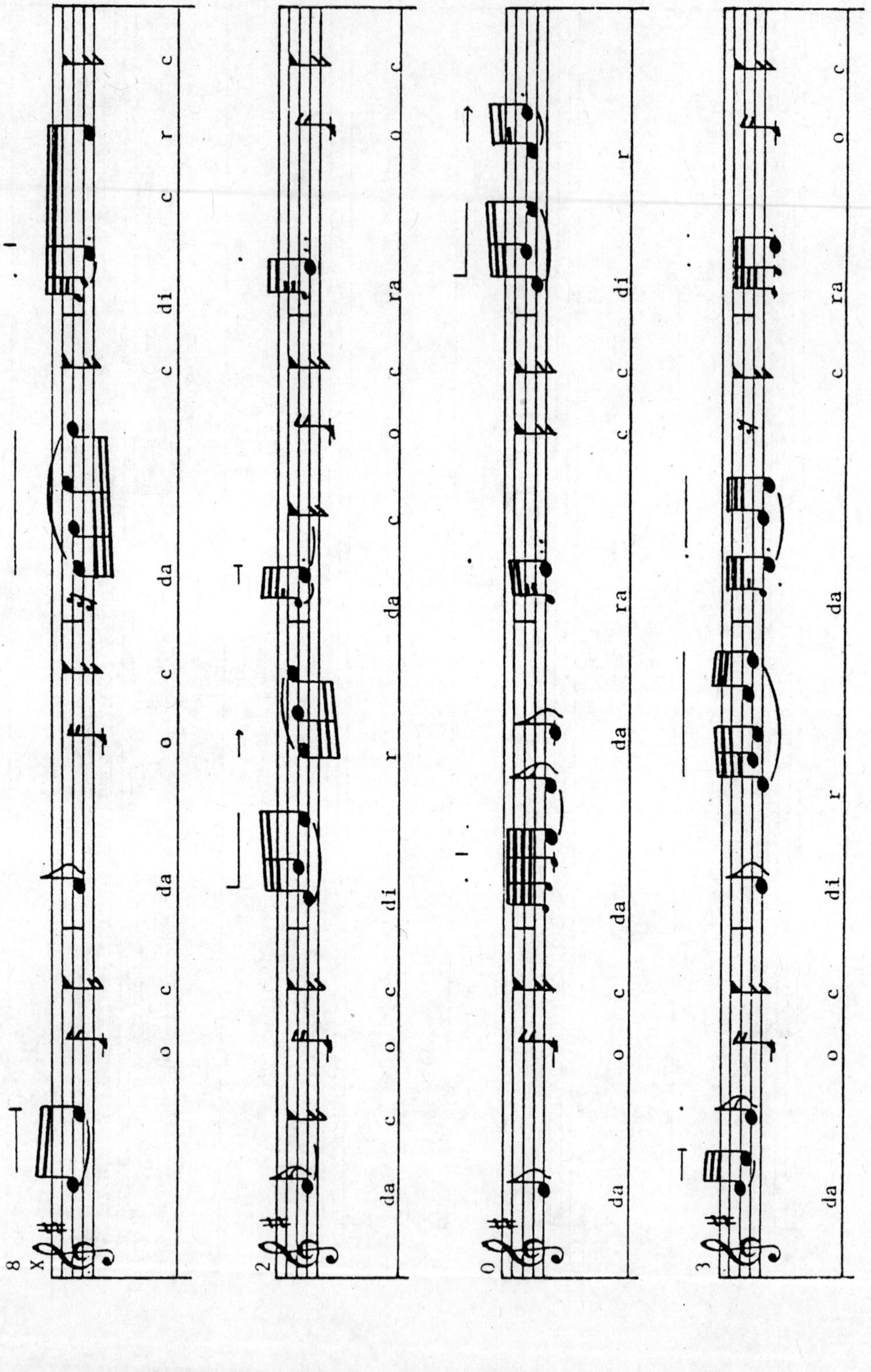
8 X
da o c da o c da c di c r c
2
da c o c di r da c o c ra o c
0
da o c da da ra c c di r c
3
da o c di r da c ra o c

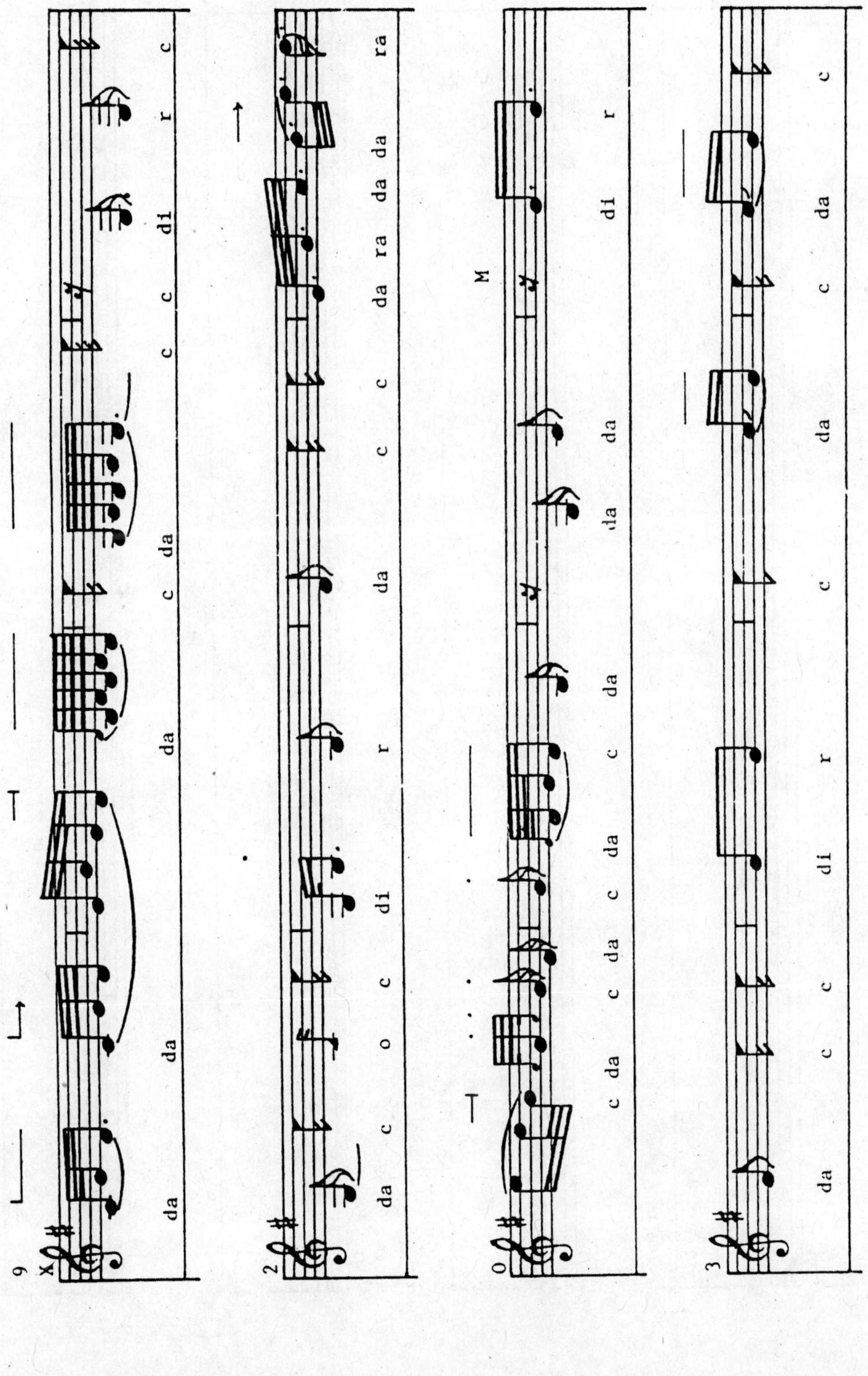

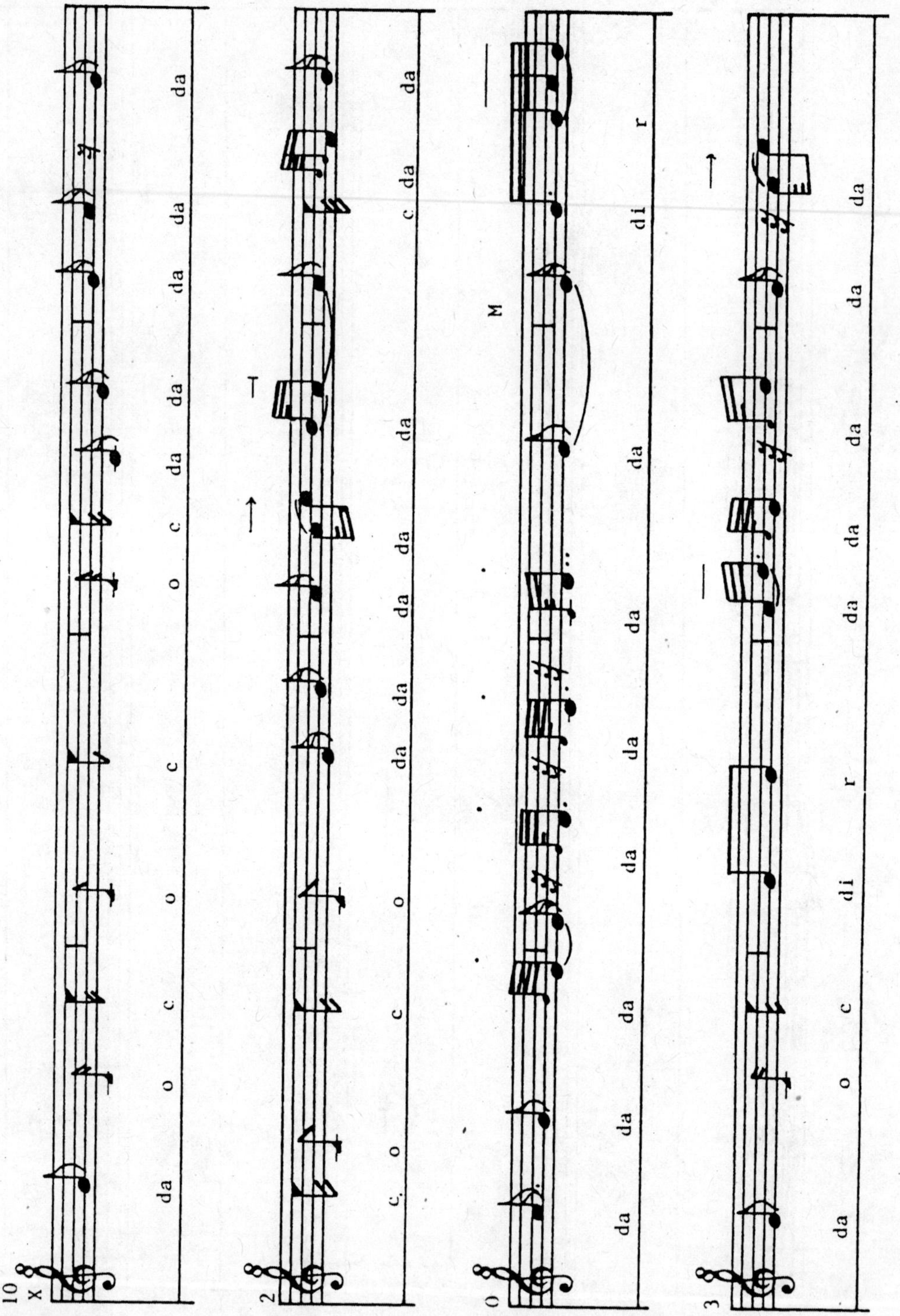
10
X
da o c o c o c da da da da da
2
c o c o da da da da da c da da
0
M
da da da da da da da da di r
3
da o c di r da da da da da

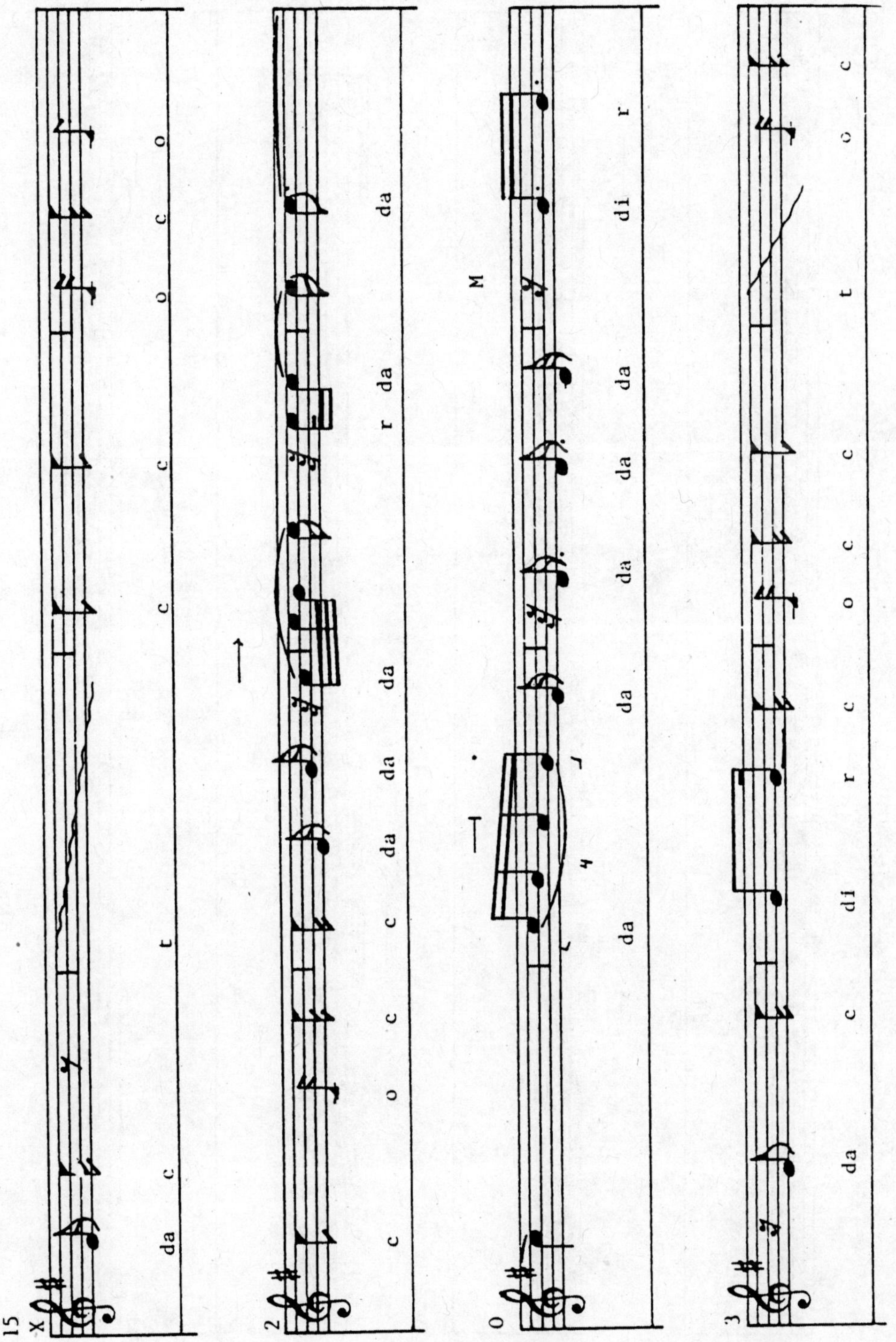
15 X
da c t c c o c o
2
c o c c da da da da r da da
0
da da da da da dI r
3
da c dI r c o c c t o c

16 X
da da da da r da da c da
2
da da da da ra da da ra da da ra da da da
0
da r da da da da ra da ra da M di r
3
da o c di r da r da r da r da r

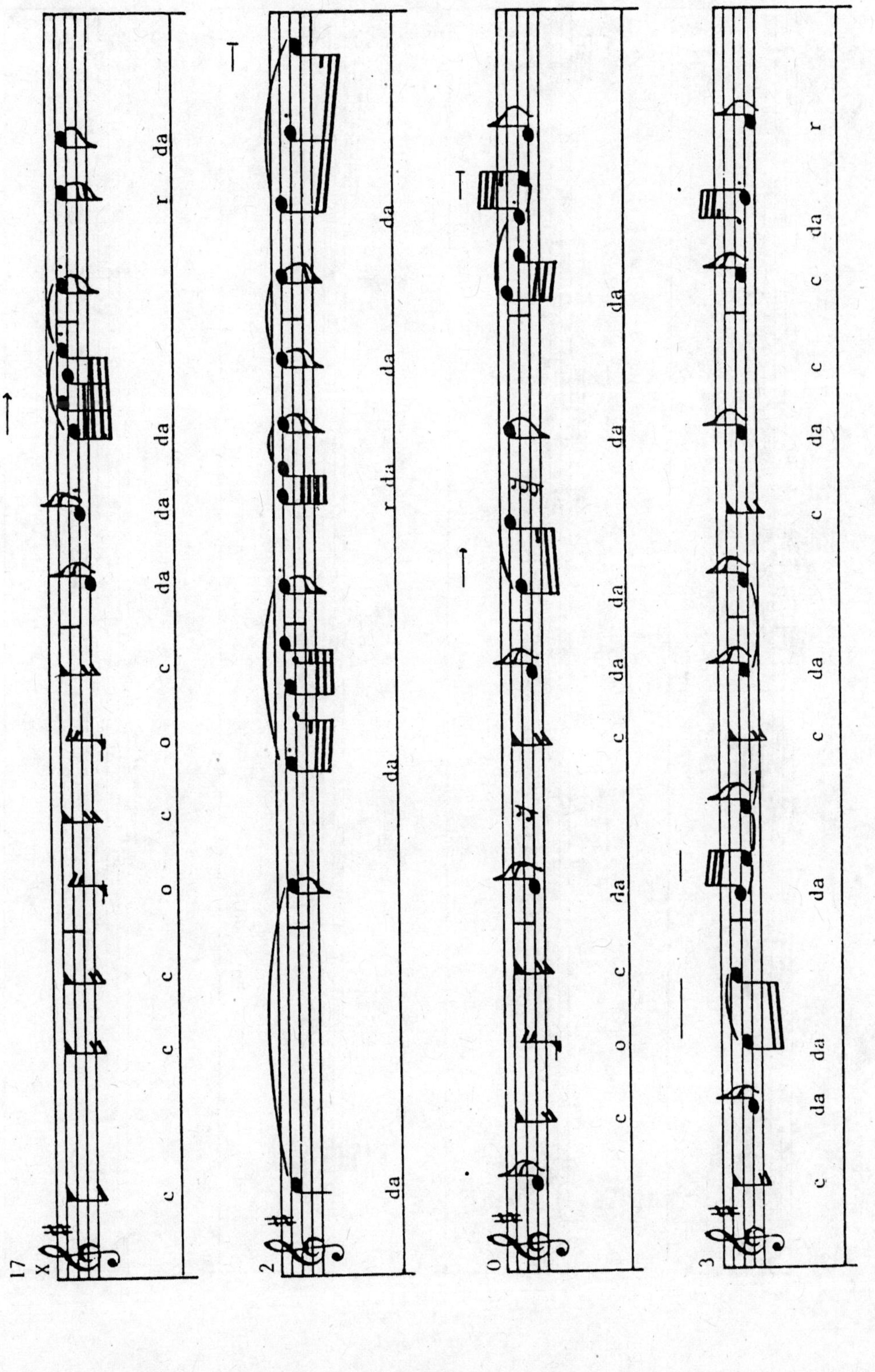
17
X
c c c o c o c da da da r da
2
da da r da da da
0
c c o c da c da da da da da
3
c da da da da c da c c da c c da r

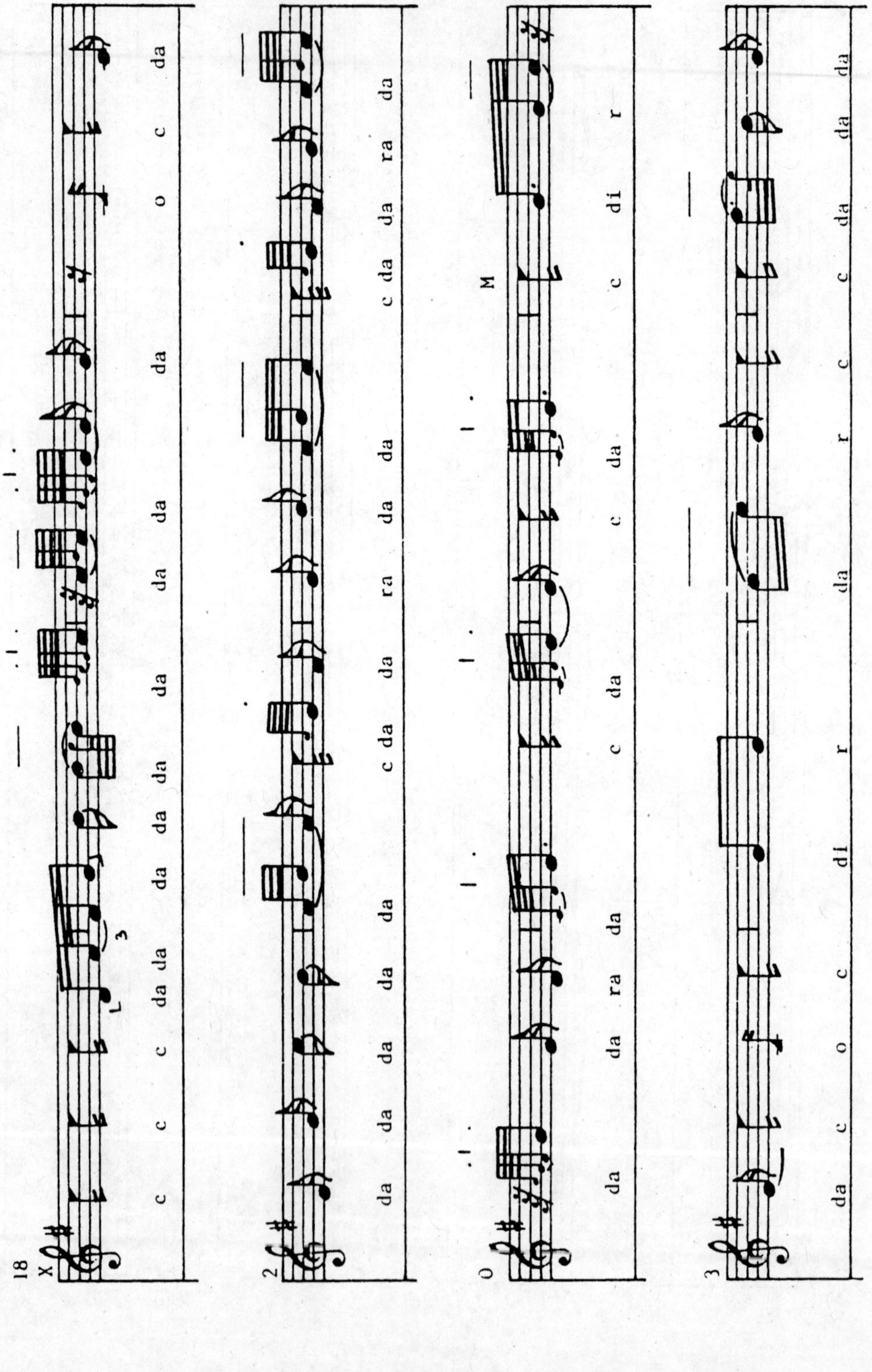
18 X
c c c da da da da da da da da da da o c da
2
da da da da da c da da ra da da c da da ra da
0
da da ra da c da c da c di r
3
da c o c di r da r c c da da da

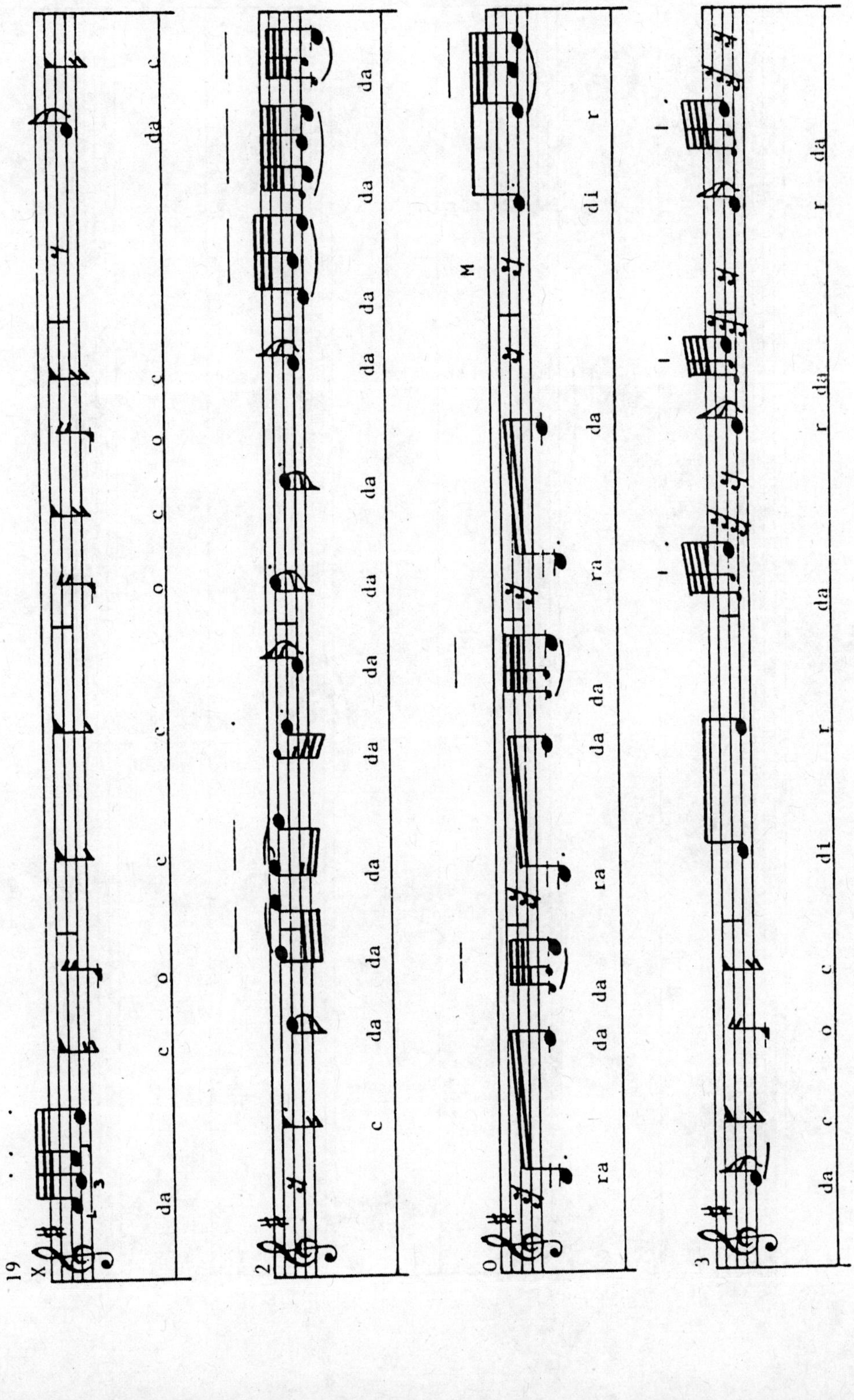

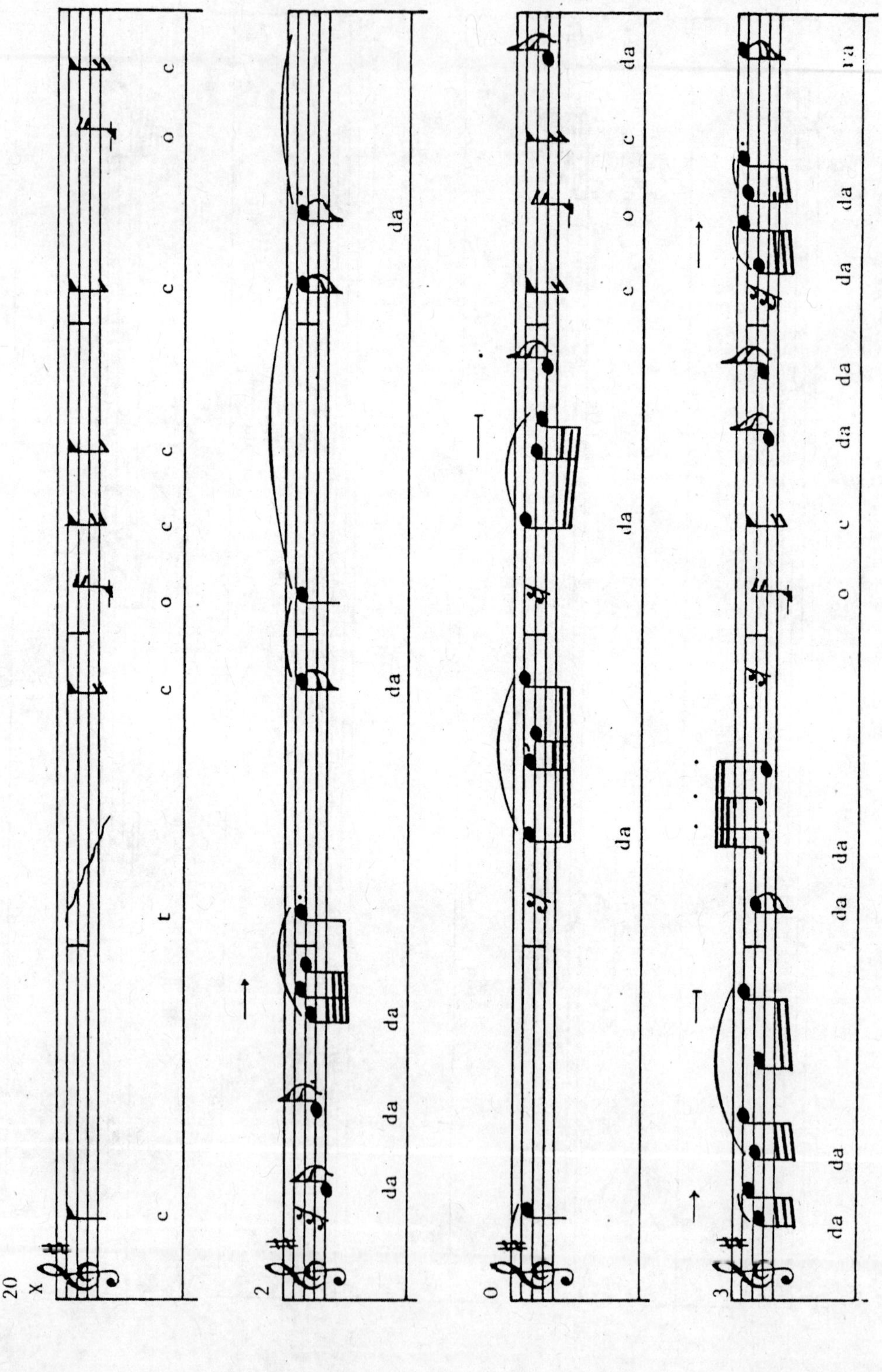

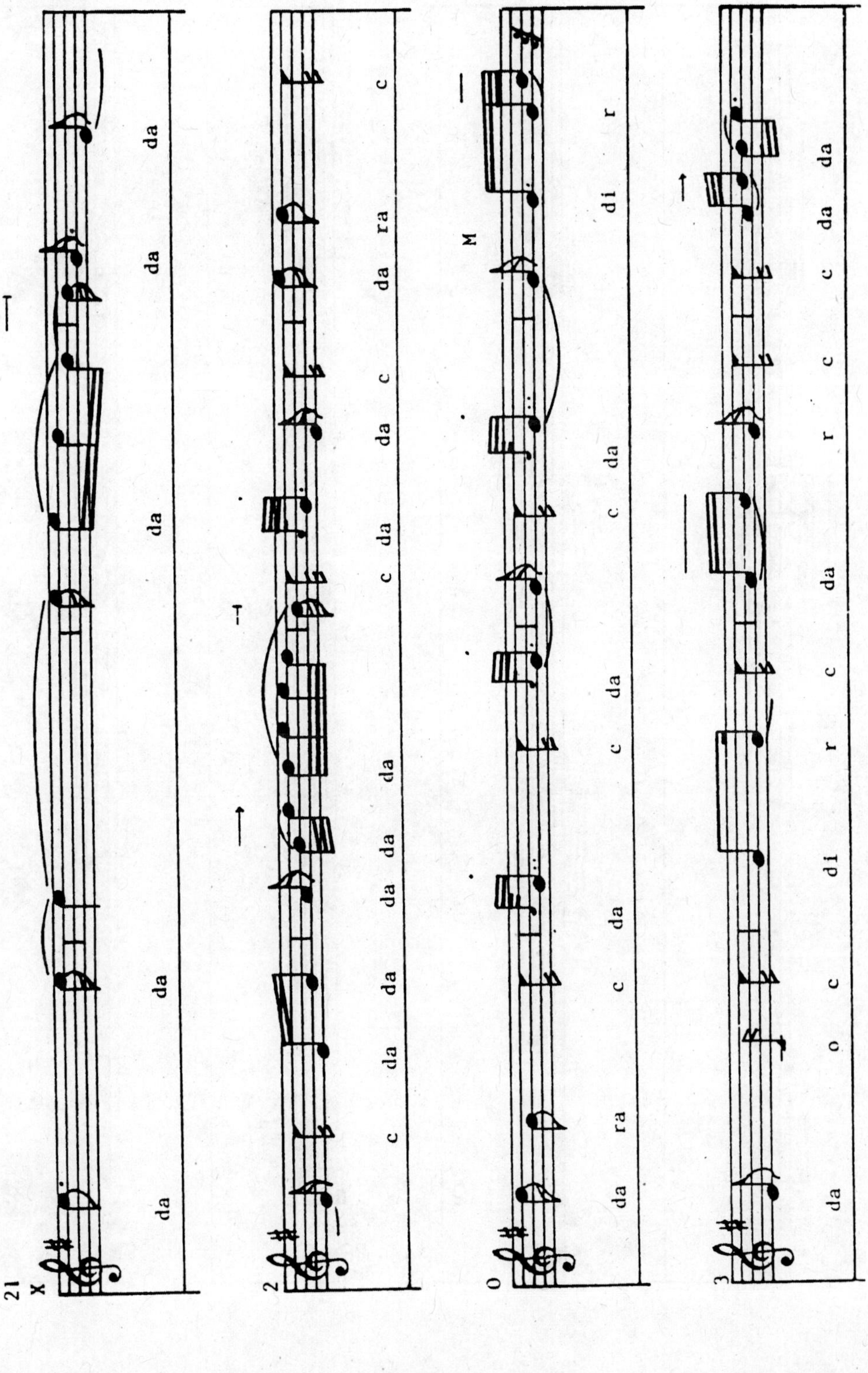
21
X
da da da da da
2
c da da da da da c da da c da ra c
0
da ra c da c da c da c da di r
3
da o c di r c da c r c c da da

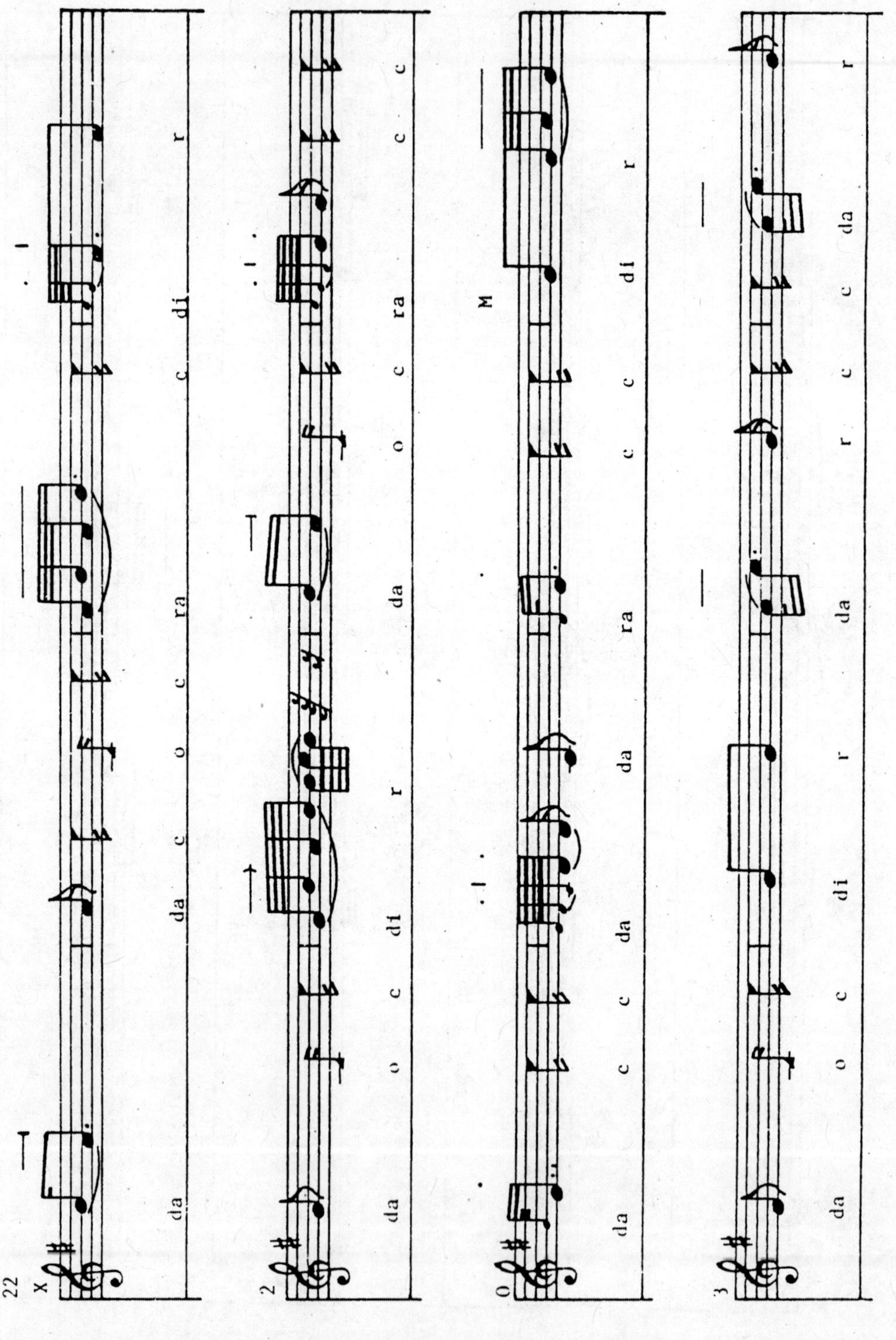
22
X
da da c o c ra c di r
2
da o c di r da o c ra c c
0
da c c da da ra c c di r
3
da o c di r da r c c da r

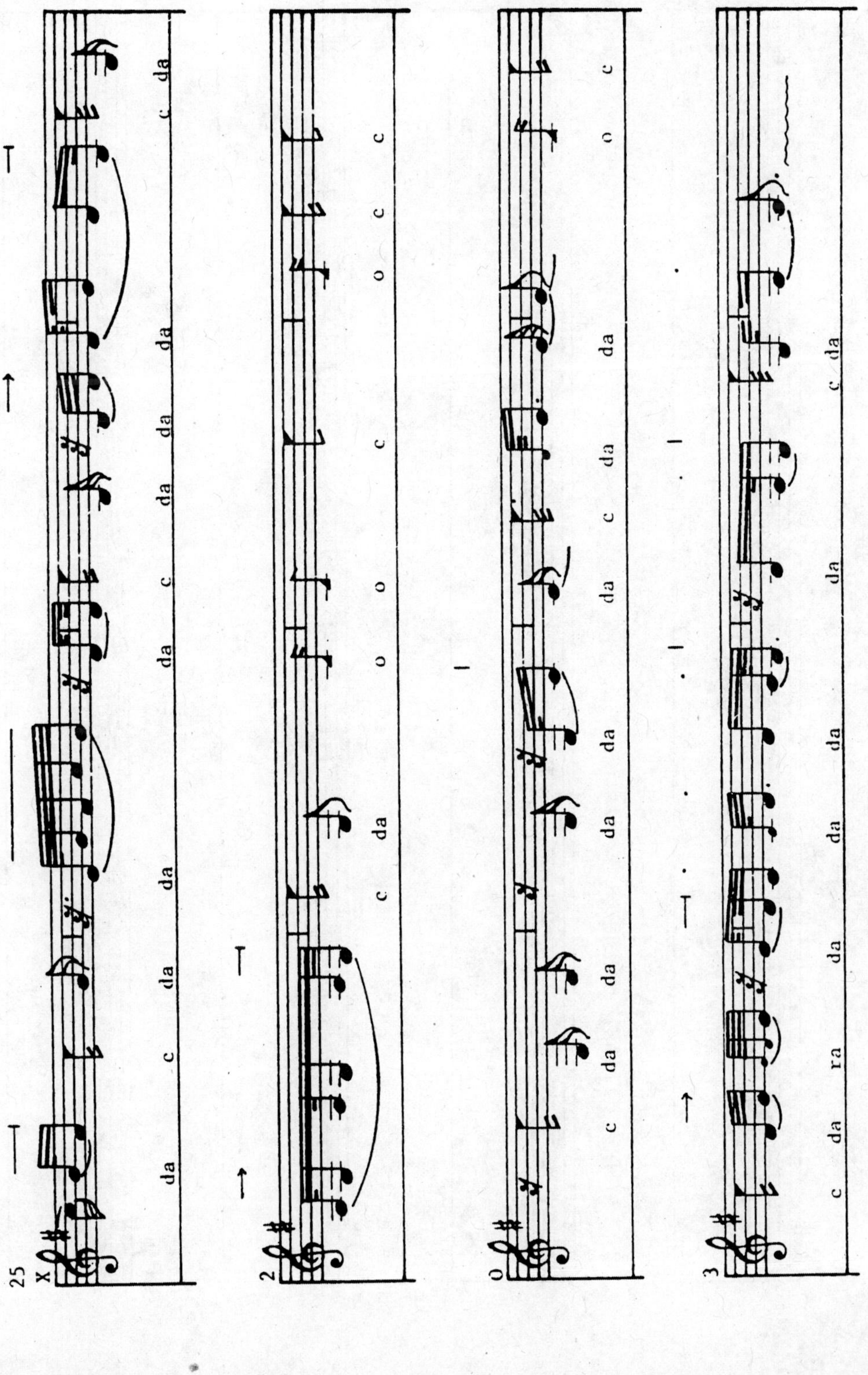
da c da da da c da da da c da
c da o o c o c c
c da da da da da c da da o c
c da ra da da da da da c da

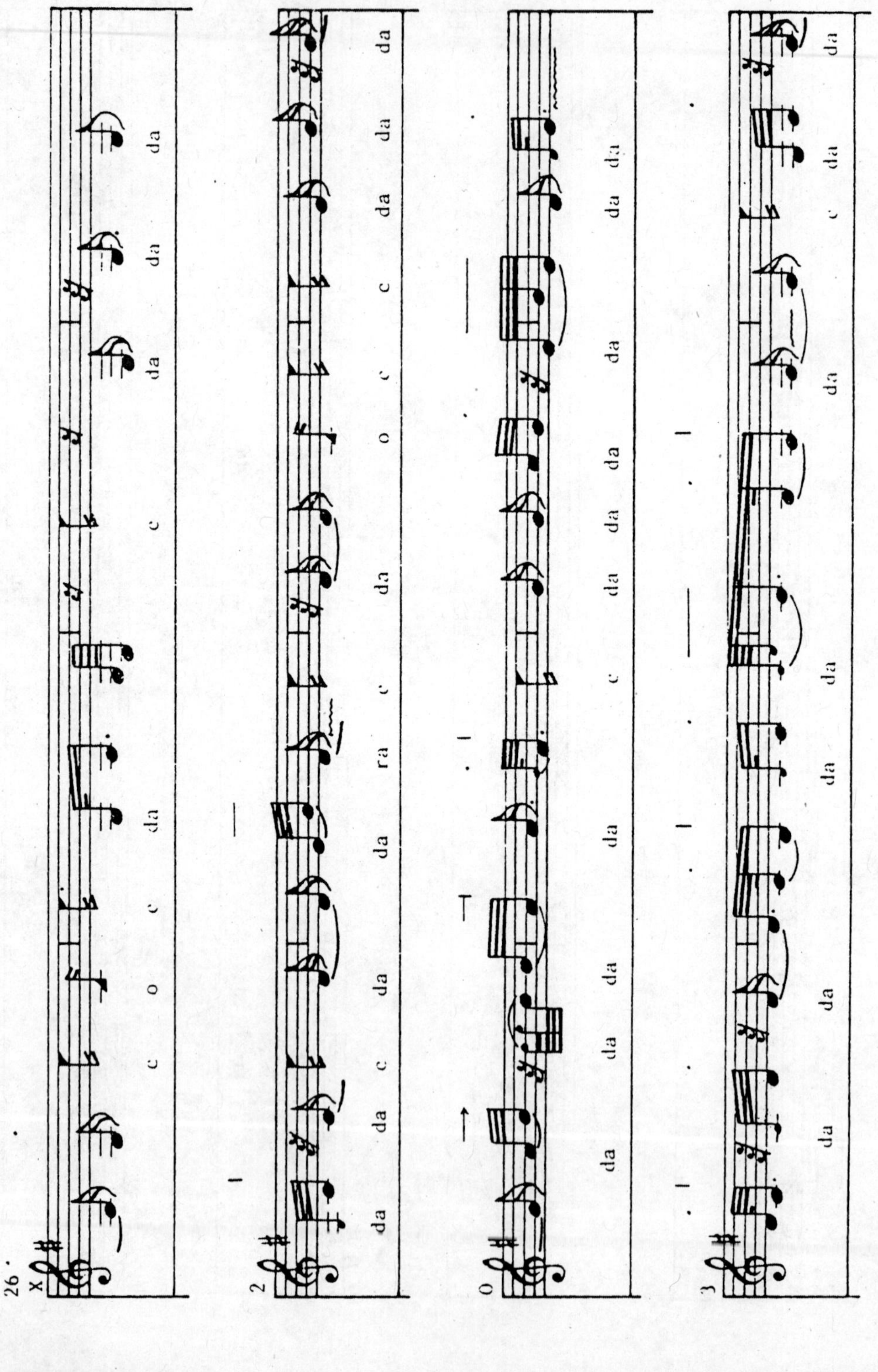

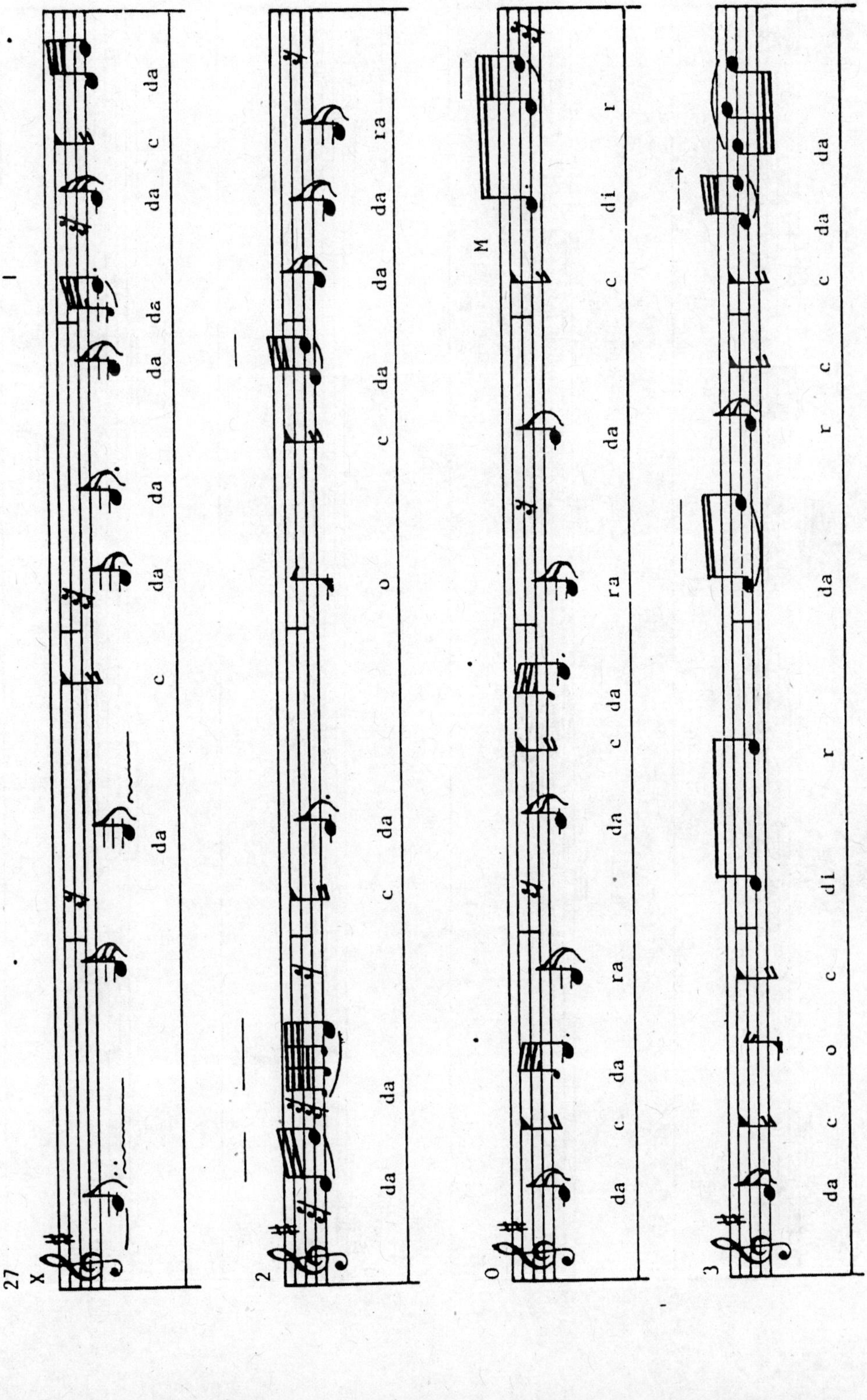
27 X
da c da da da da da c da
2
da da c da o c da da da ra
0
da c da ra da c da ra da c di r
3
da c o c di r da r c c da da

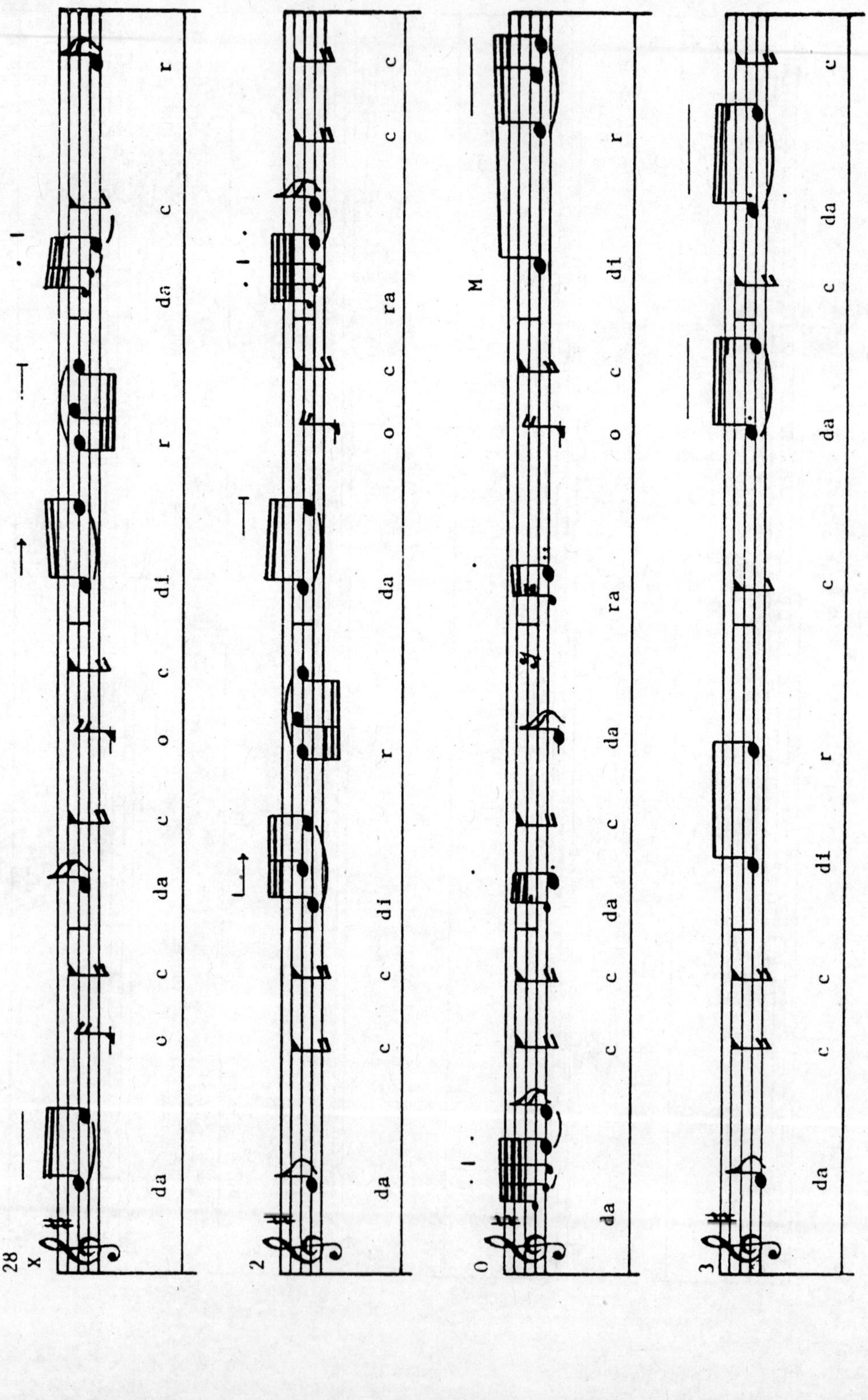
28 X
da o c da c o c dī r da c r
2
da c c dī r da o c ra c c
0
da c c da c da ra o c dī r
3
da c c dī r c da c da c

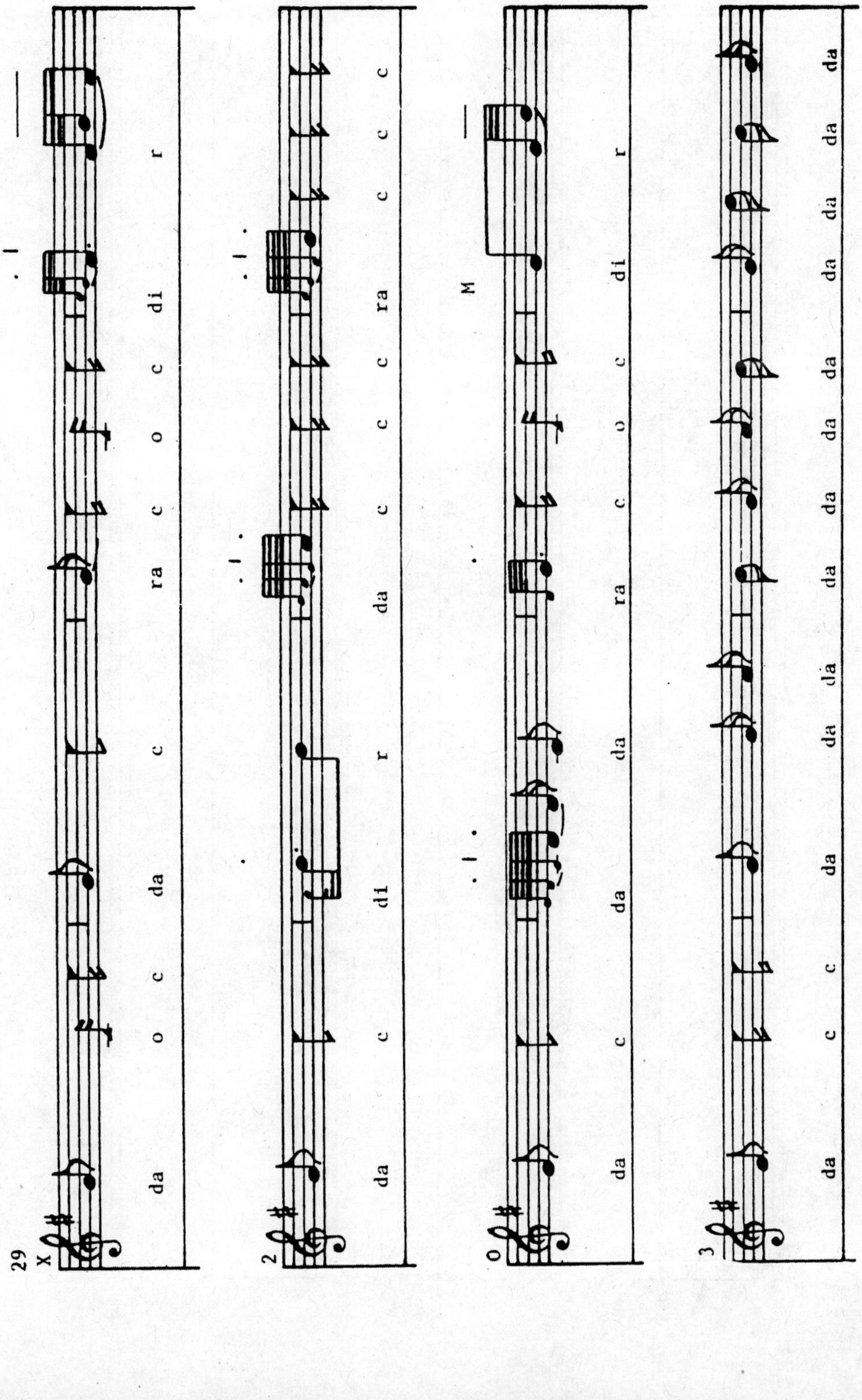
29
X
da o c da c ra c o c di r
2
da c di r da c c c ra c c c c
0
da c da da ra c o c di r
M
3
da c c da da da da da da da da da da da

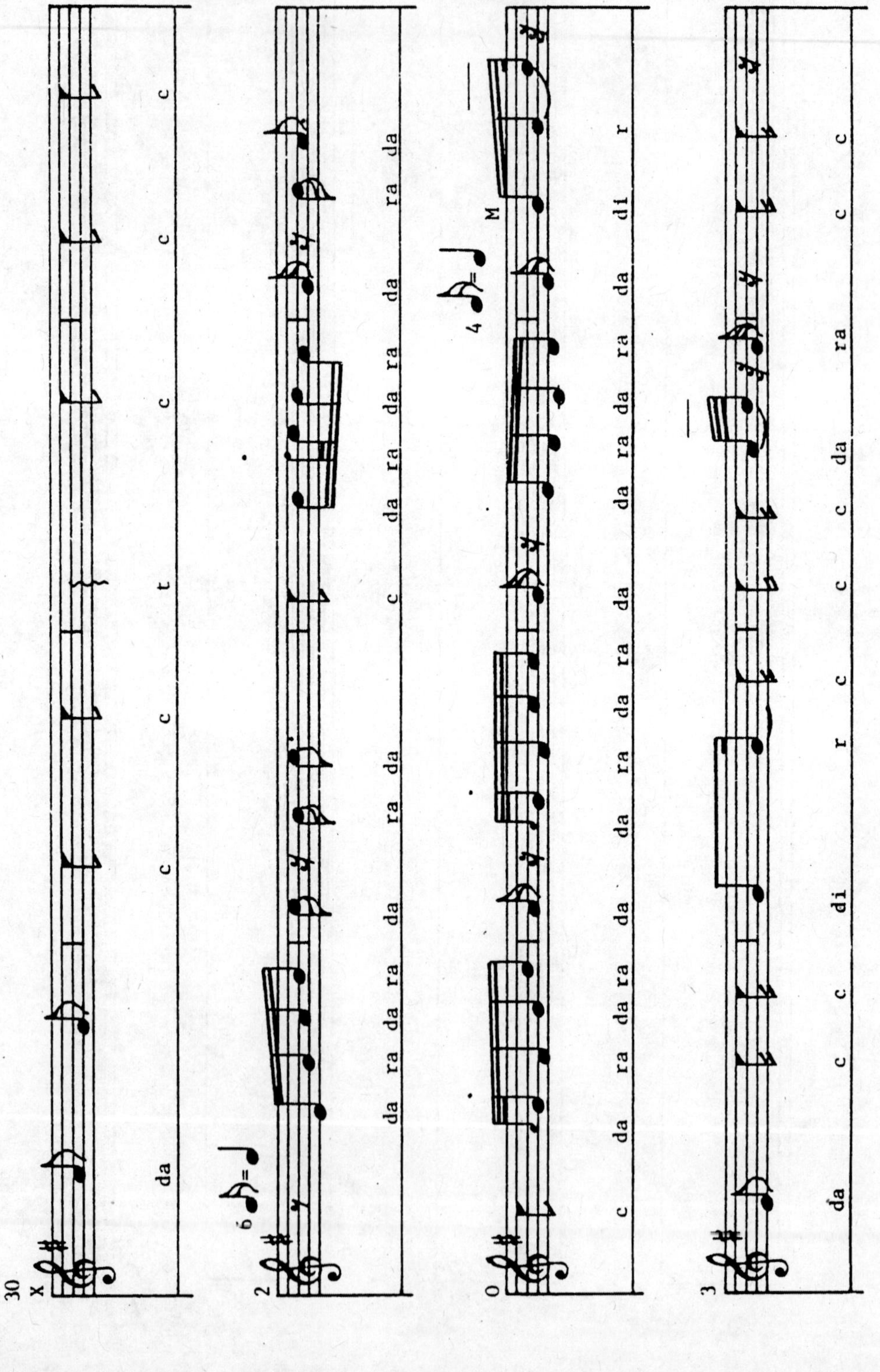
30
X
da c c c t c c c
2
6
da ra da ra da ra da c da ra da ra da ra da
0
4
M
c da ra da ra ra da da ra da ra da da ra da ra da ra da di r
3
da c c di r c c c da ra c c

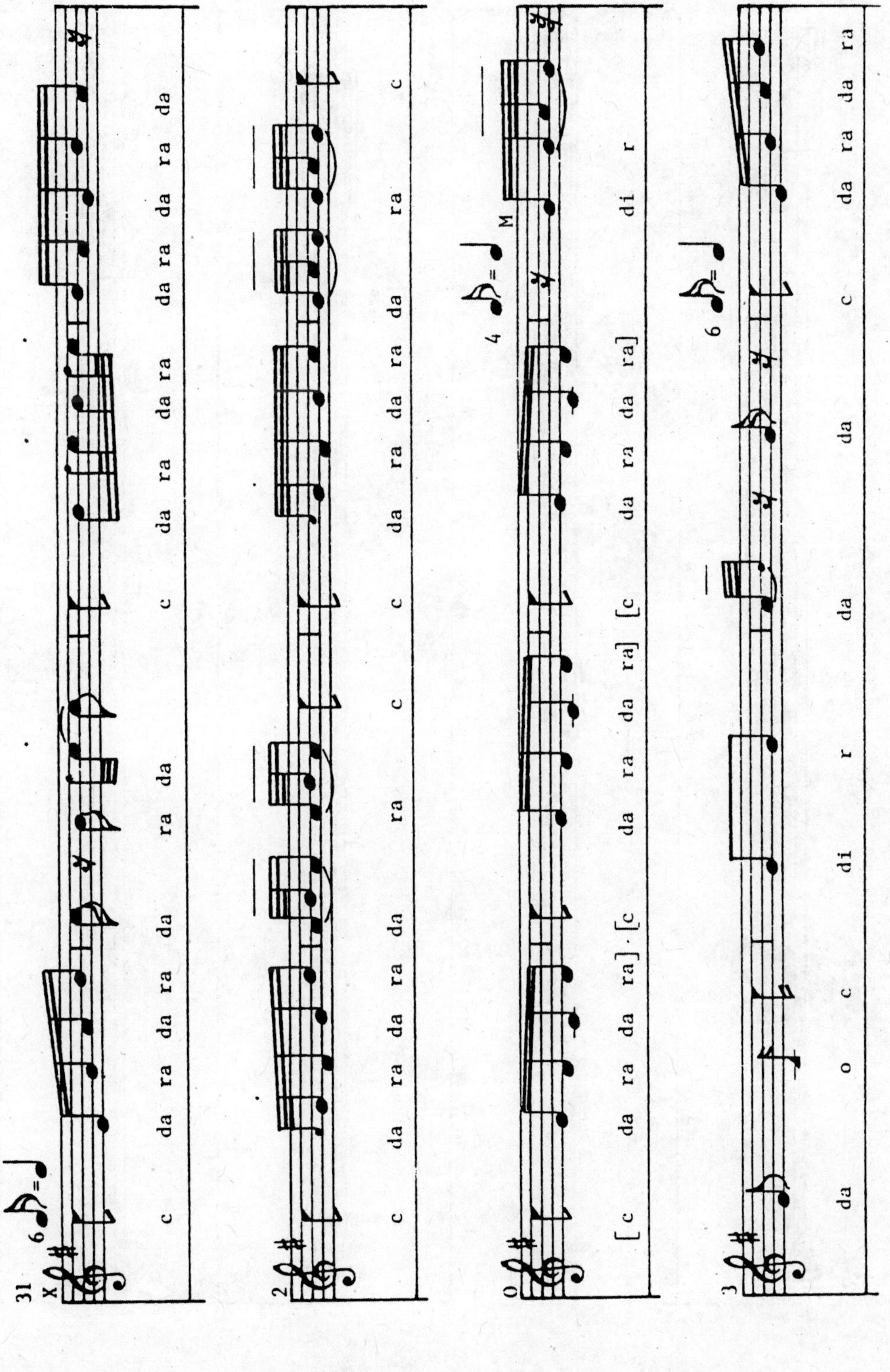
31
X
c da ra da ra da ra da c da ra da ra da ra da ra da
2
c da ra da ra da ra c c da ra da ra da ra c
0
[c da ra da ra] [c da ra da ra] [c da ra da ra] di r
M
3
da o c di r da da c da ra da ra da ra

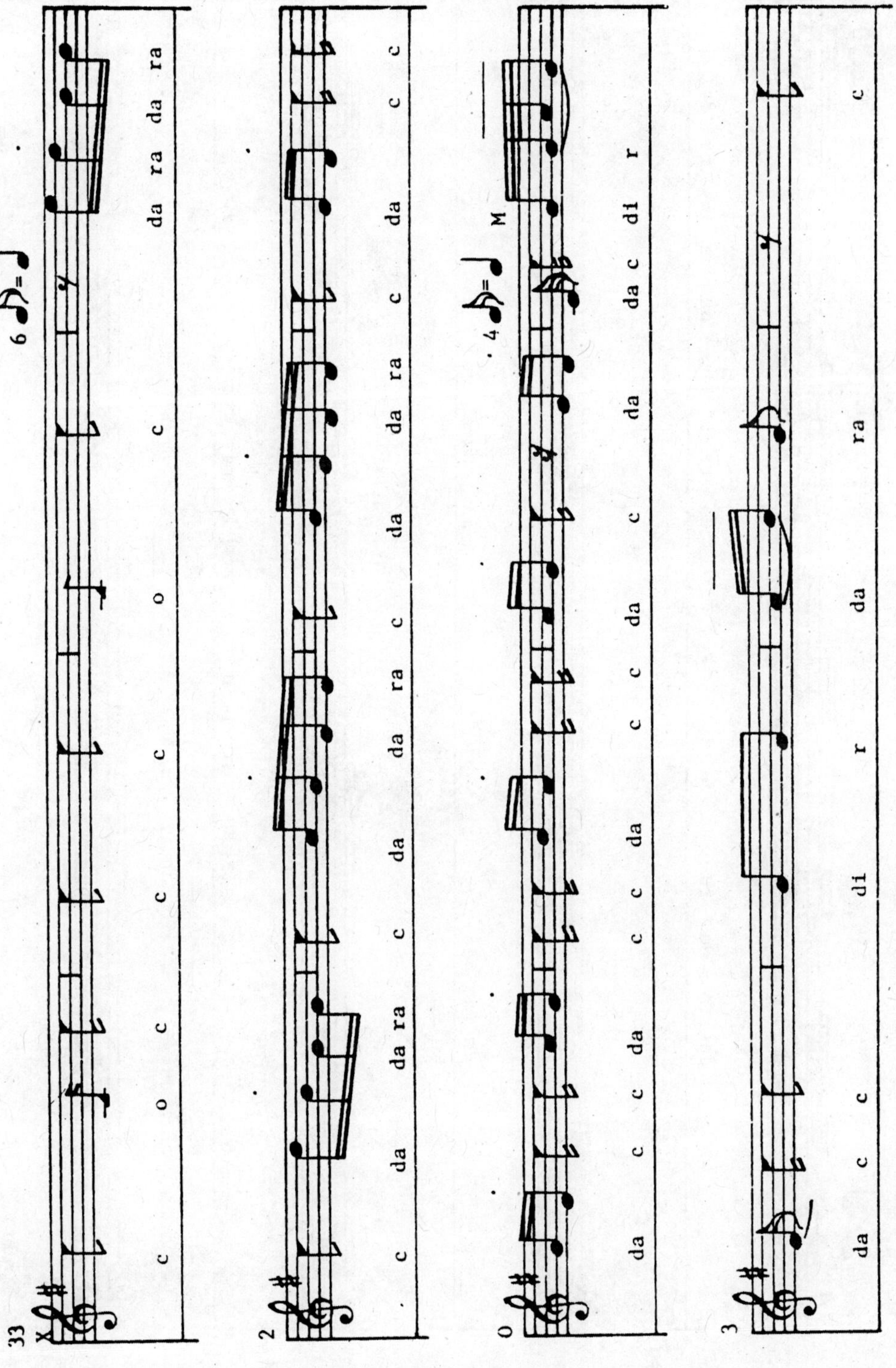
33
c o c c c o c da ra da ra
2
c da da ra c da da ra c da da ra c da c c
0
da c c da c c da c c da c da da c di r
3
da c c di r da ra c

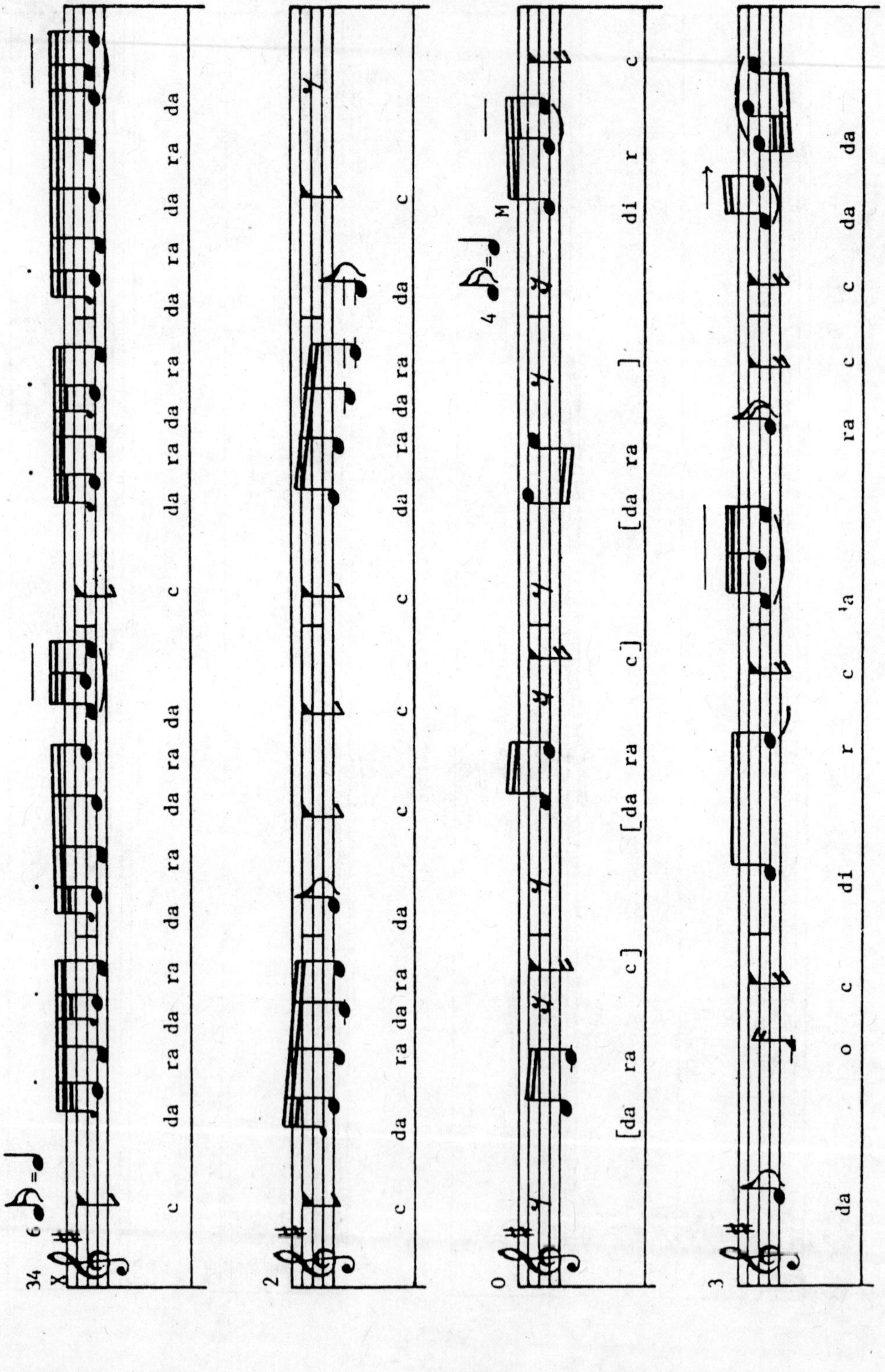
c da ra da ra da ra da ra da c da ra da ra da ra da ra da
c da ra da ra da c c c da ra da ra da c
[da ra c] [da ra c] [da ra] di r c
da o c di r c 'a ra c c da da

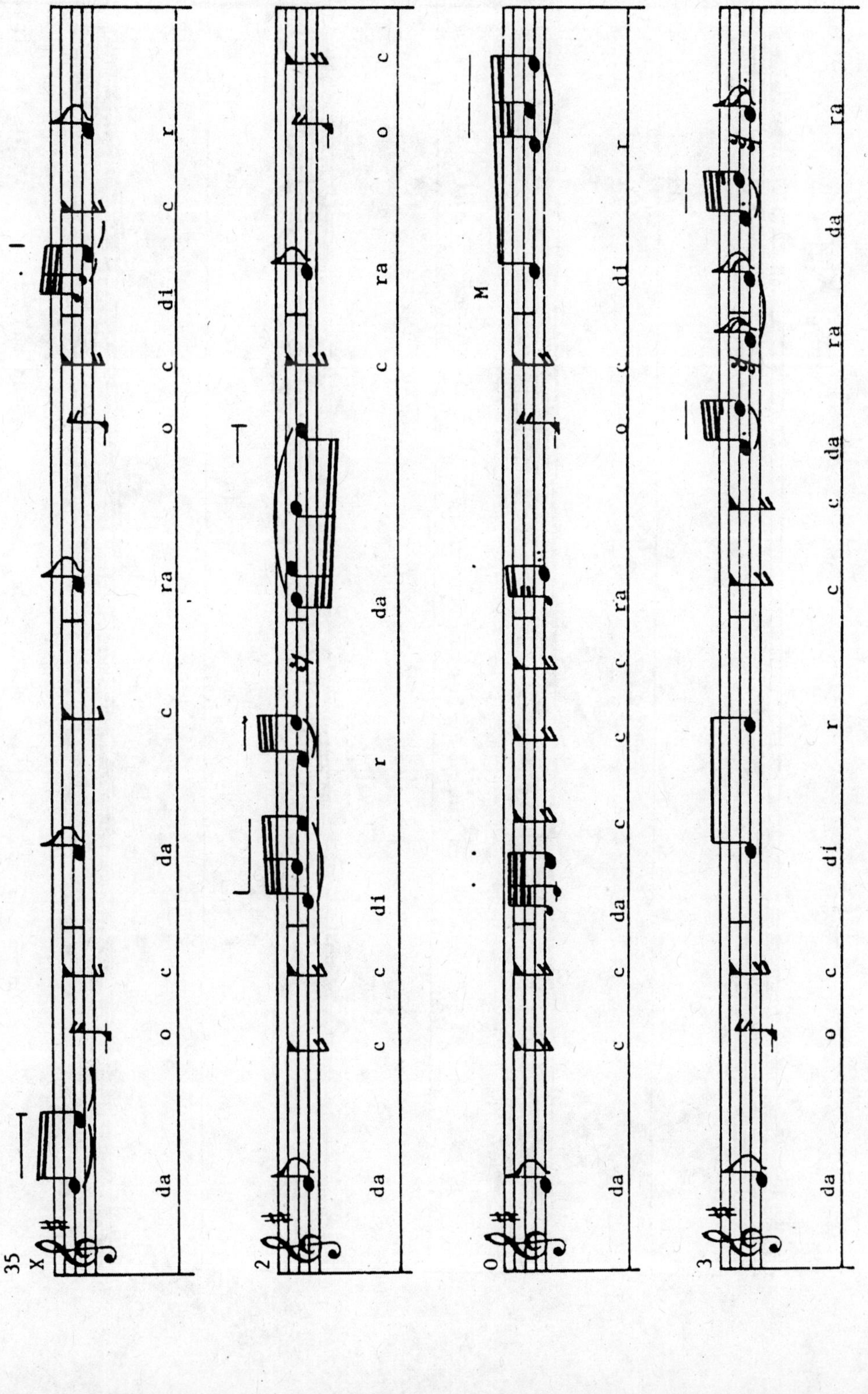
35
X
da o c da c ra o c dl c r
2
da c c dl r da c ra o c
0
da c c da c c c ra o c dl r
3
da o c dl r c c da ra da ra

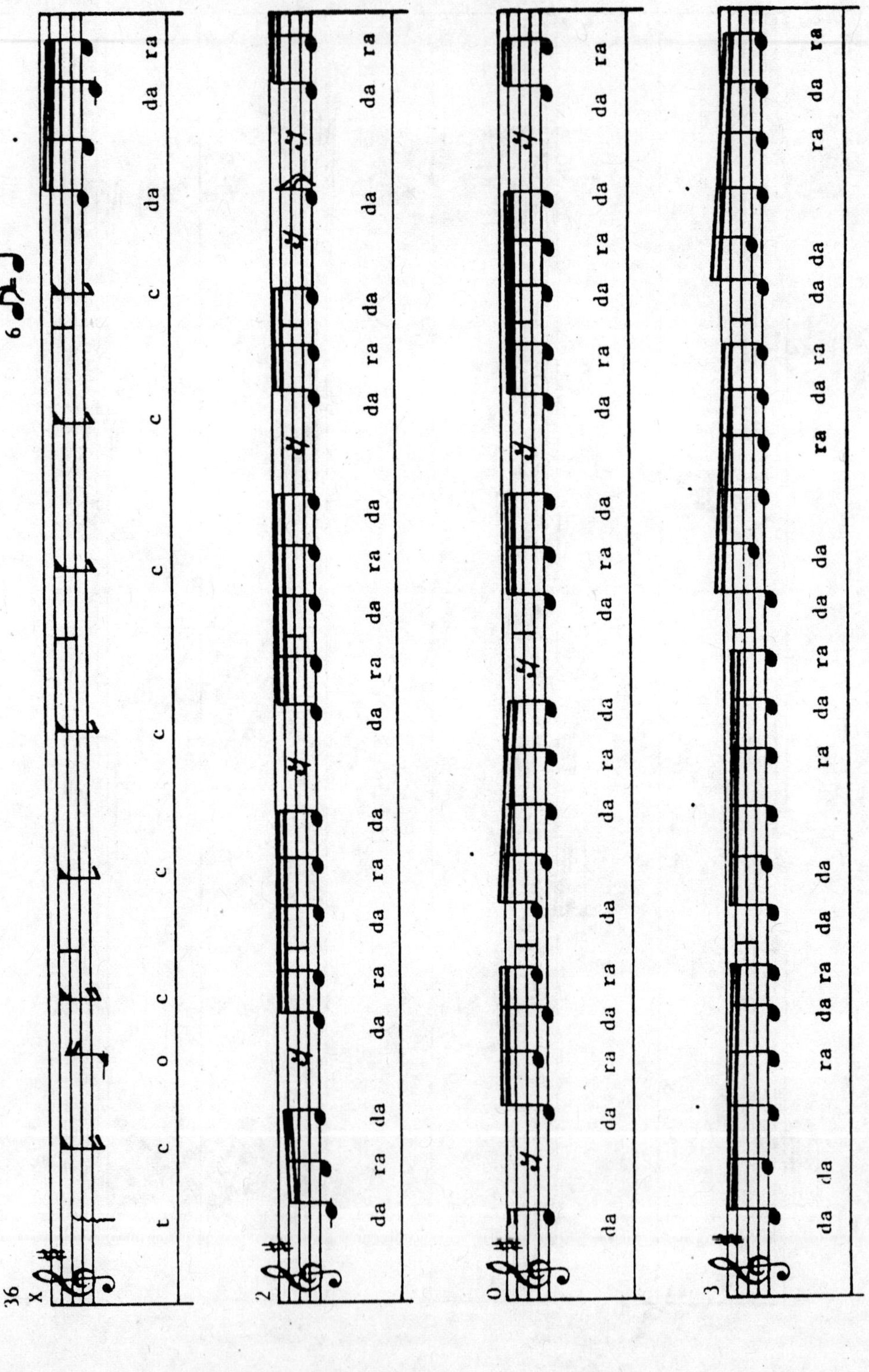
36
x
t c o c c c c c c da da ra
2
da ra da da ra da ra da da ra da ra da da ra da da da ra
0
da da ra da ra da da ra da da ra da da ra da ra da da ra
3
da da ra da ra da da ra da ra da da ra da ra da da ra da ra

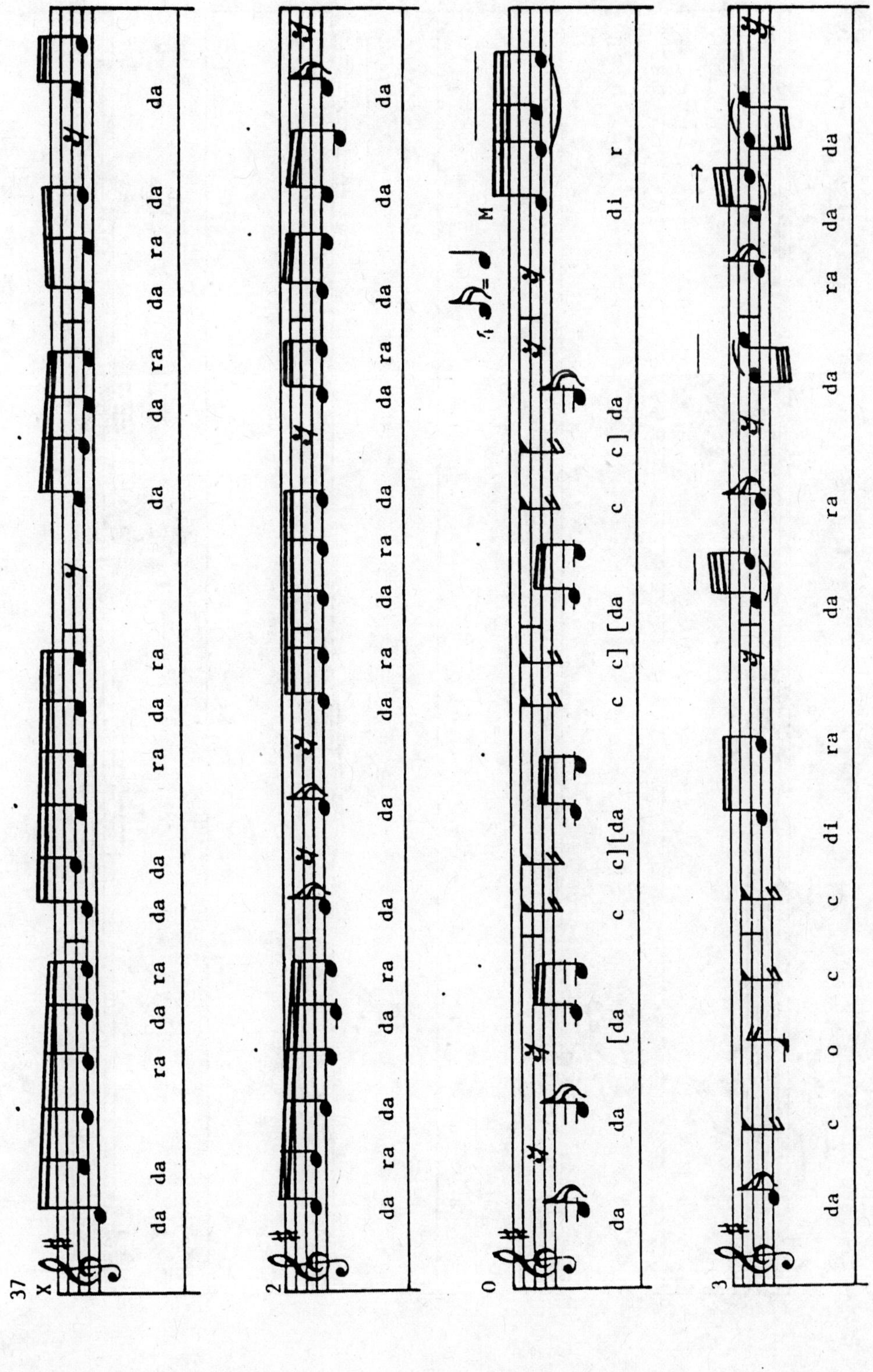
37
X
da da ra da ra da da ra da ra da da ra da ra da da
2
da ra da da ra da da da ra da ra da da ra da da da
0
M
da da [da c c][da c c] [da c c] da di r
3
da c o c c di ra da ra da ra da da

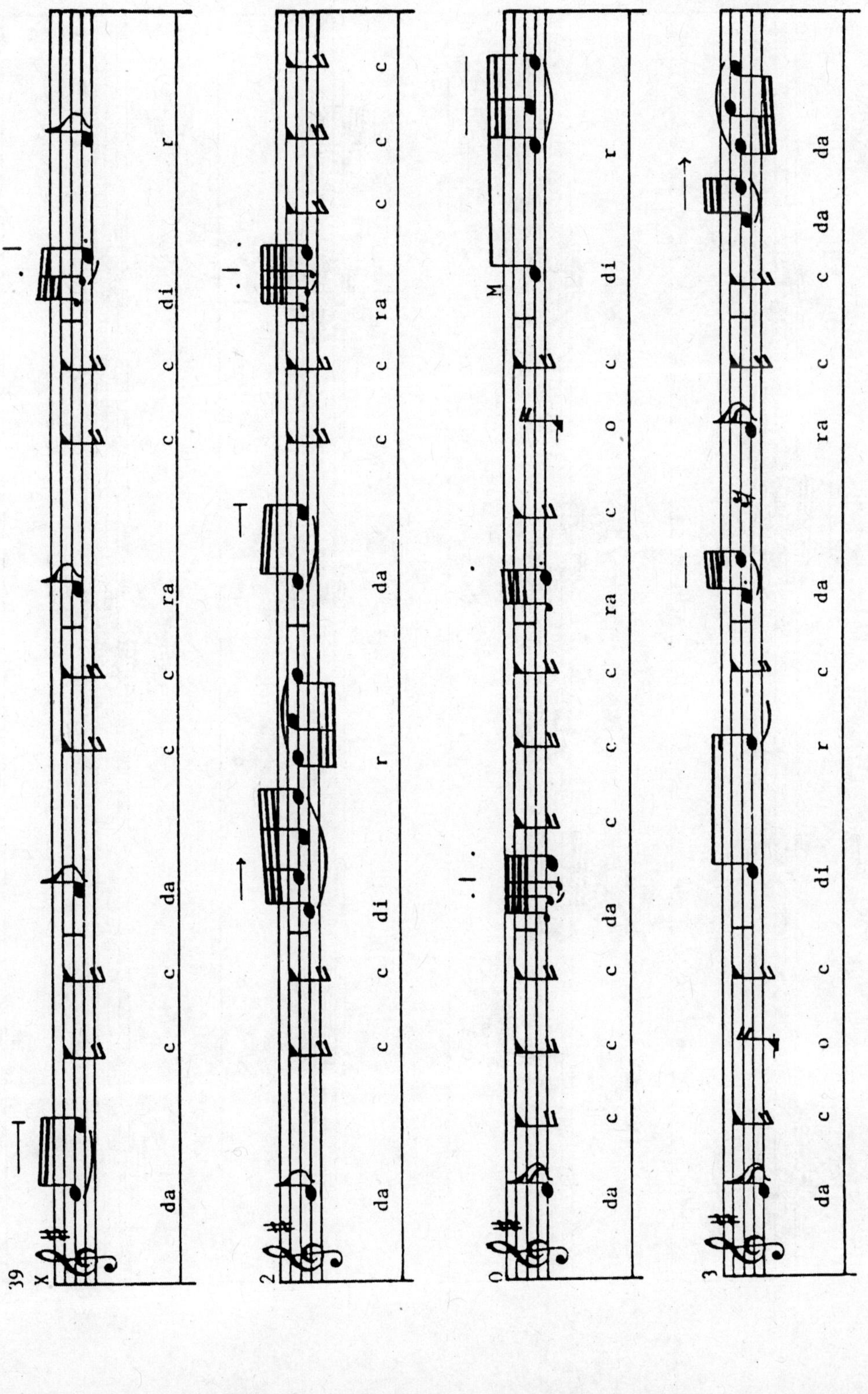
39
da c c da c c ra c c di r
da c c di r da c c ra c c c
da c c c da c c c ra c o c di r
da c o c di r c da ra c c da da

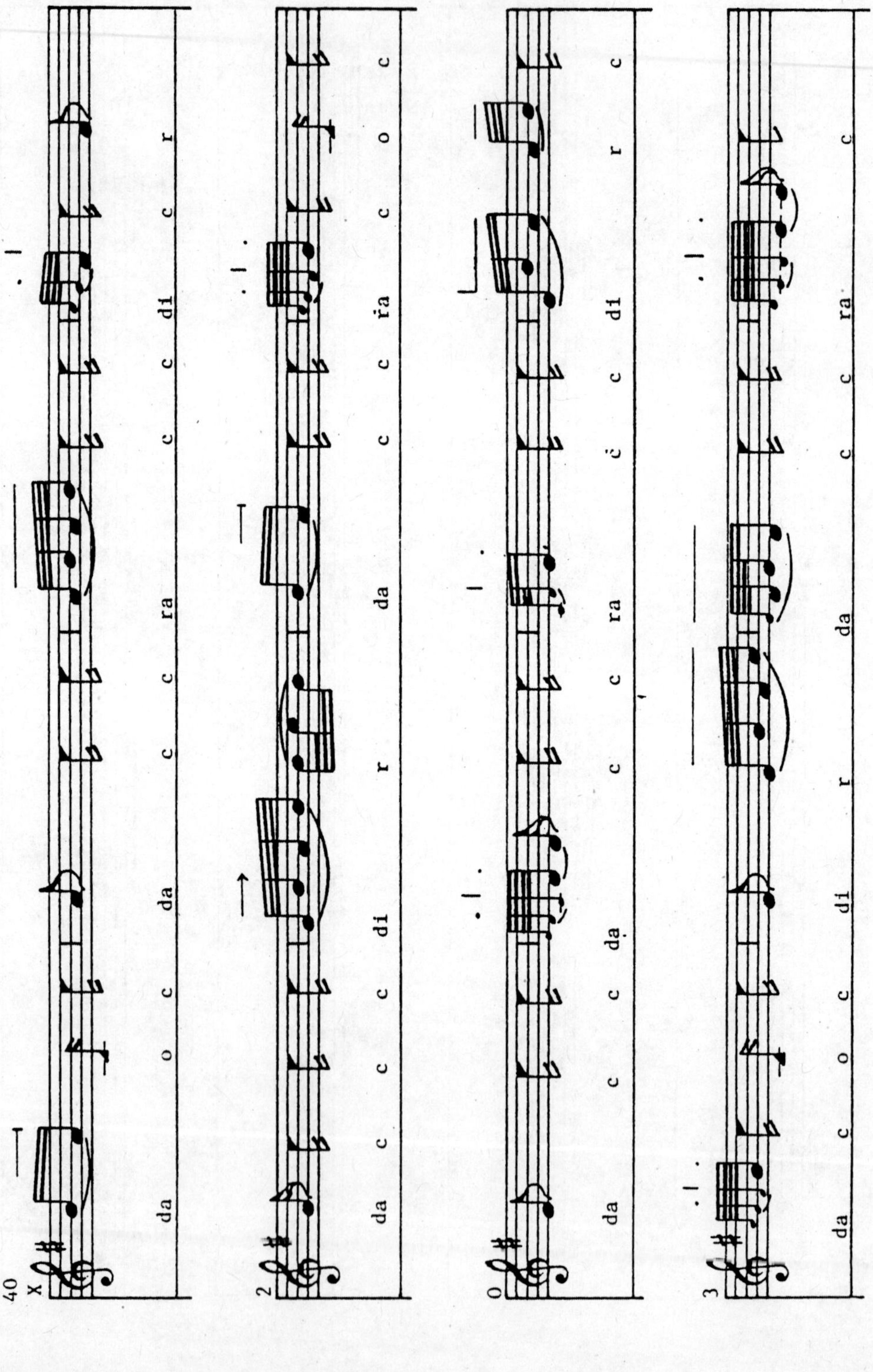
40 X
da o c da c c ra c c dī c r
2
da c c c dī r da c c ṙa c o c
0
da c c ḍa c c ra c̀ c dī r c
3
da c o c dī r da c c ra c c

41 X
da da ra c dl r
2
da o c da c c da c da da da
0
da c da da ra c da r da c M dl r
3
da c da c da c da c da da c da da

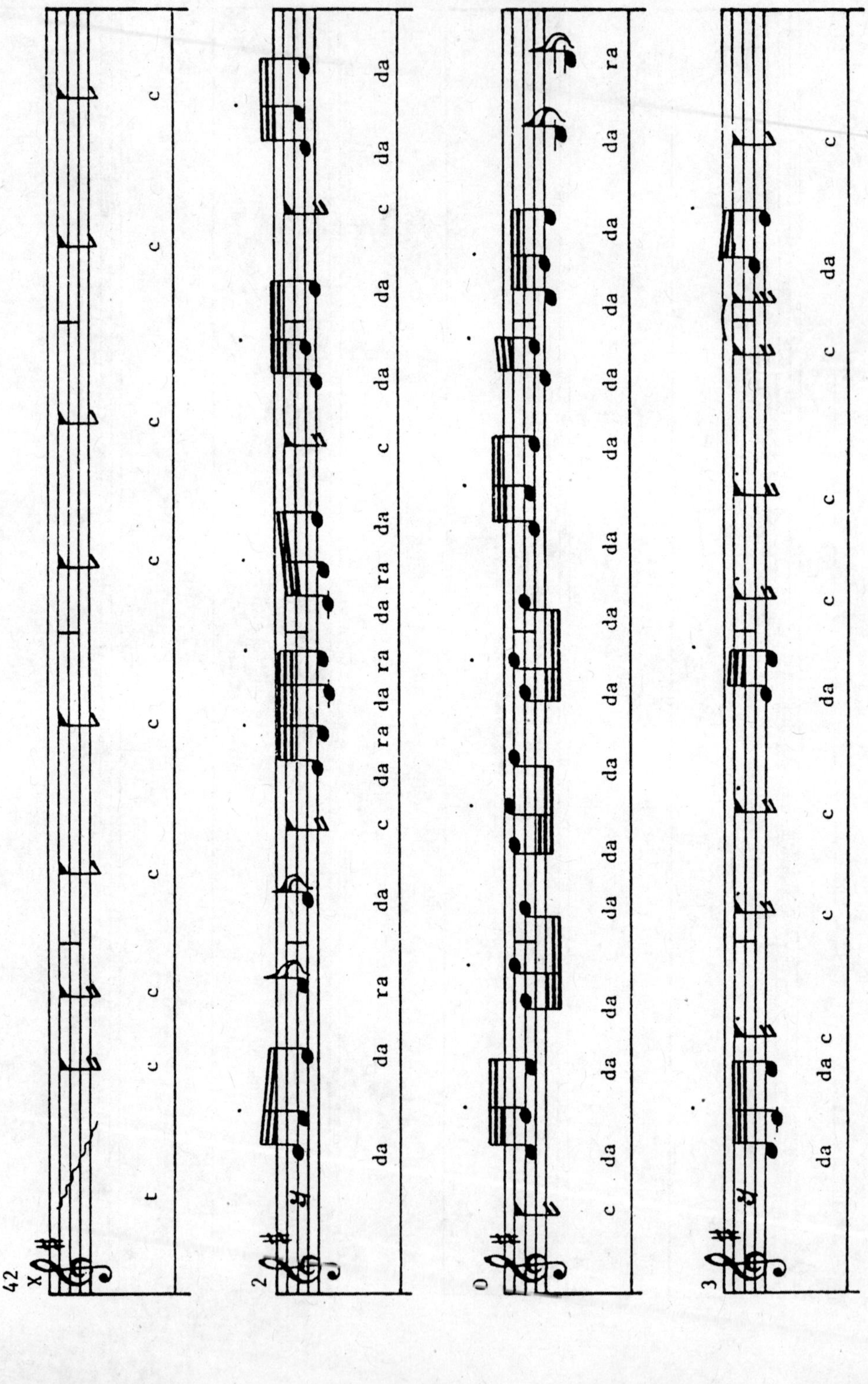
42
X
t c c c c c c c c
2
da da ra da c da ra da ra da ra da c da da c da da
0
c da da da da da da da da da da da da da da ra
3
da da c c c da c c c da c

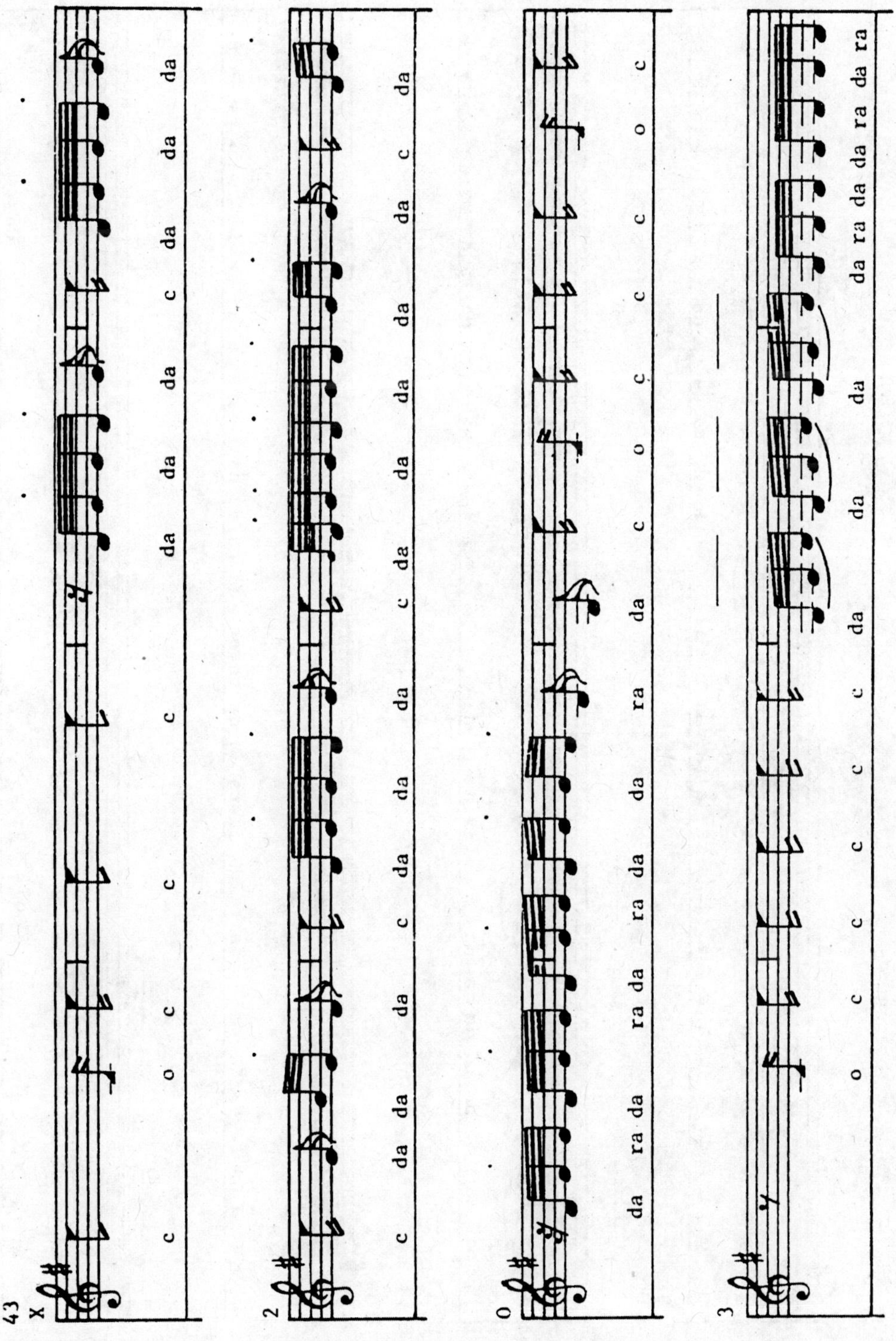
43 X
c o c c c da da da c da da da
2
c da da da c da da da c da da da da da c da
0
da ra da ra da ra da da ra da c o c c c o c
3
o c c c c c da da da da ra da da ra da ra

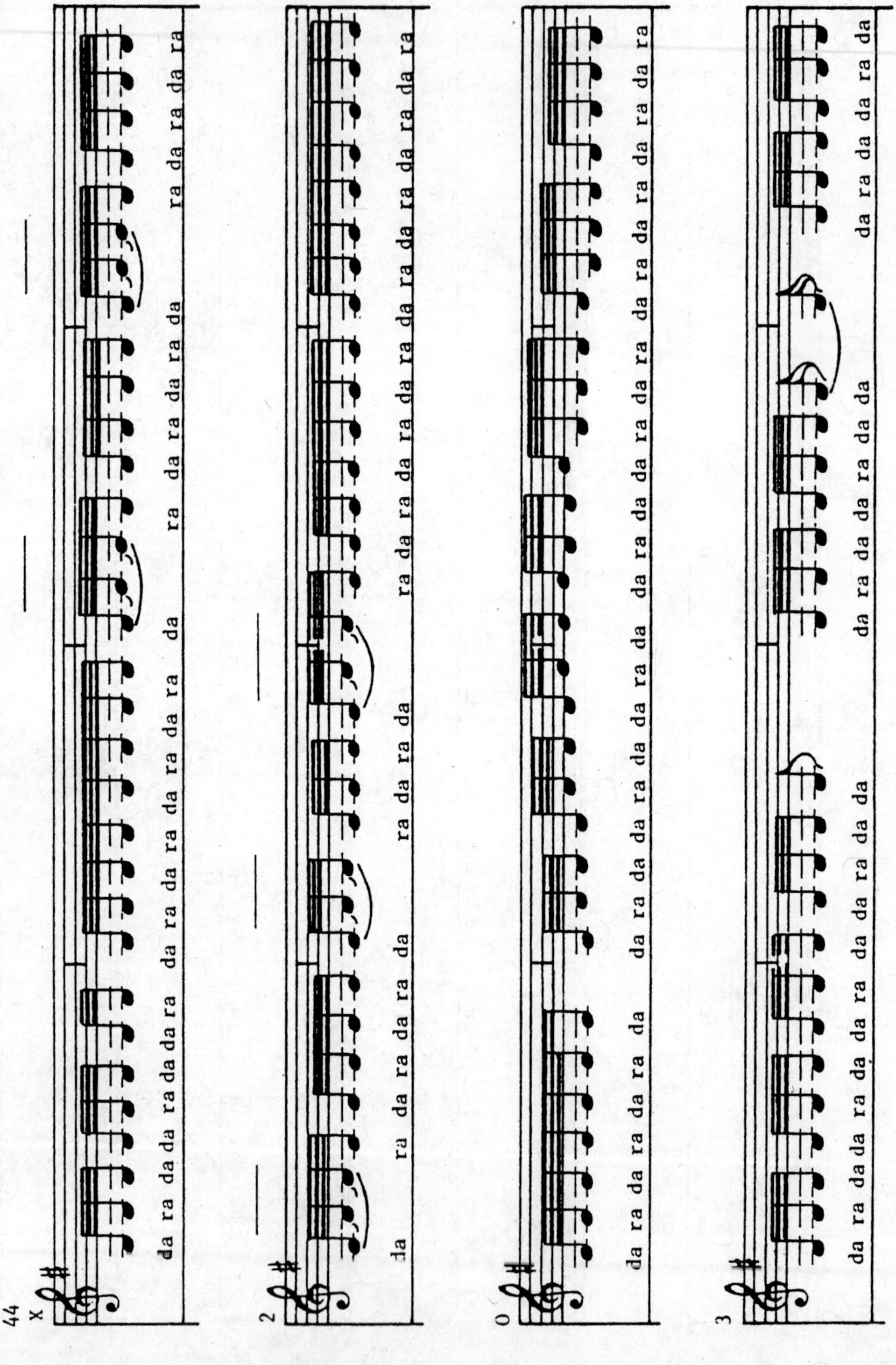

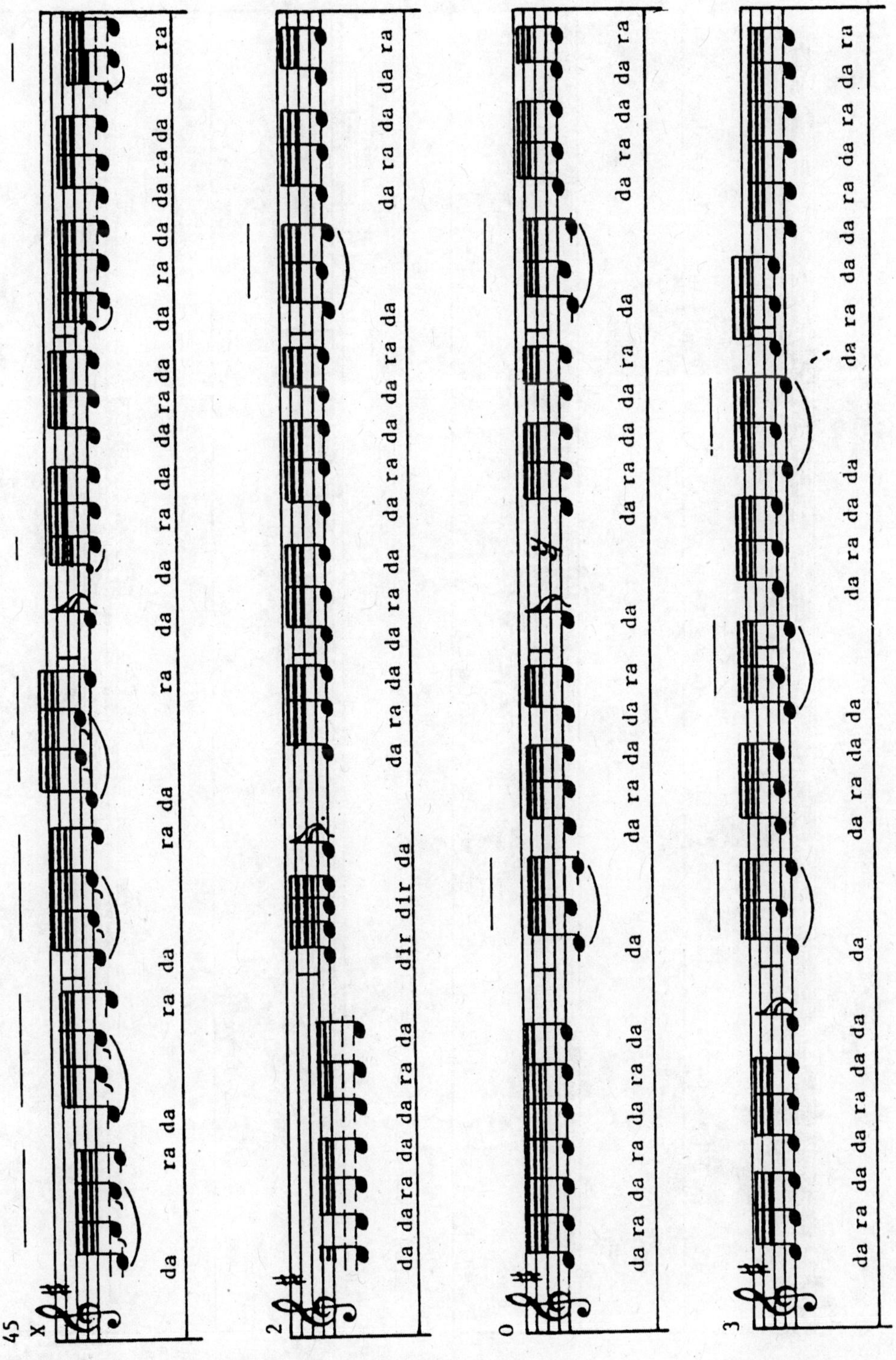
45
X
da ra da ra da ra da ra da da ra da da ra da da ra da da ra da da ra da da ra
2
da da ra da da ra da dir dir da da ra da da ra da da ra da da ra da da ra da da ra
0
da ra da ra da ra da da da ra da da ra da da ra da da ra da da ra da da ra
3
da ra da da ra da da da da ra da da da ra da da da ra da da ra da ra da ra

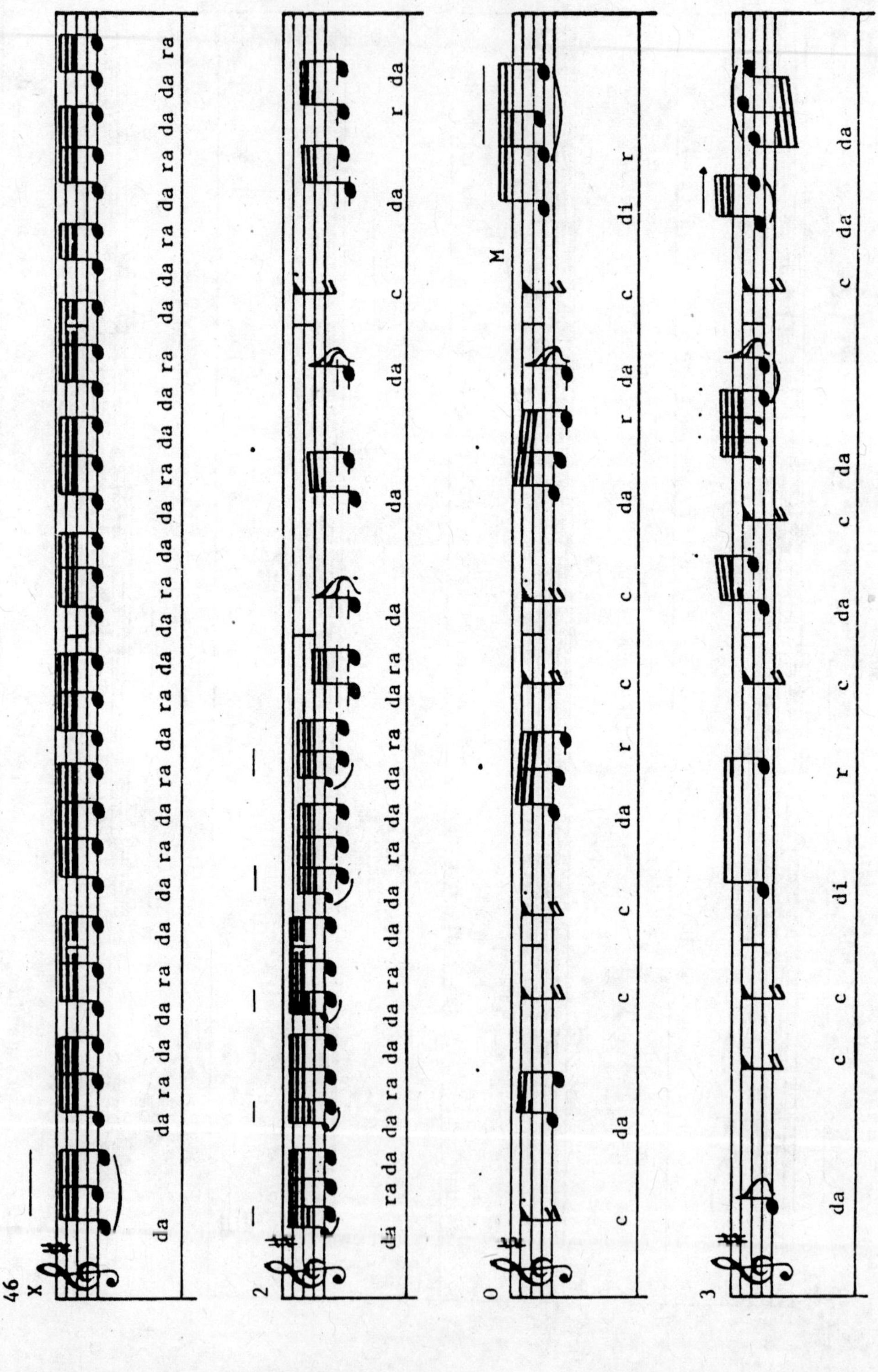
46
X
da da ra da da ra da ra da ra da ra da ra da da ra da ra da ra da ra da ra
2
di ra da da ra da da ra da da ra da da ra da da c da r da
0
c da c c c da r c c da r da c di r
M
3
da c c c di r c da c da c da da

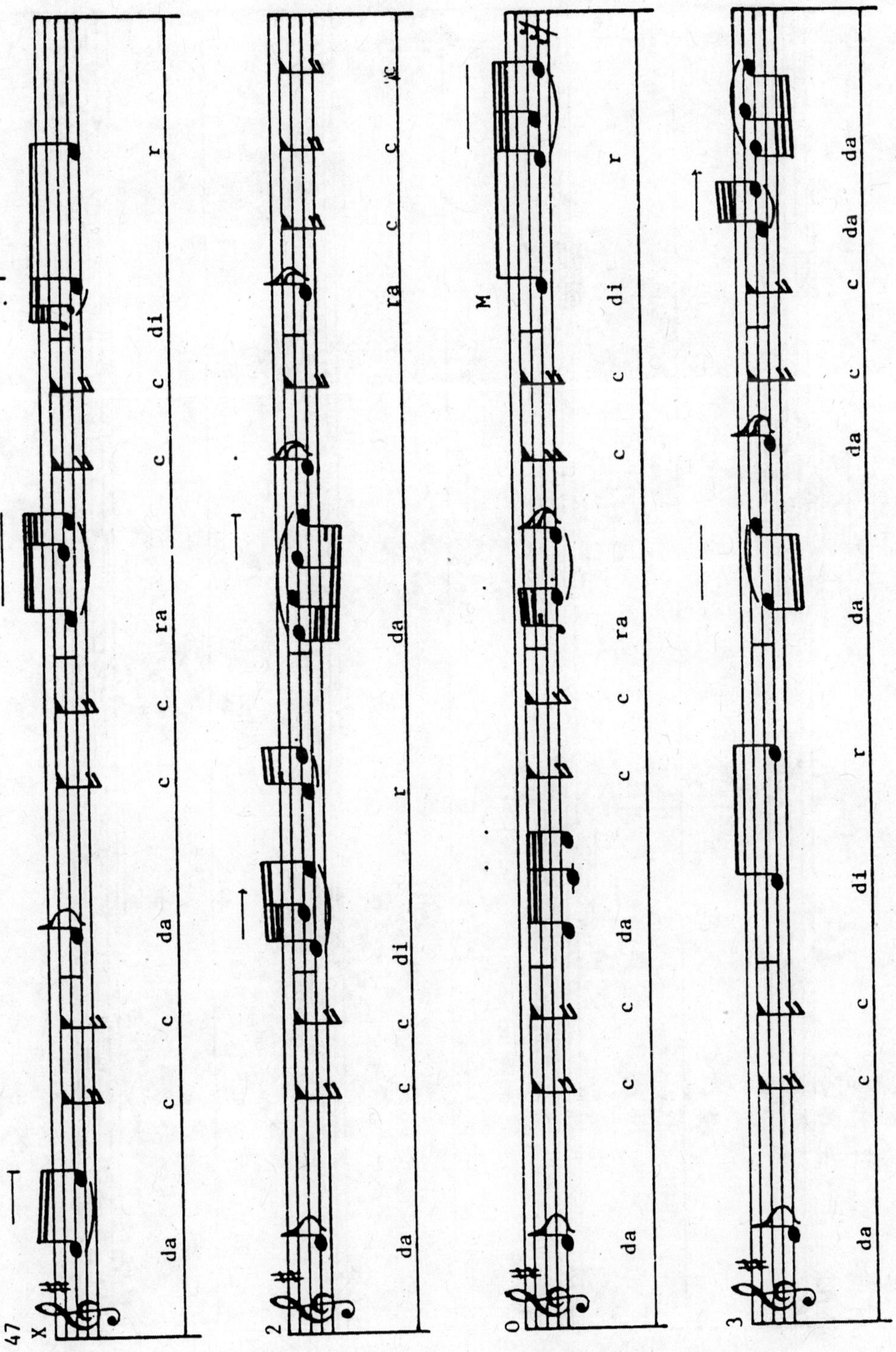
47 X
da c c da c c ra c c di r
2
da c c di r da ra c c c
0
da c c da c c ra c c di r
3
da c c di r da da c c da da

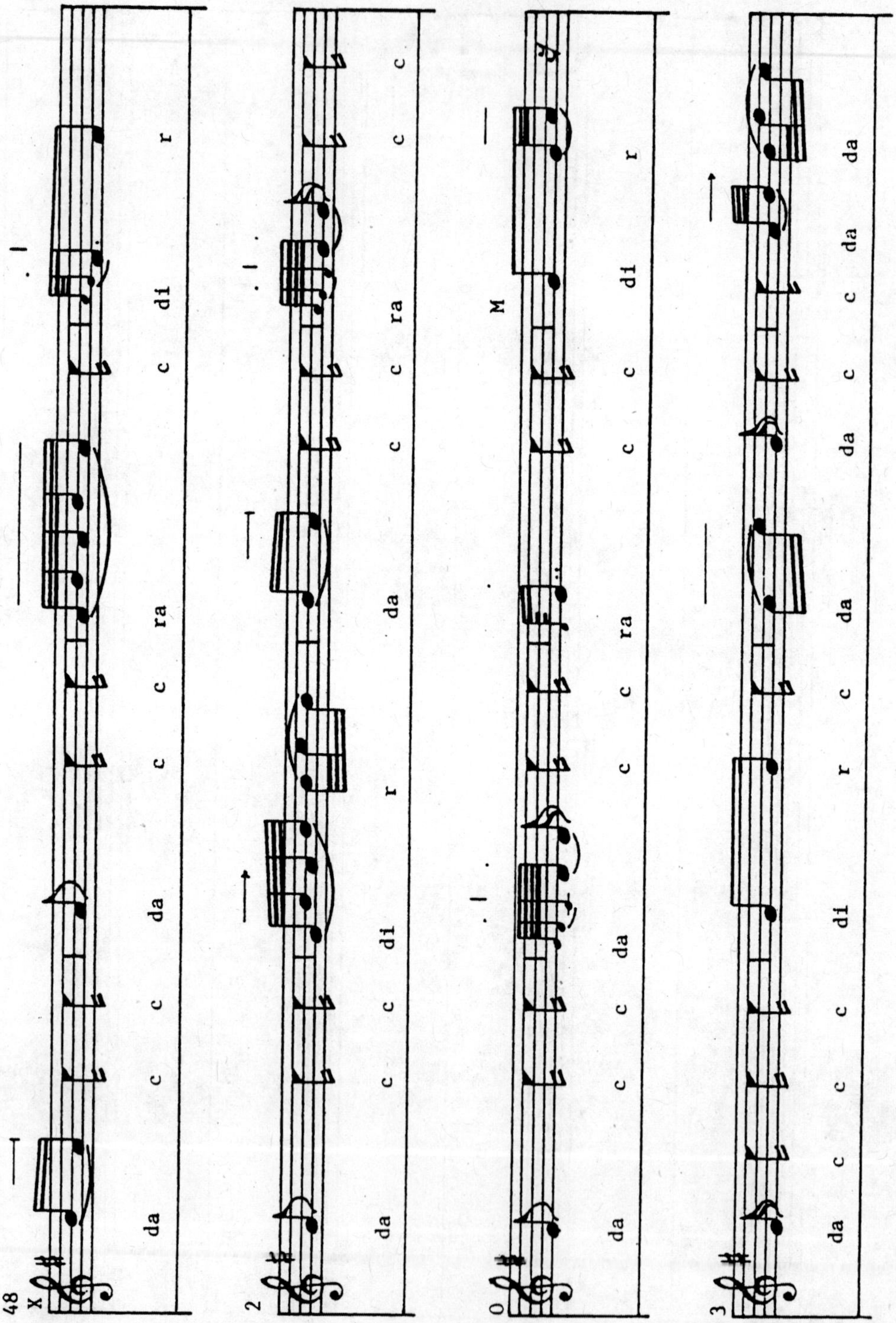
48
X
da c c da c c ra c di r
2
da c c di r da c c ra c c
0
M
da c c da c c ra c c di r
3
da c c c di r c da da c c da da

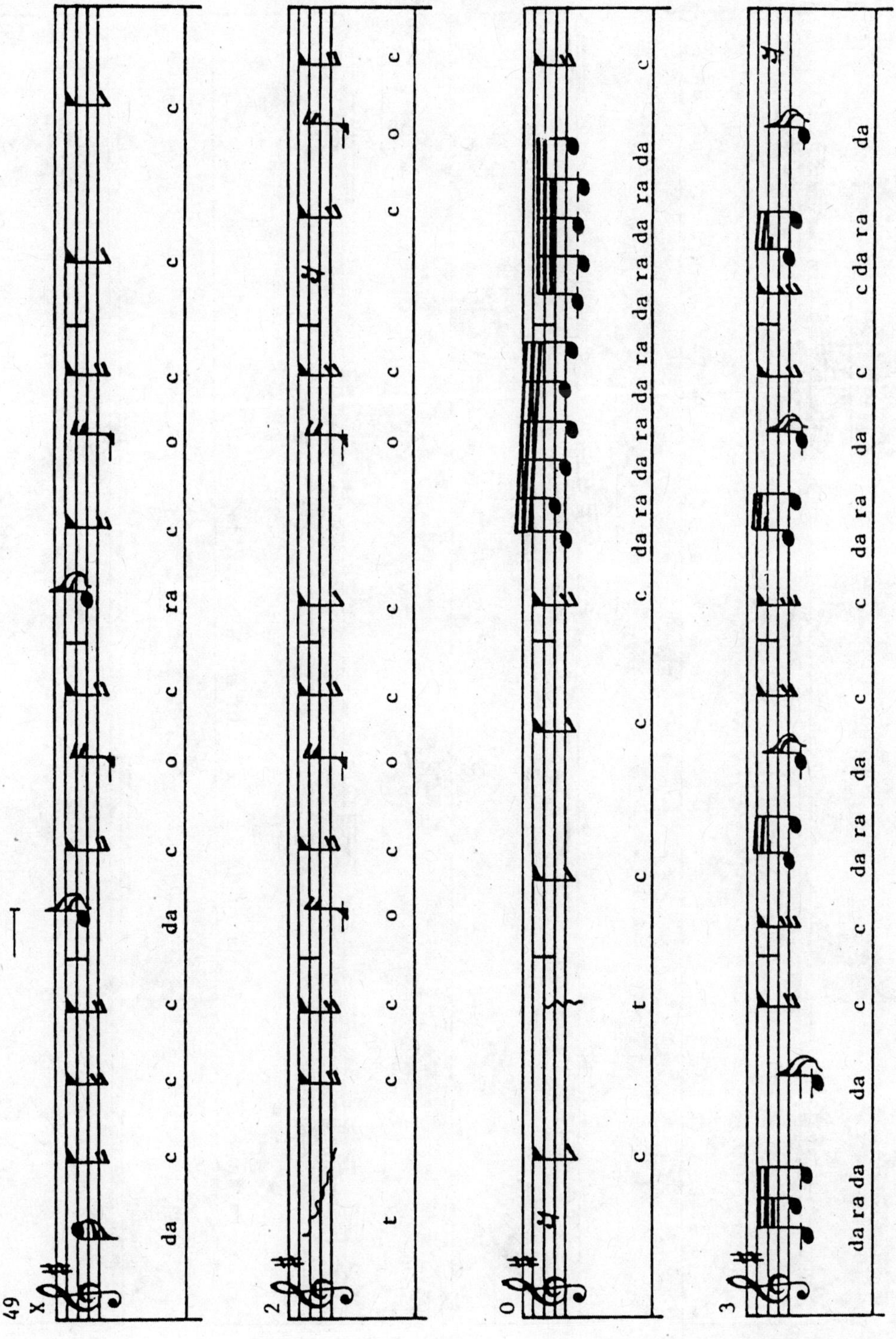
49
X
I
da c c c da c c o c ra c o c c c
2
t c c c o c c o c c c o c o c
0
c t c c c da ra da ra da ra da ra da ra da ra da c
3
da ra da da c c da ra da c c da ra da c c da ra da

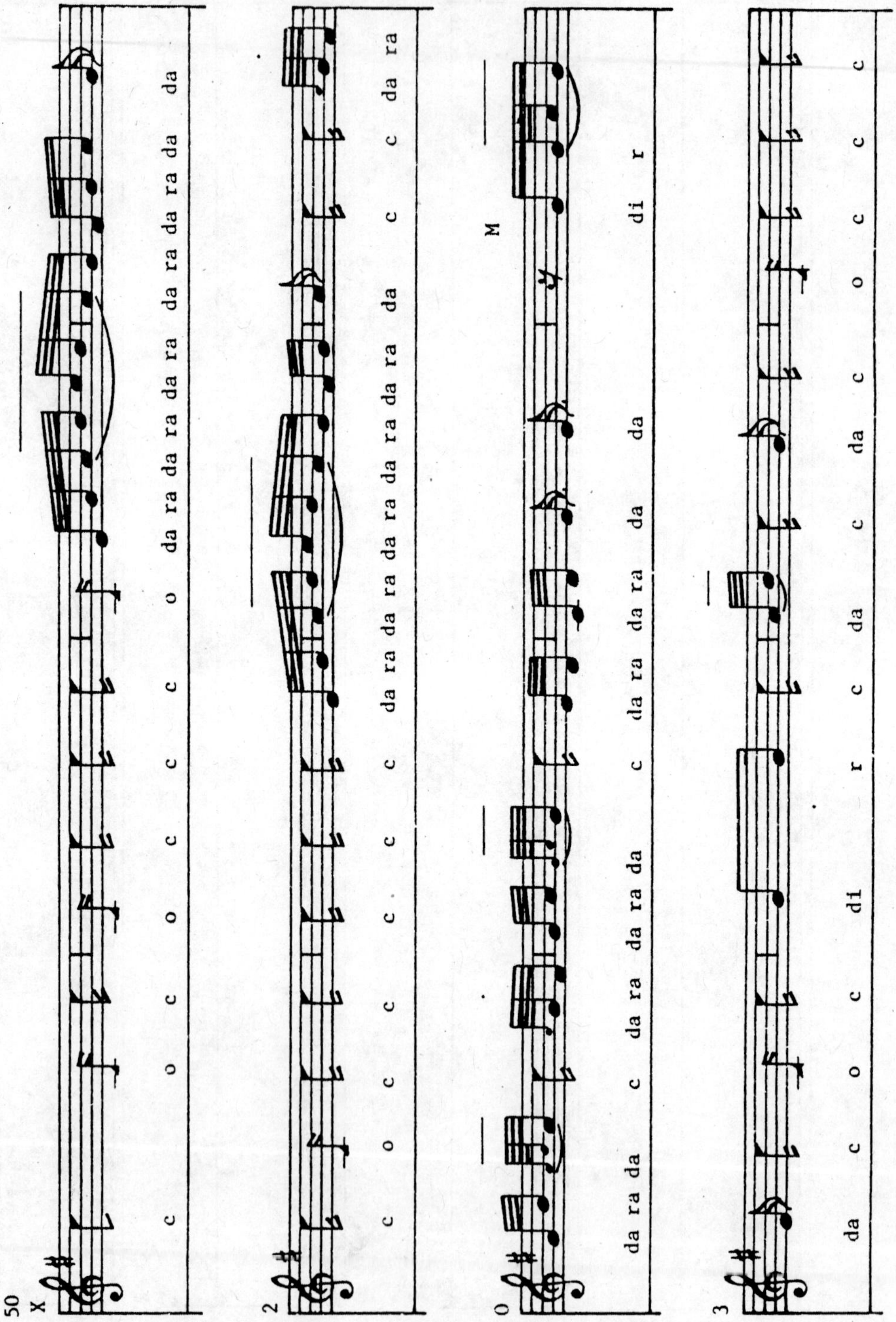

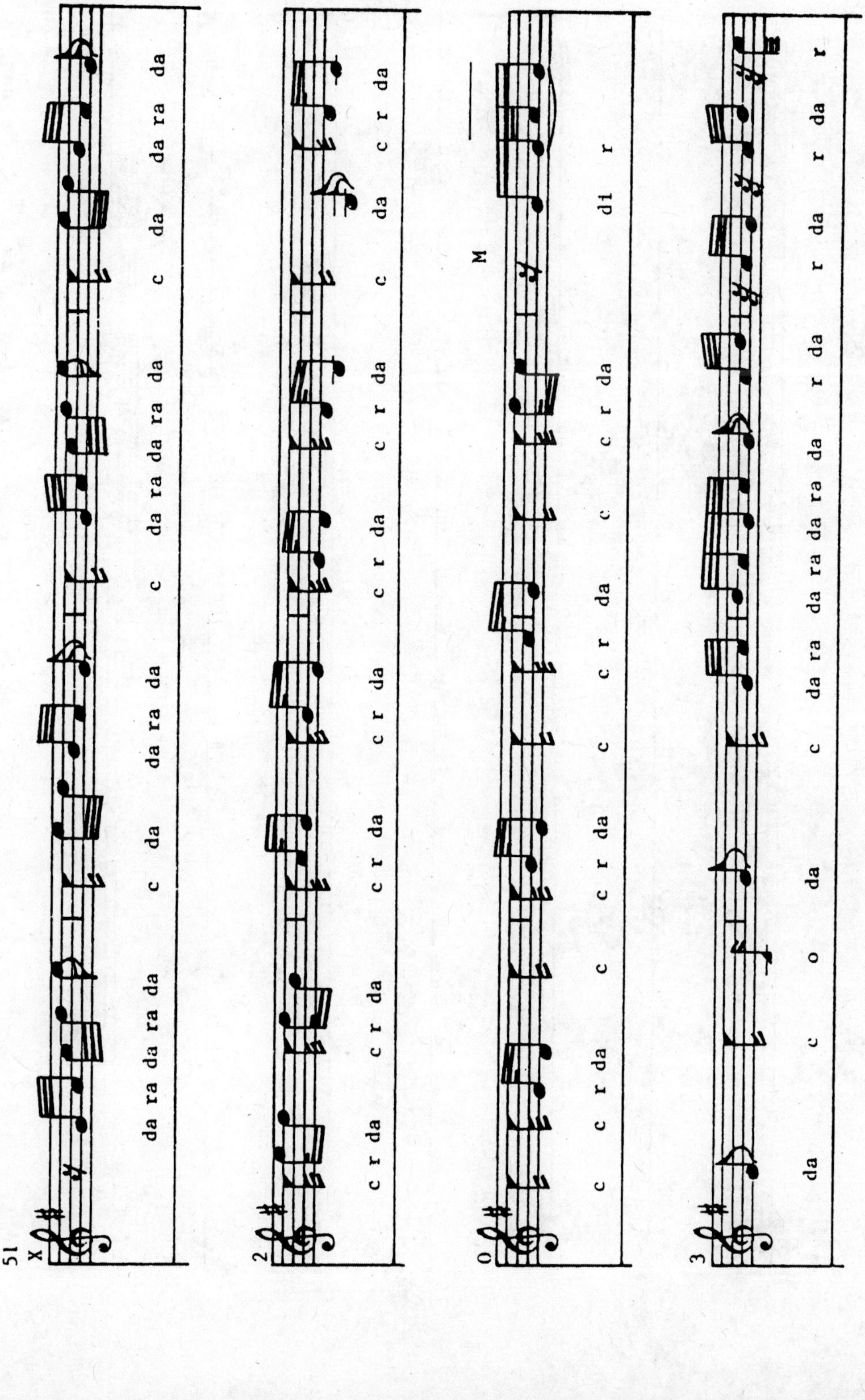
51
X
da ra da ra da c da da ra da c da ra da ra da c da da ra da
2
c r da c r da c r da c r da c r da c r da c da c r da
0
c c r da c c r da c c r da c c r da dl r
M
3
da c o da c da ra da ra da r da r da r

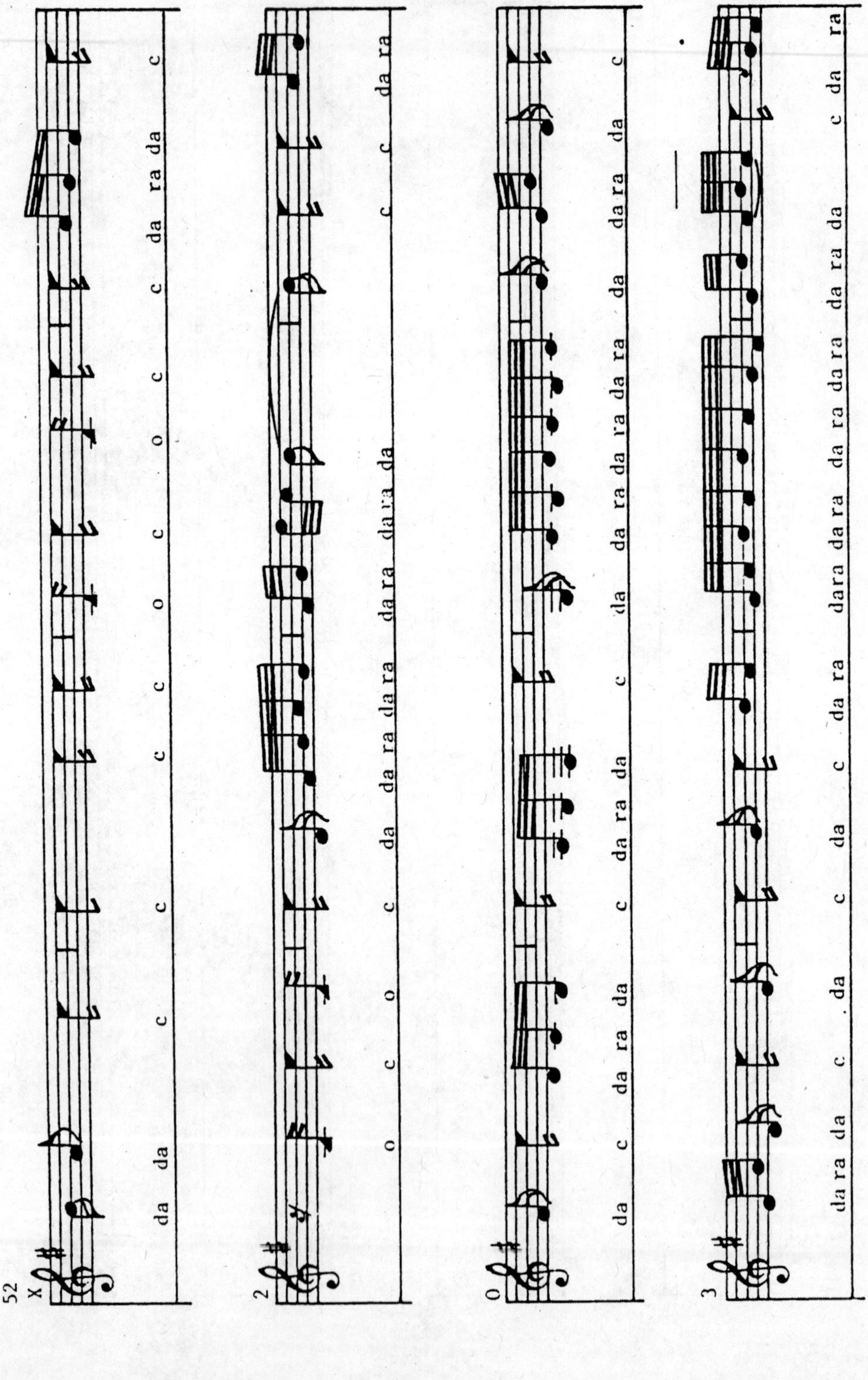

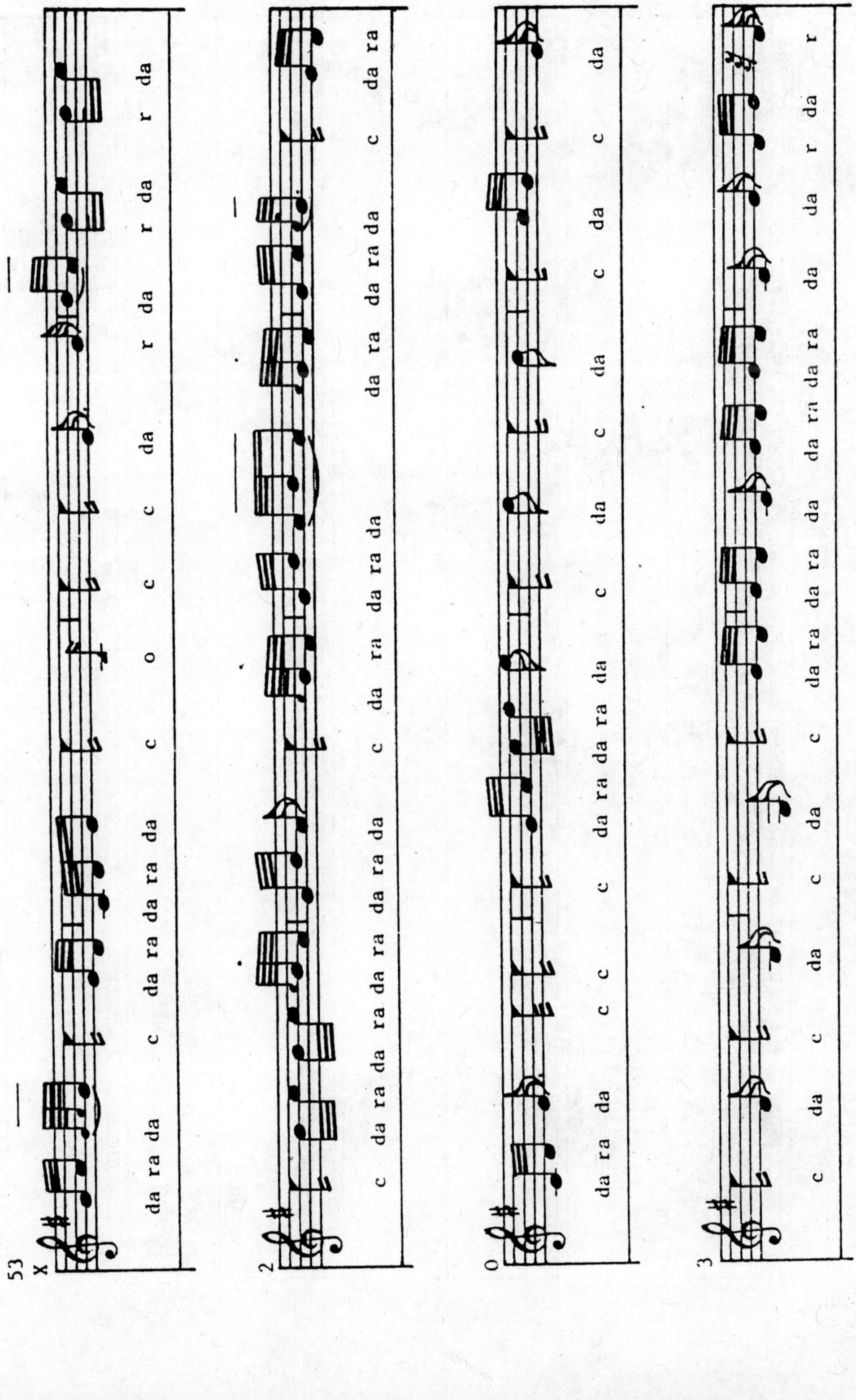
53 X
da ra da c da ra da ra da ra da c o c c da r da r da r da
2
c da ra da ra da ra da ra da ra da c da ra da ra da ra da da ra da ra da c da ra
0
da ra da c c c da ra da ra da ra da c da c da c da c da c da
3
c da c da c da ra da ra da ra da da ra da ra da ra da da r da r

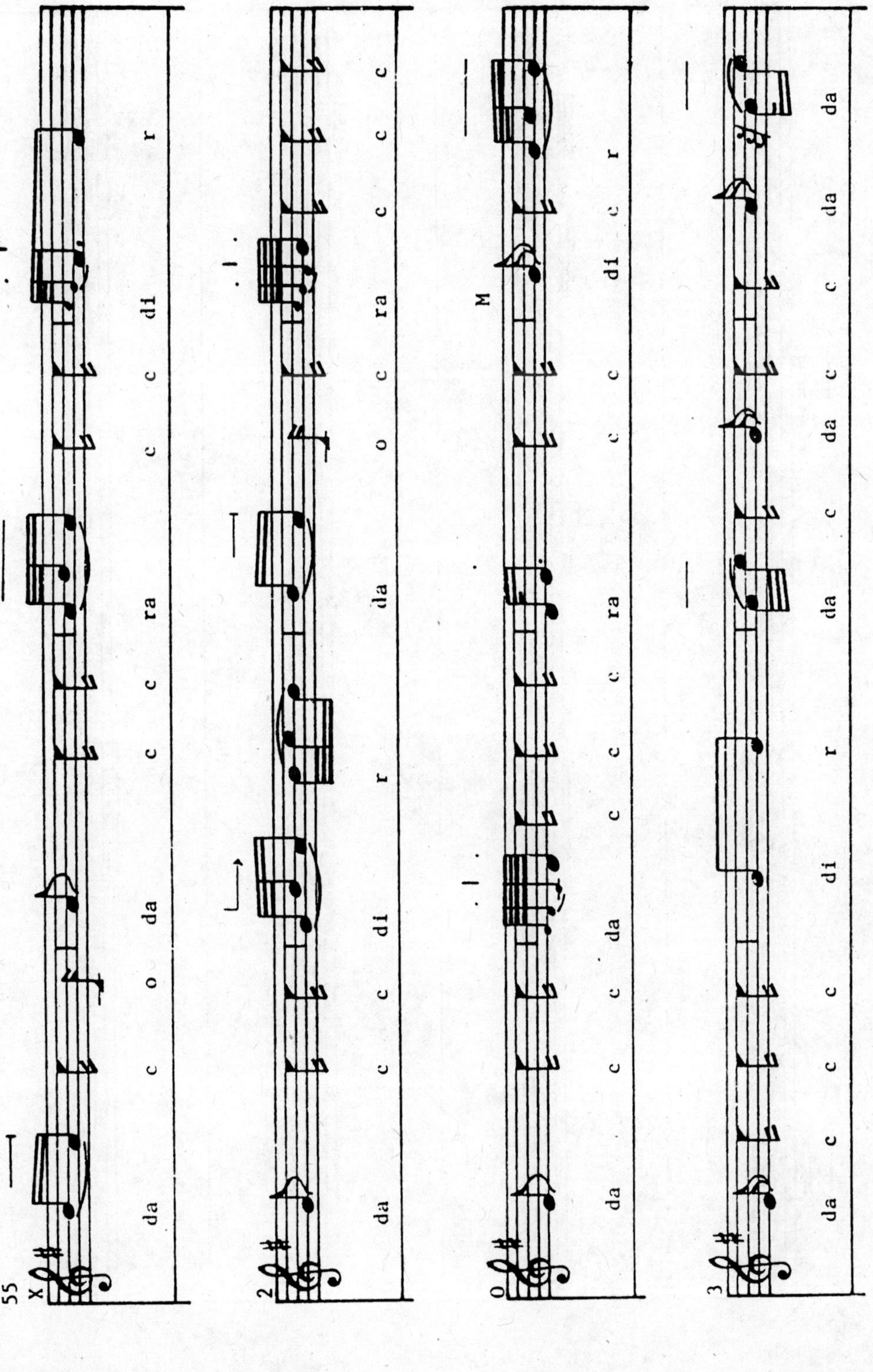
55 X
da c o da c c ra c c dl r
2
da c c dl r da o c ra c c c
0
M
da c c da c c c ra c c dl c r
3
da c c c di r da c da c da da

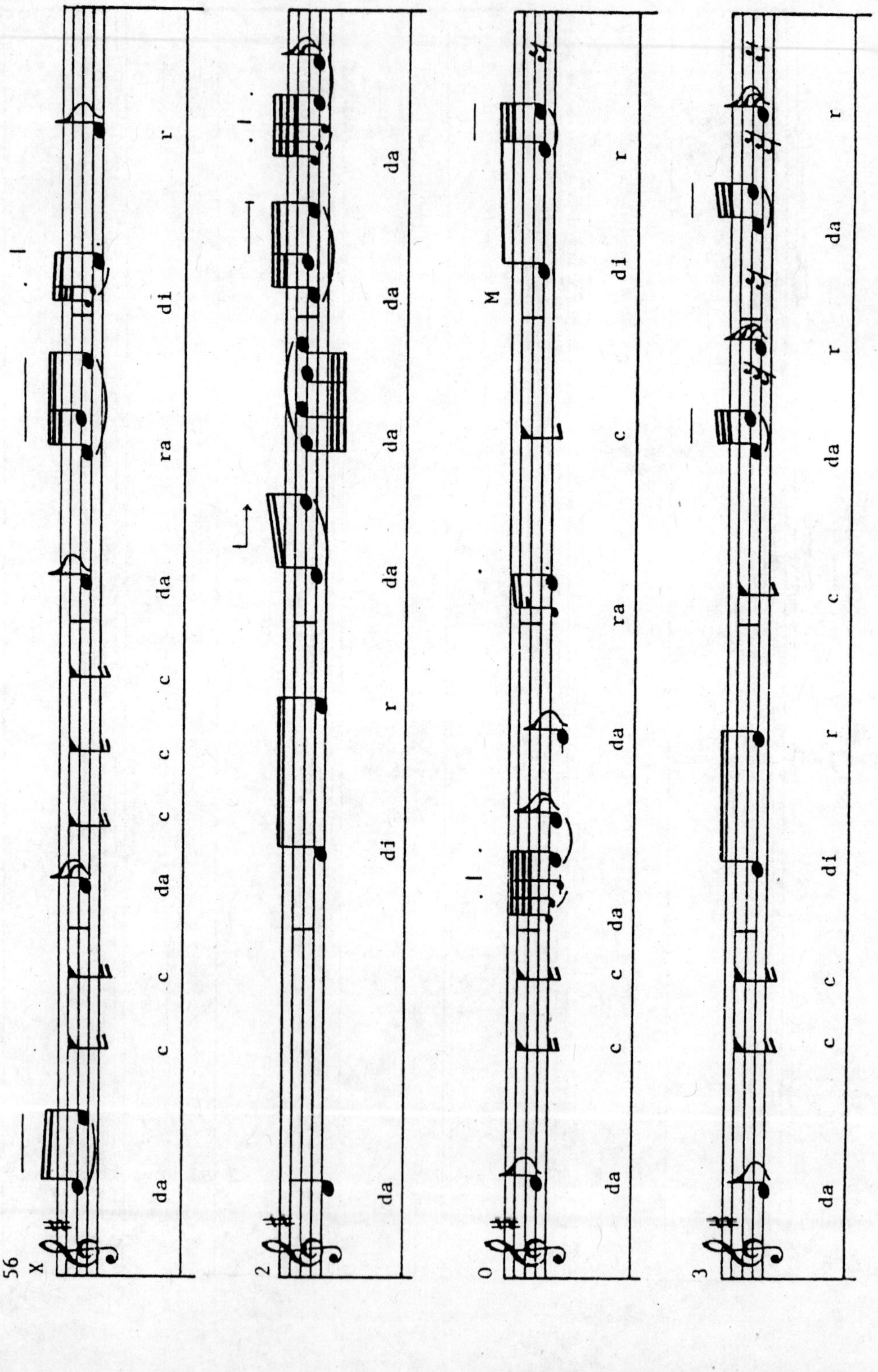
56
X
da c c da c c c da ra di r
2
da di r da da da da
0
da c c da da ra c di r
M
3
da c c di r c da r da r

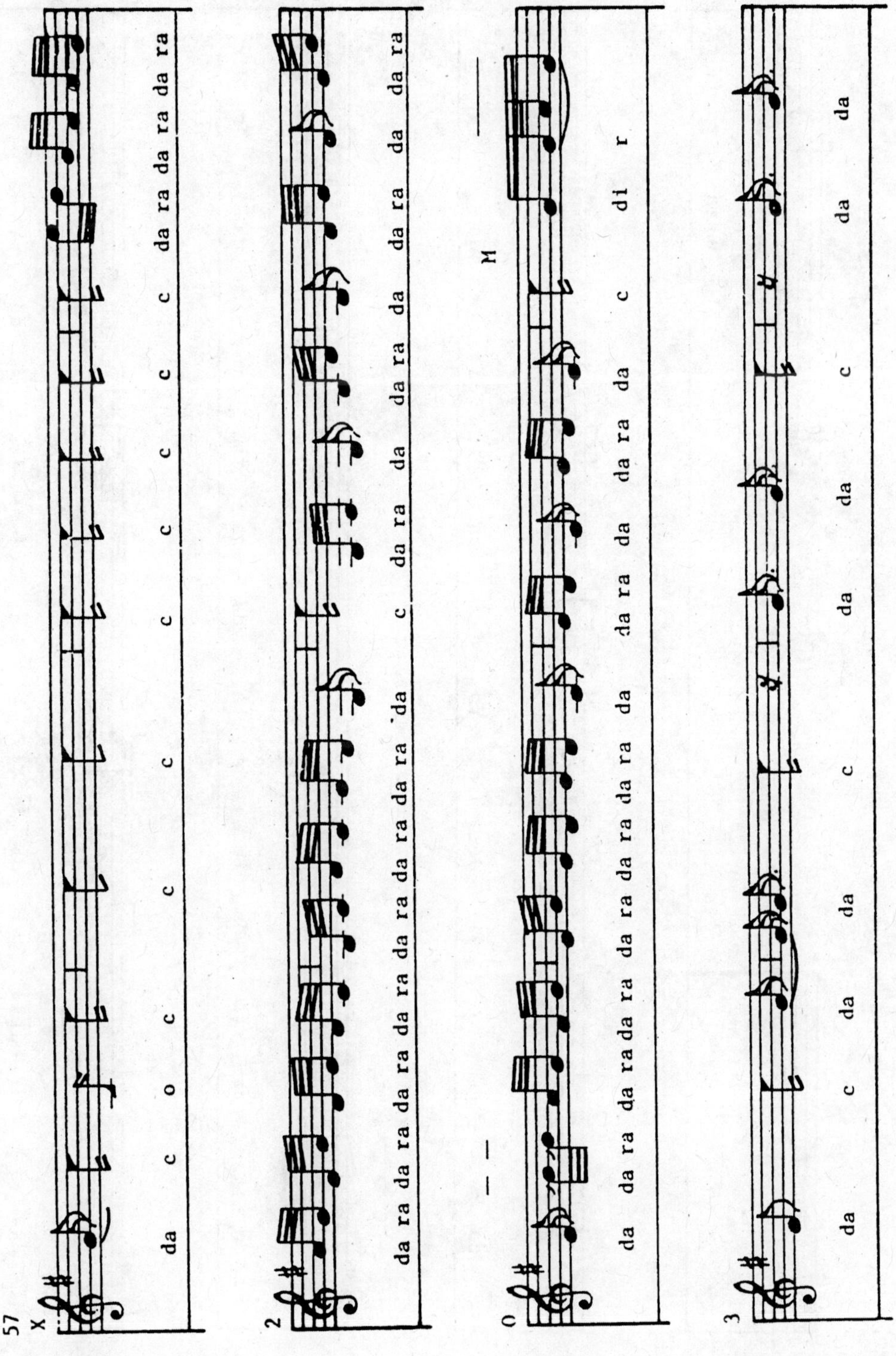
57
X
da c o c c c c c c c c da ra da ra da ra da ra
2
da ra da ra da ra da ra da ra da ra da ra da ra 'da c da ra da da ra da da ra da ra da da ra
0
da da ra da ra da ra da ra da ra da ra da da ra da da ra da c di r
M
3
da c da da c da da c da da

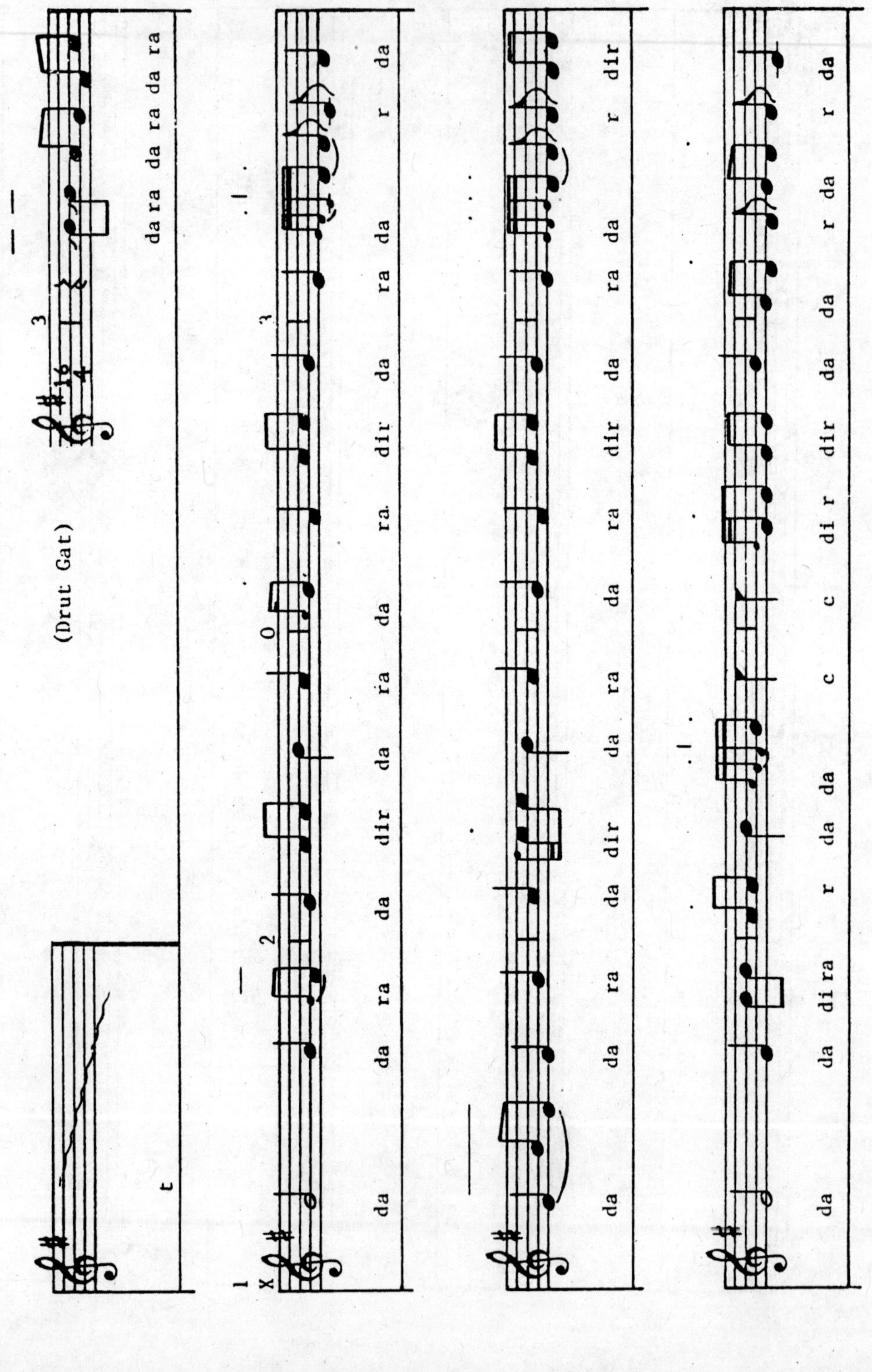
(Drut Gat)
t
da ra da ra da ra da ra
da da ra da dir da ra da ra da dir ra da ra da r da
da da ra da dir da ra da ra da dir da ra da r dir
da da di ra r da da c c di r dir da da r da r da

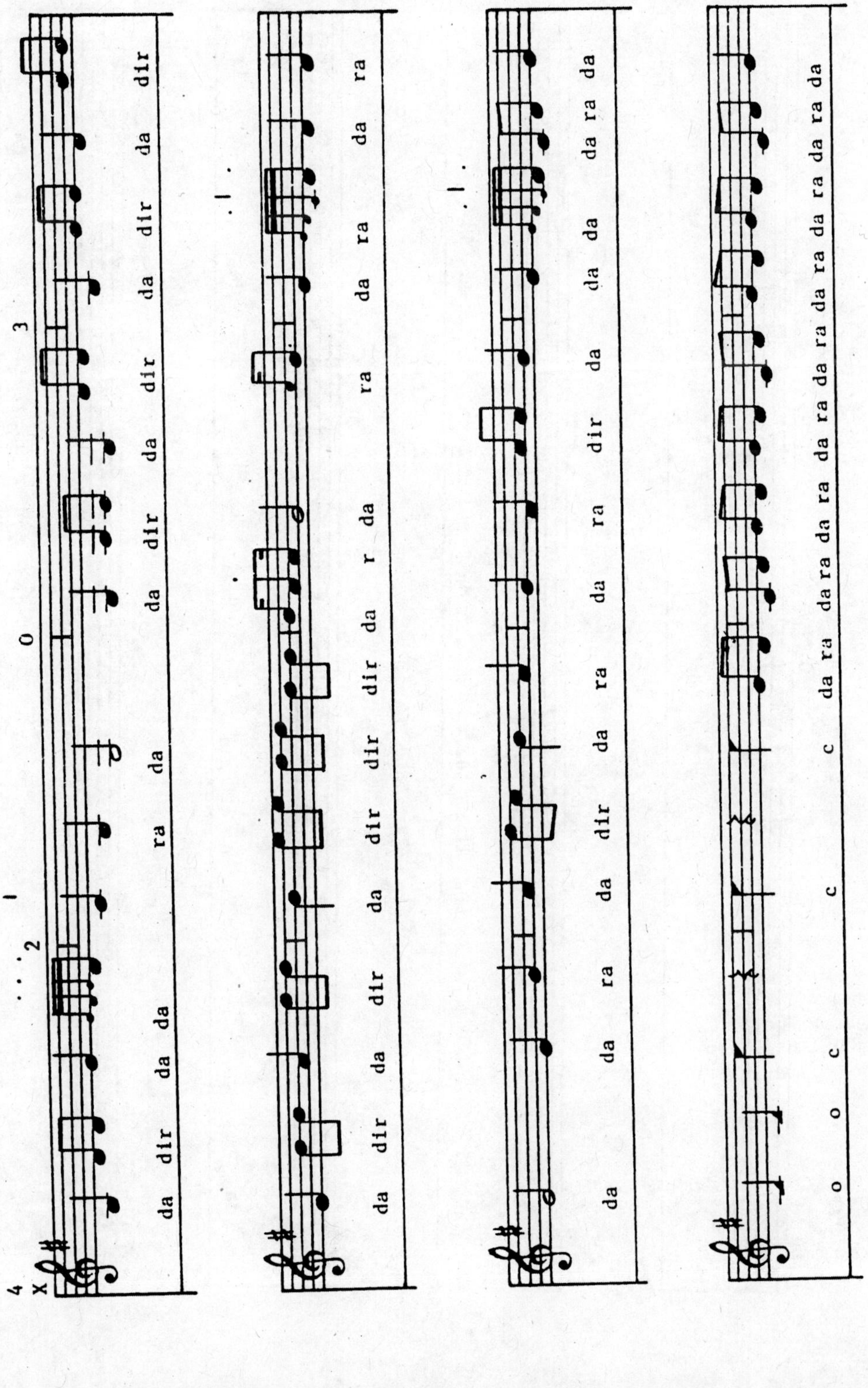
4
X
2
1
0
3
da dir da da ra da da dir da dir da dir da dir
da dir da dir da dir dir dir da r da ra da ra da ra
da da ra da dir da ra da ra dir da da da da ra da
o o c c c da ra da ra da ra da ra da ra da ra da ra da ra da

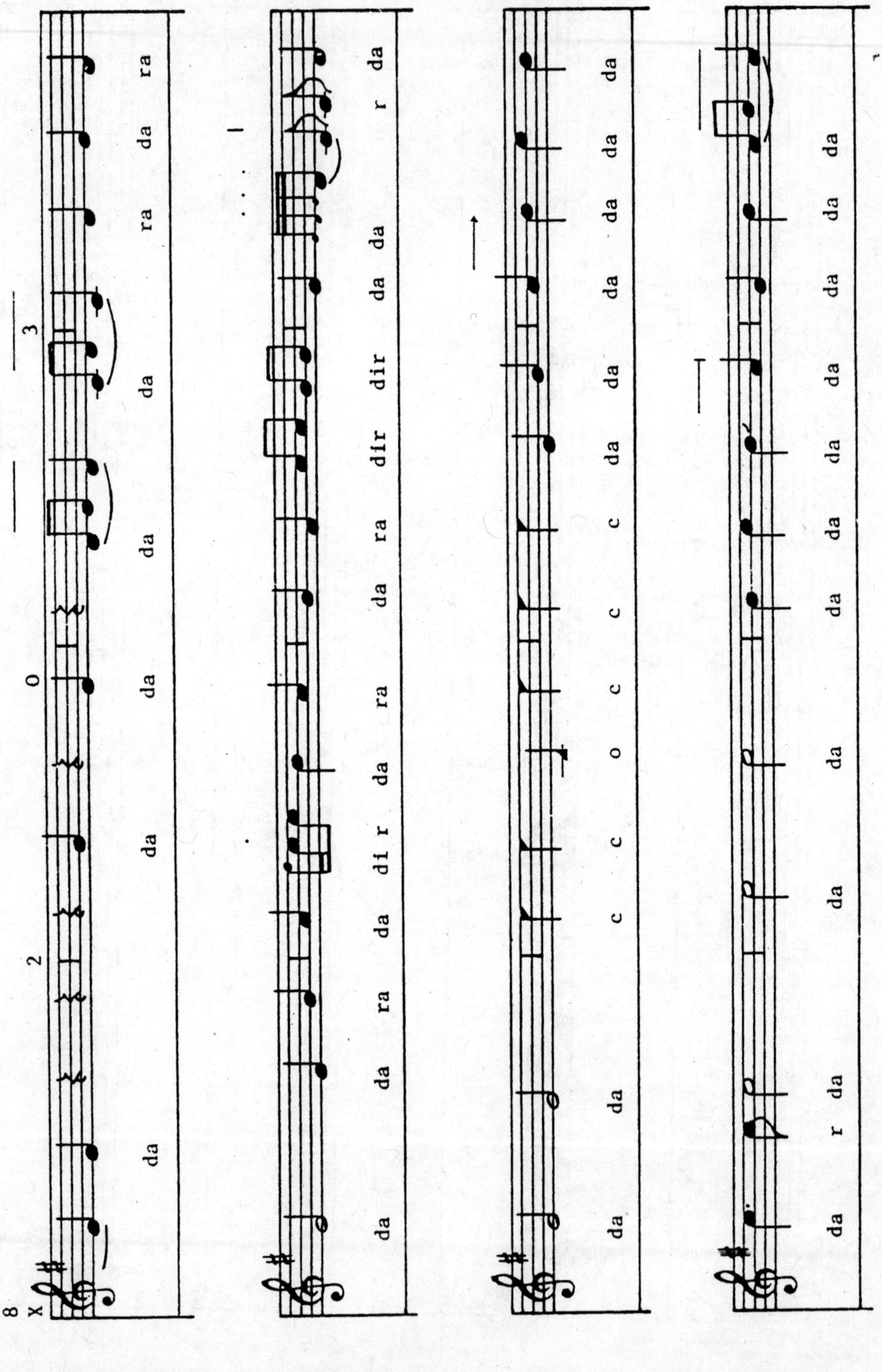
X
8
da
da
2
da
0
da
da
3
da
ra
da
ra
da
da
ra
da
dir
da
ra
da
ra
dir
dir
da
da
r
da
da
da
c
c
o
c
c
c
da
da
da
da
da
da
da
r
da
da
da
da
da
da
da
da
da
da

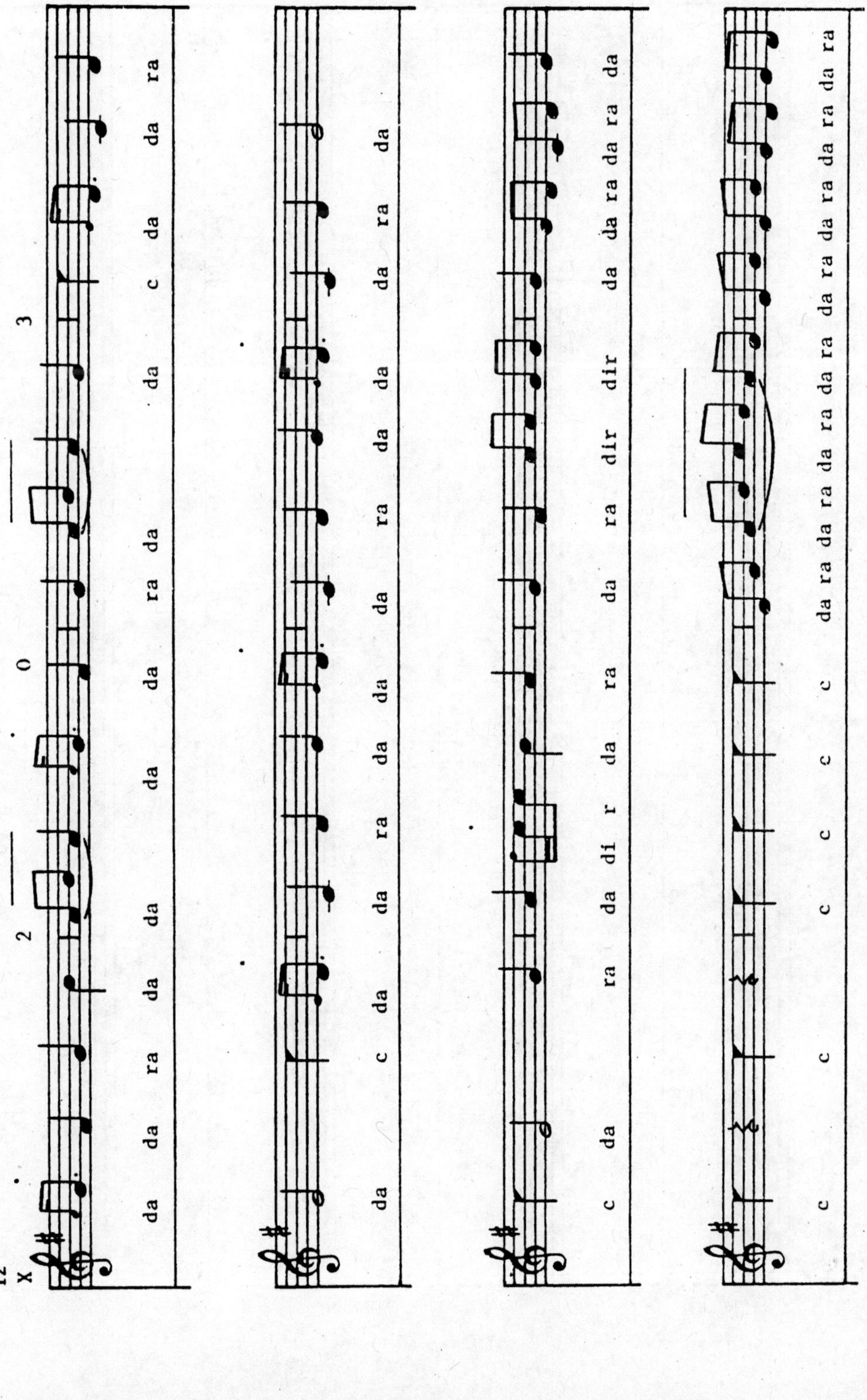
12
X
2
0
3
da da ra da da da da ra da da c da da ra
da da c da da ra da da da ra da da da ra da
c da ra da di r da ra da ra dir dir da da ra da ra da ra da
c c c c c c da ra da ra da ra da ra da ra da ra da ra da ra da ra da ra

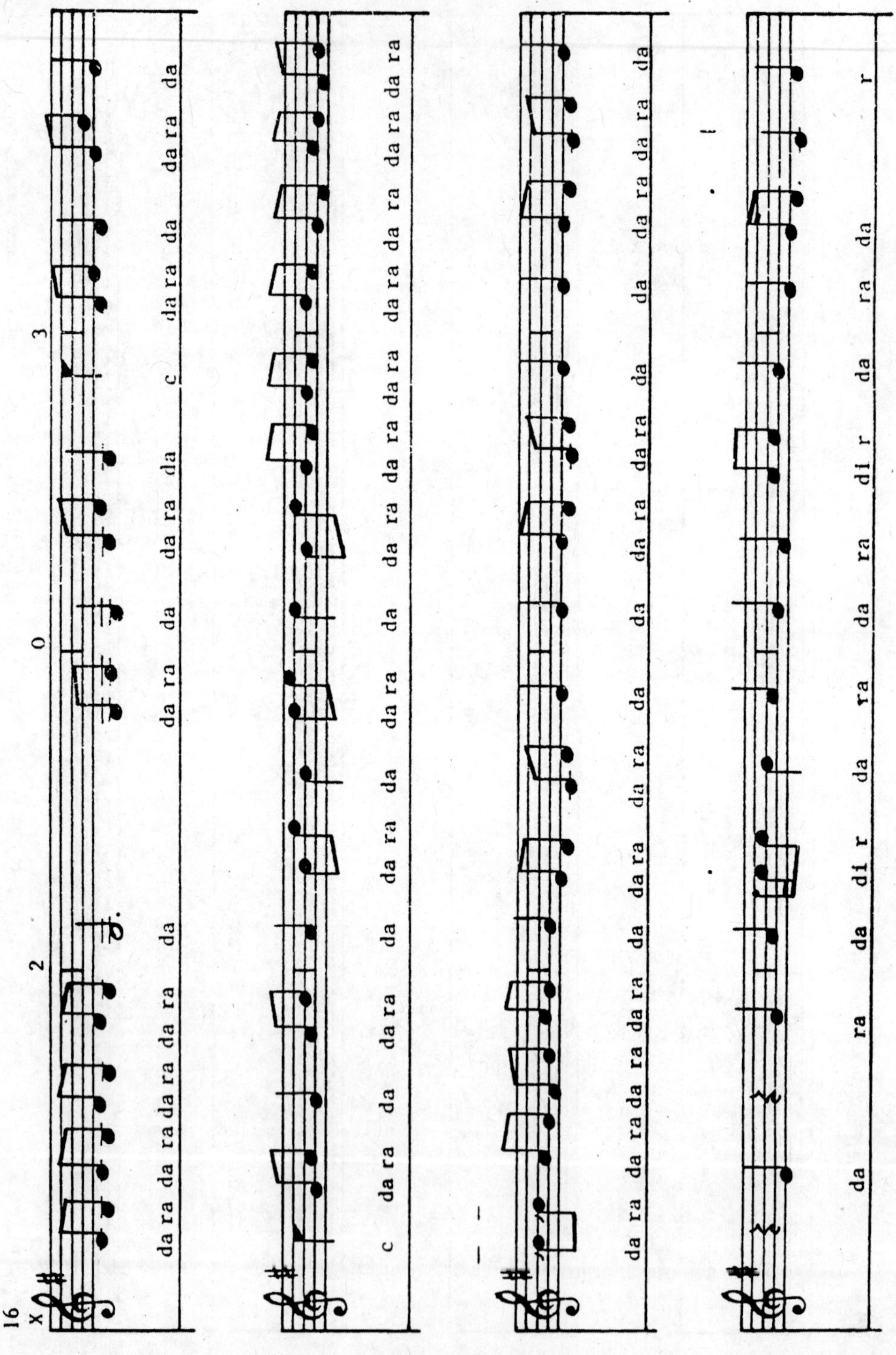
16
X
2
0
3
da ra da ra da ra da ra da ra da
da ra da da ra da c da ra da da ra da
c da ra da da ra da da ra da da ra da ra da ra da ra da ra da ra da ra da ra da ra
da ra da ra da ra da ra da ra da da ra da ra da ra da da da da ra da ra da ra da da da ra da ra da ra da
da ra da di r da ra da ra di r da ra da r

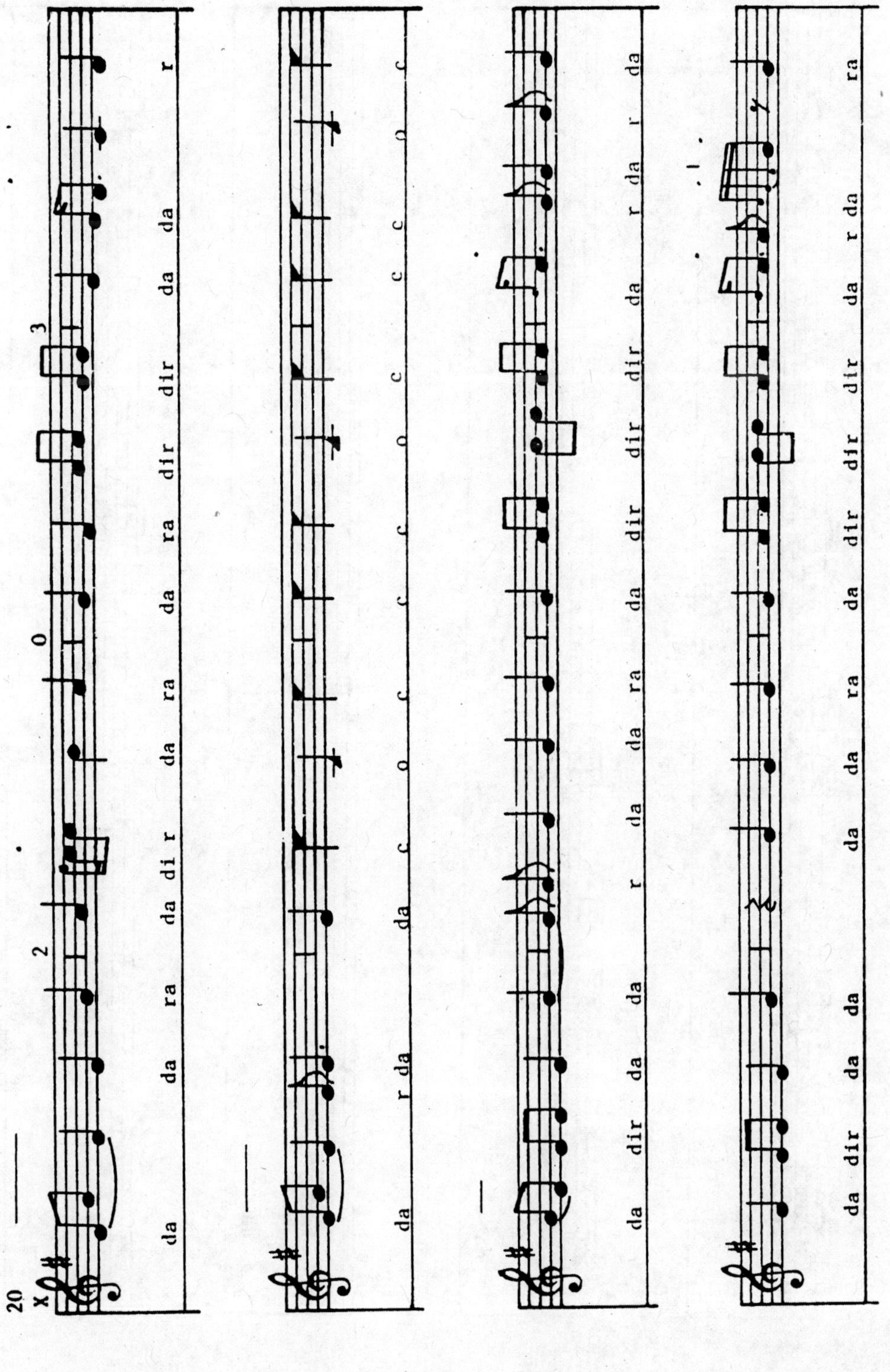

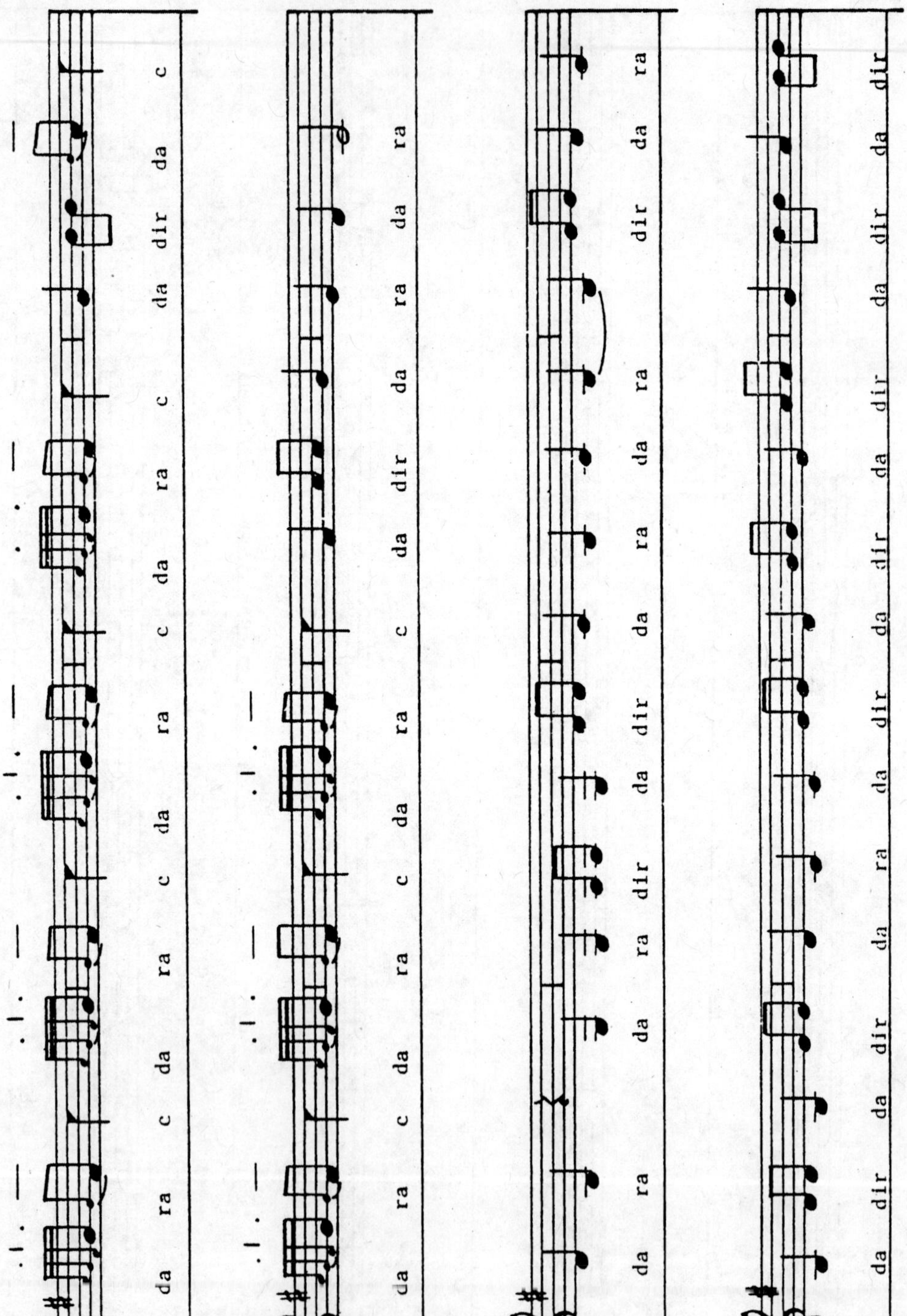
24
X
da ra c da ra c da ra c da ra c da dir da c
da ra c da ra c da ra c da dir da ra da ra
da ra da ra dir da dir da ra da ra ra da dir da ra
da dir da dir da ra da da dir da dir da dir da dir da dir

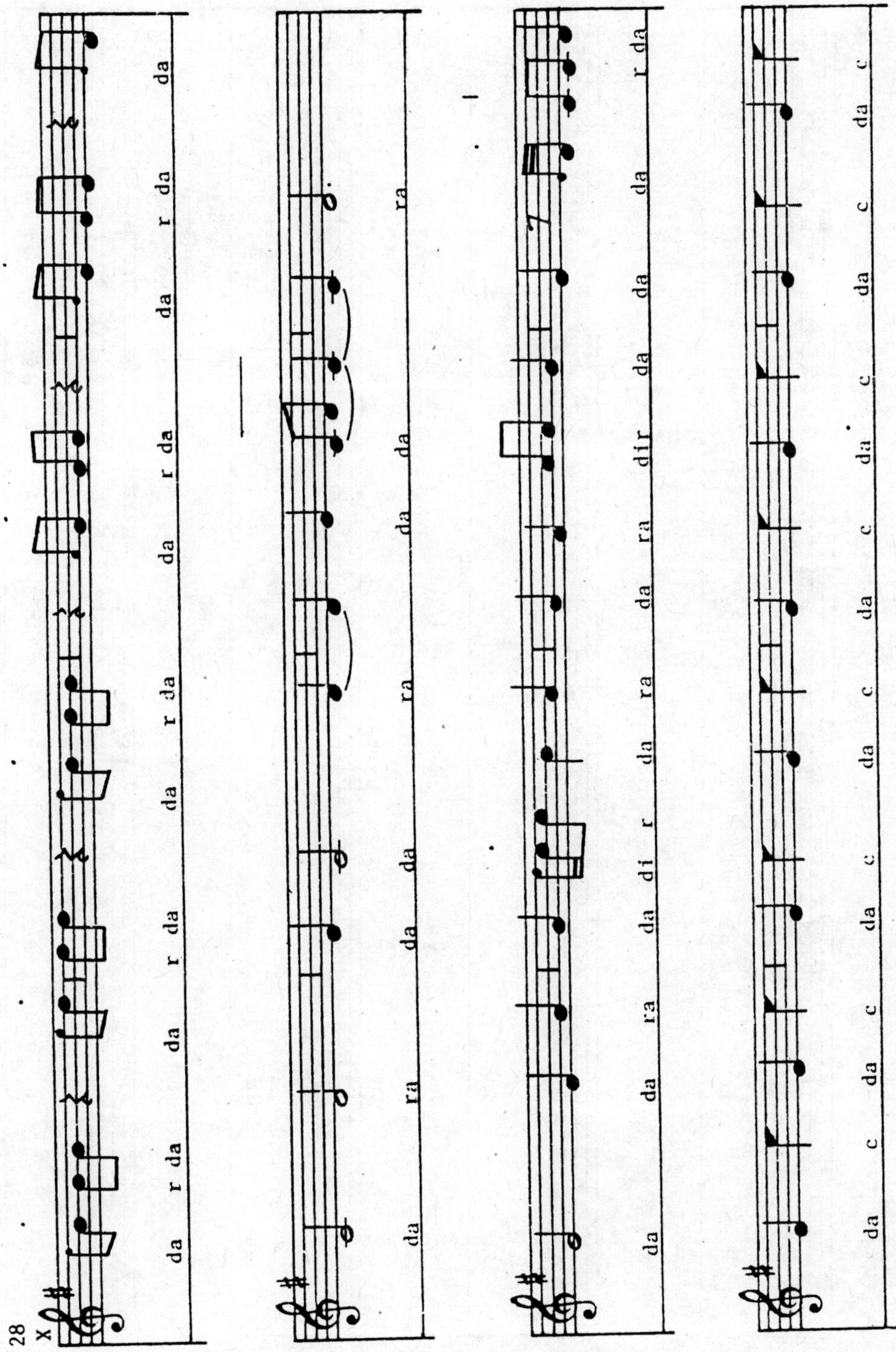
28
X
da r da da r da da r da da r da da r da da
da ra da da ra da da ra
da da ra da di r da ra da ra dir da da da r da
da c da c da c da c da c da c da c da c

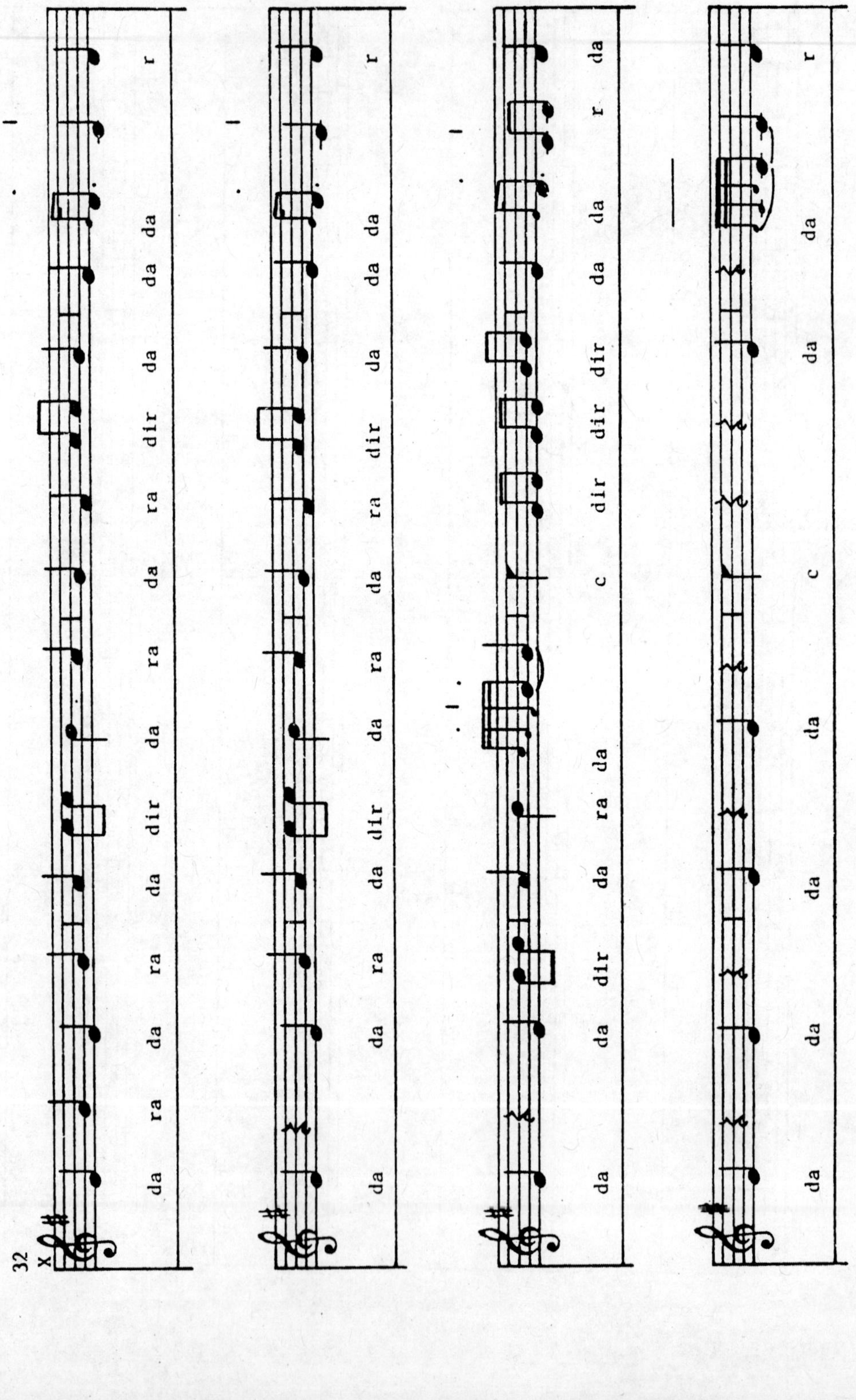
32
X
da ra da ra da dir da ra da ra dir da da da r
da da ra da dir da ra da ra dir da da da r
da da dir da ra da c dir dir dir da da r da
da da da da c da da r

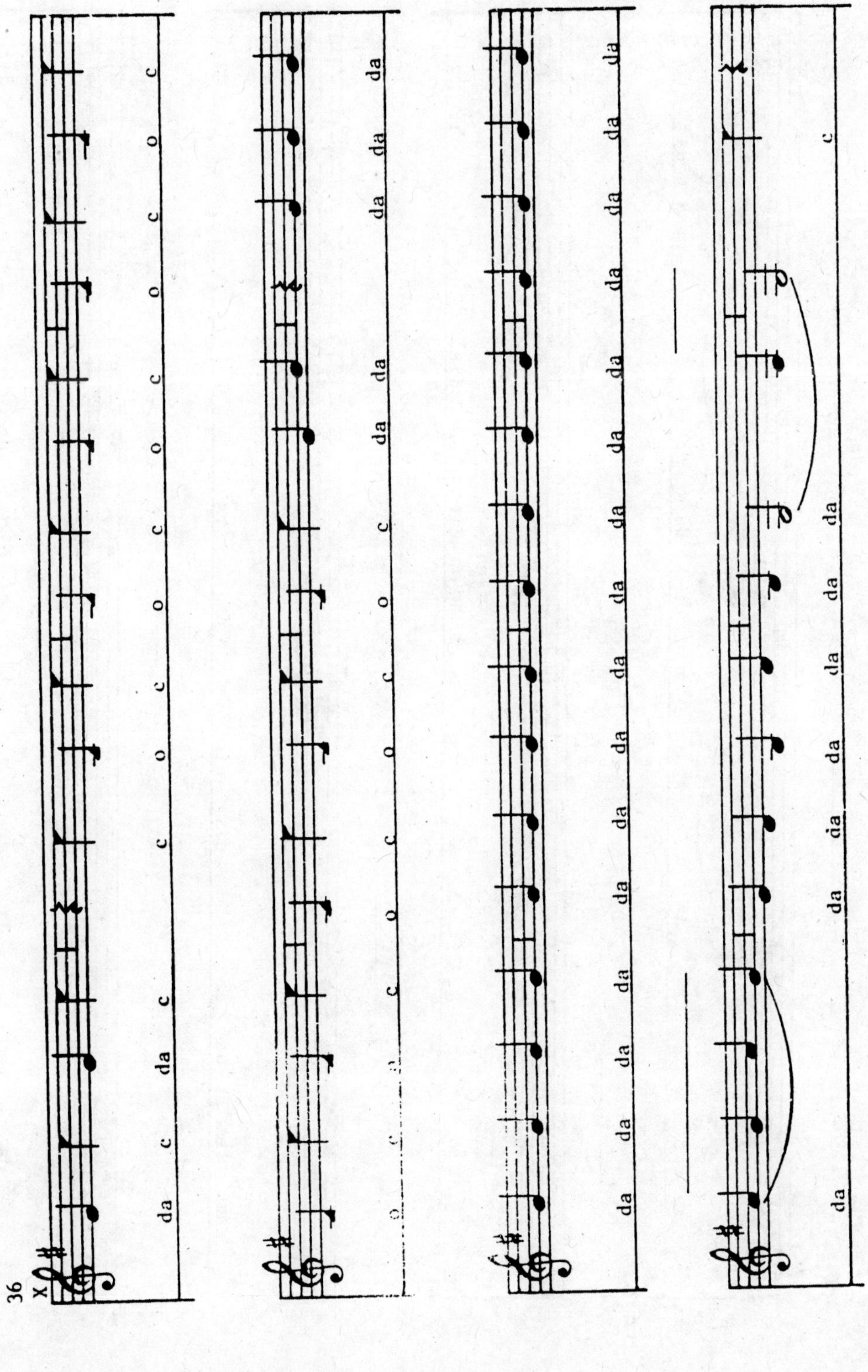
36
X
da c da c c o c o c o c o c o c
o c o c o c o c o c da da da da da
da da da da da da da da da da da da da da da da
da da da da da da da da c

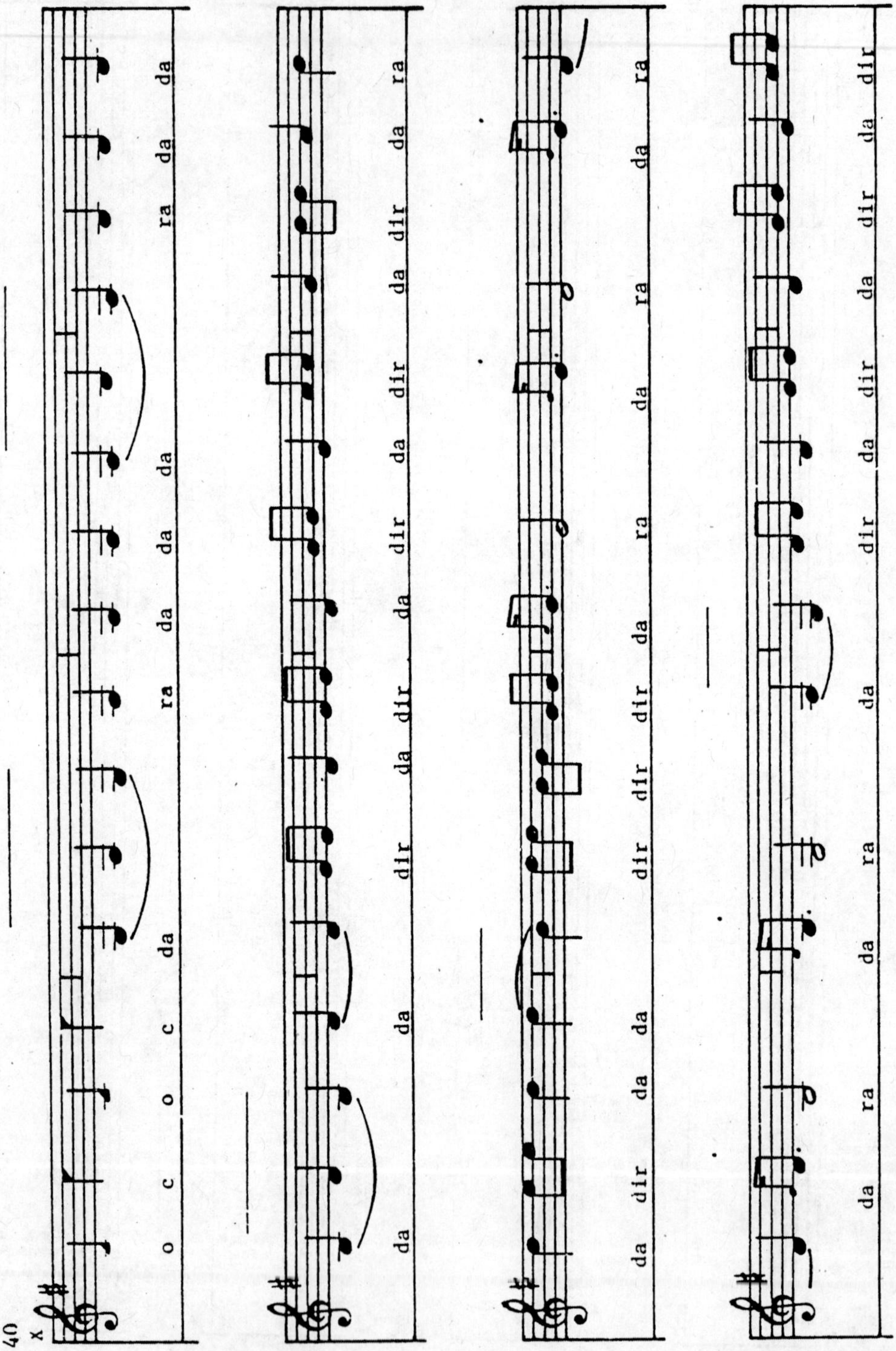
o c o c da ra da da da ra da da
da da dir da dir da dir da dir da dir da ra
da dir da da dir dir dir da ra da ra da ra
da ra da ra da dir da dir da dir da dir

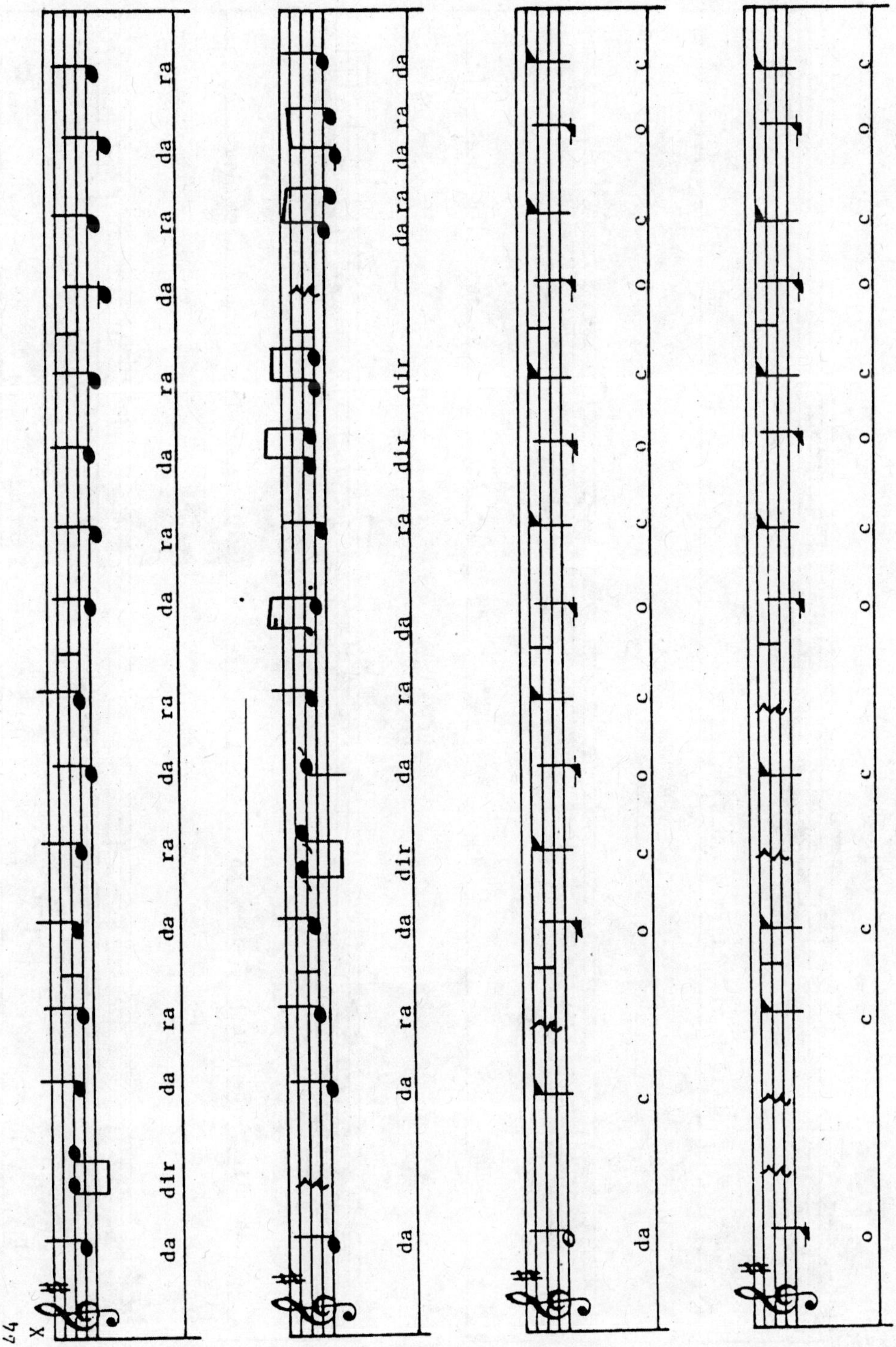
X
da d1r da ra da ra da ra da ra da ra da ra da ra
da da ra da d1r da ra da ra d1r d1r da ra da ra da ra da
da c o c o c o c o c o c o c
o c c c c o c o c o c o c

48

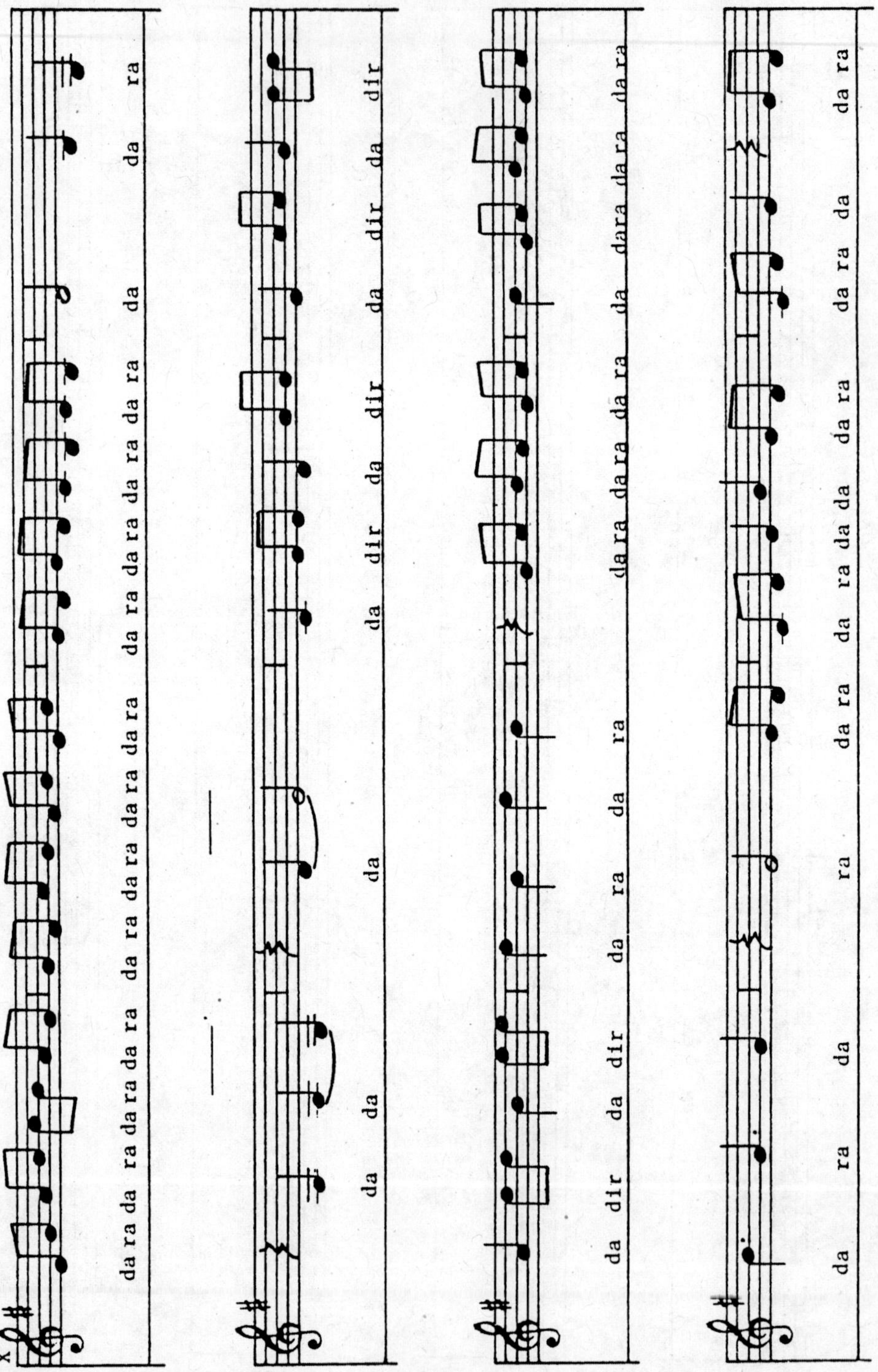
X
da ra da ra da ra da ra da ra da ra da ra da ra da ra da ra da ra da ra da ra da ra da ra da ra da ra da da ra
da da da da dir da dir da da dir da dir da dir
da dir da dir da da ra da ra da ra dara dara dara dara dara da dara dara dara
da ra da ra da ra da ra da ra da da ra da ra da ra da ra da ra

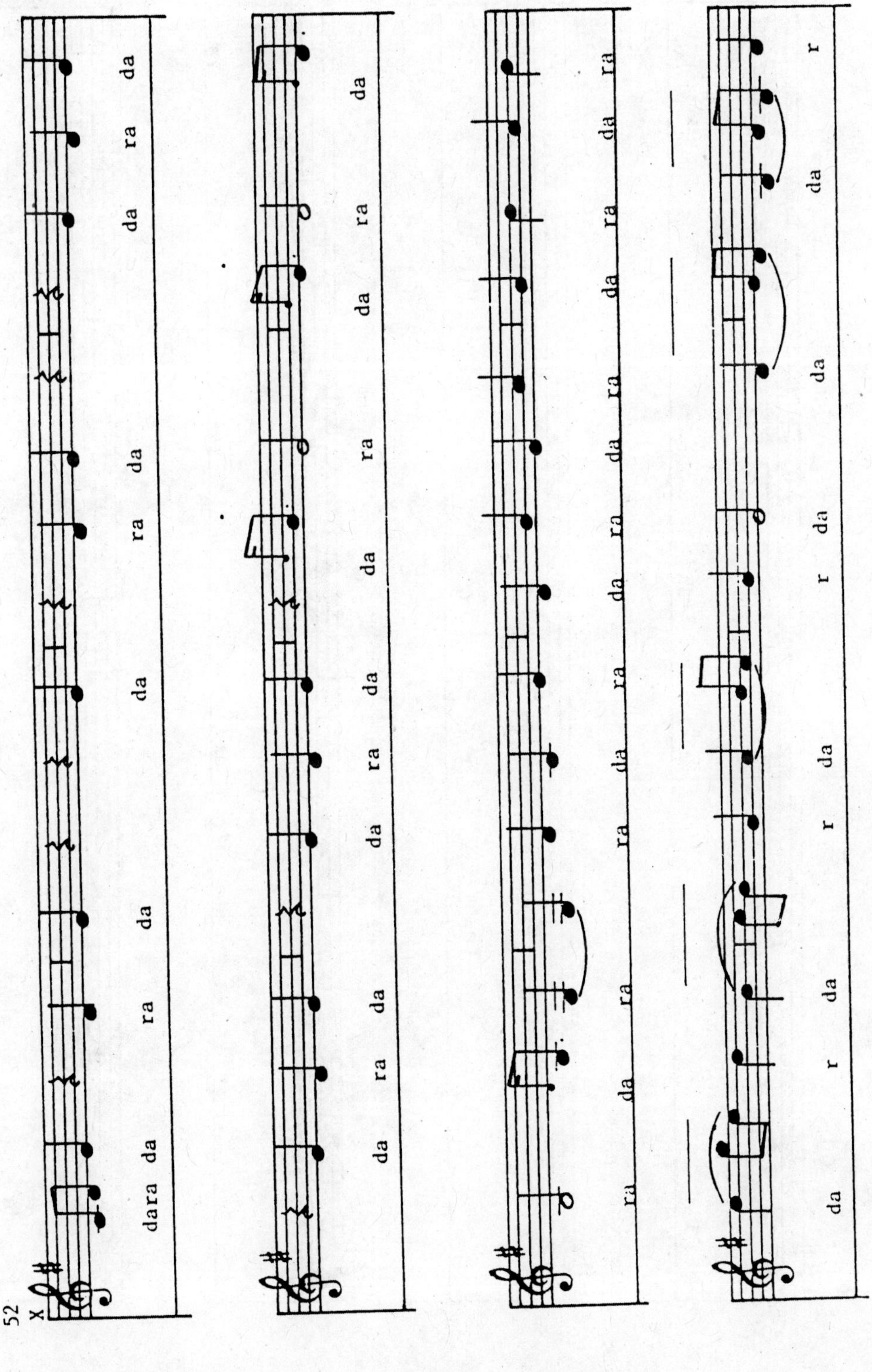
52
X
dara da ra da da ra da da ra da
da ra da ra da da ra da da ra da
ra da ra ra da ra da ra da ra da ra da ra
da r da r da r da da da r

56 X

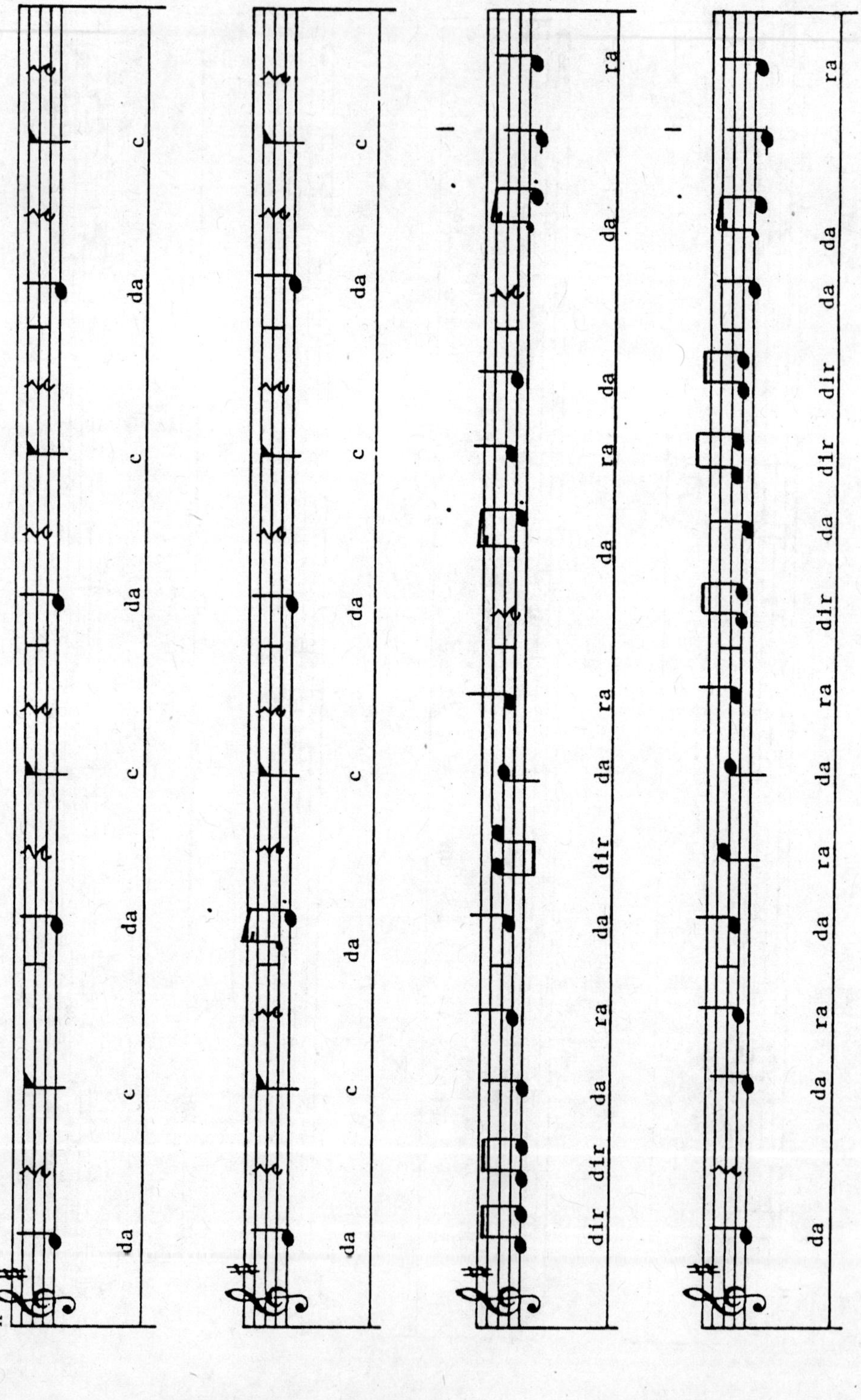
da c da c da c da c
da c da c da c da c
dir dir da ra da dir da ra da ra da da ra
da da ra da ra da ra dir da dir dir da da ra

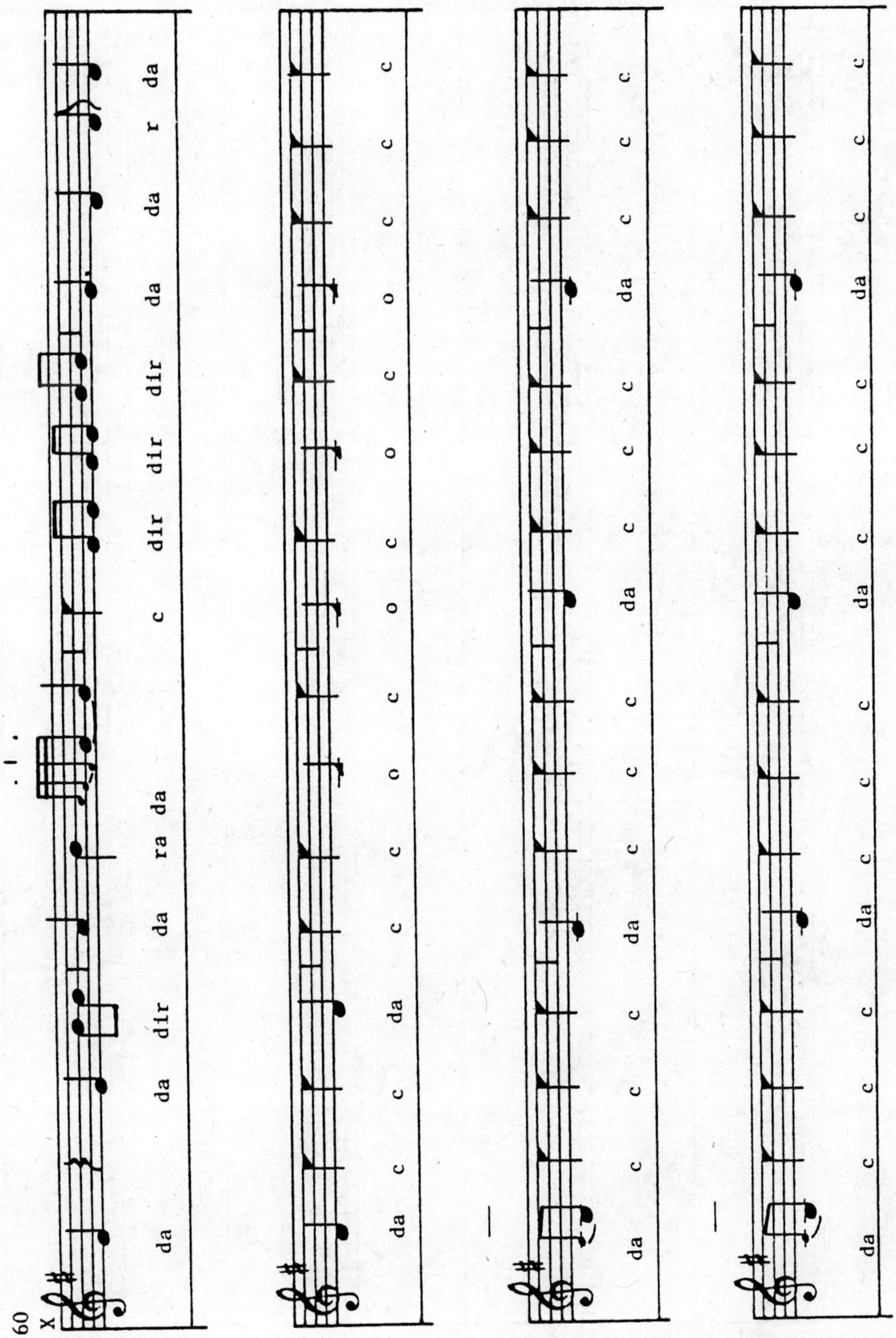
60
X
da da dir da ra da c dir dir dir da da r da
da c c da c c o c o c o c o c c c
da c c c da c c c da c c c da c c c
da c c c da c c c da c c c da c c c

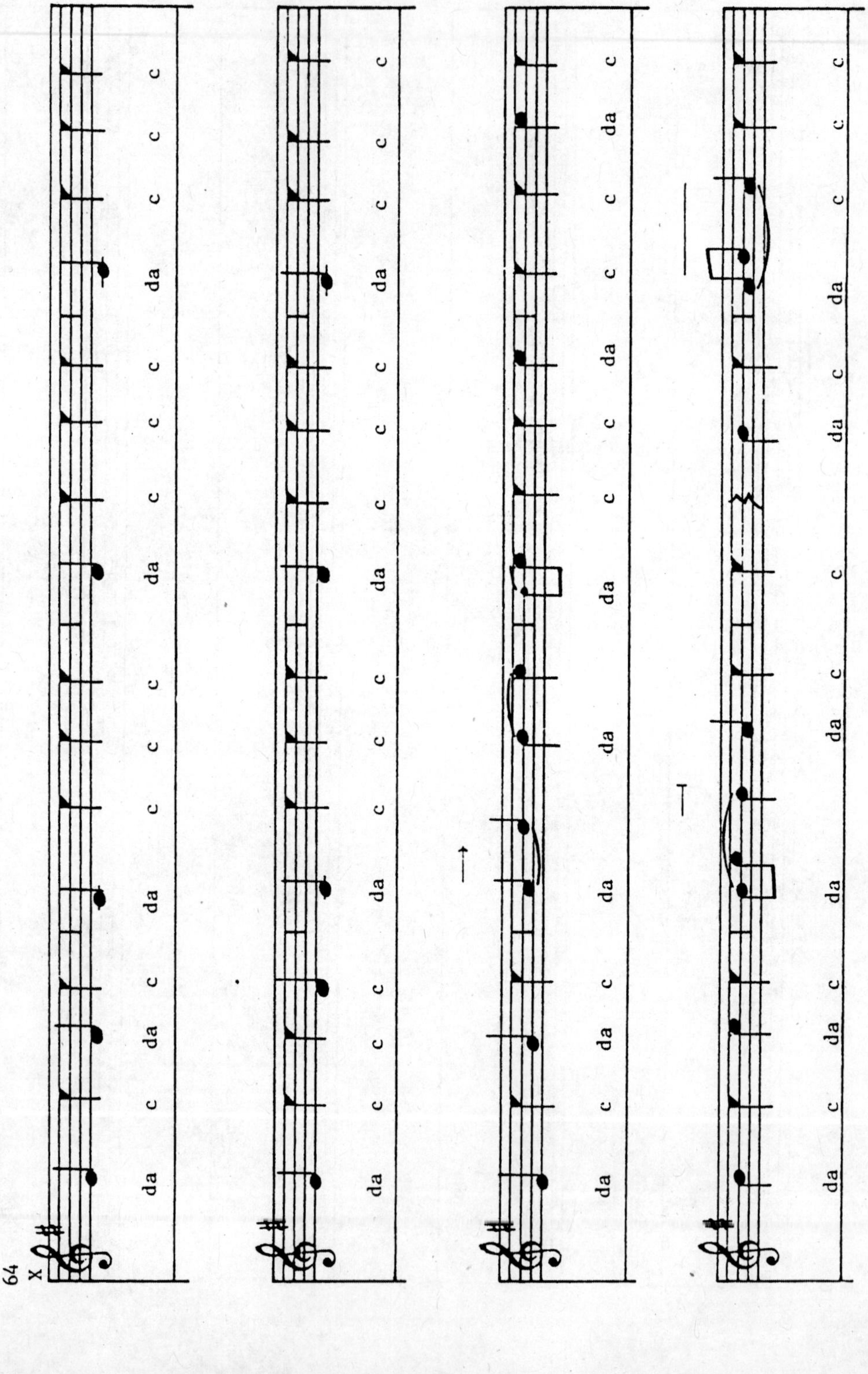
64
X
da c da c da c c c da c c c da c c c
da c c c da c c c da c c c da c c c
da c da c da da da c c da c c da c
da c da c da da c c da c da c c c

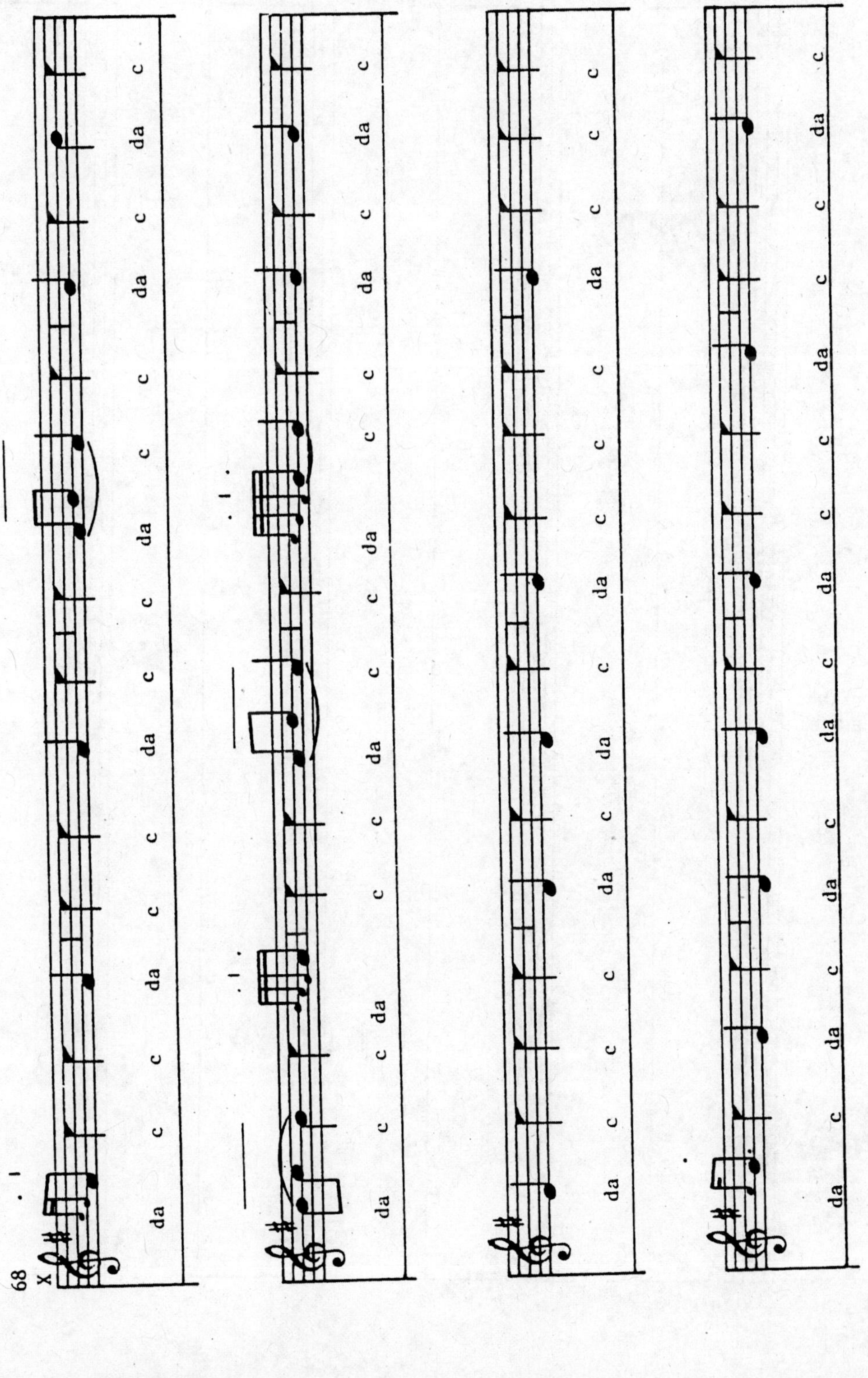
X 68
da c c da c c da c c da c c da c da c
da c c da c c da c c da c c da c da c
da c c c da c da c da c c c da c c c
da c da c da c da c da c c da c c da c

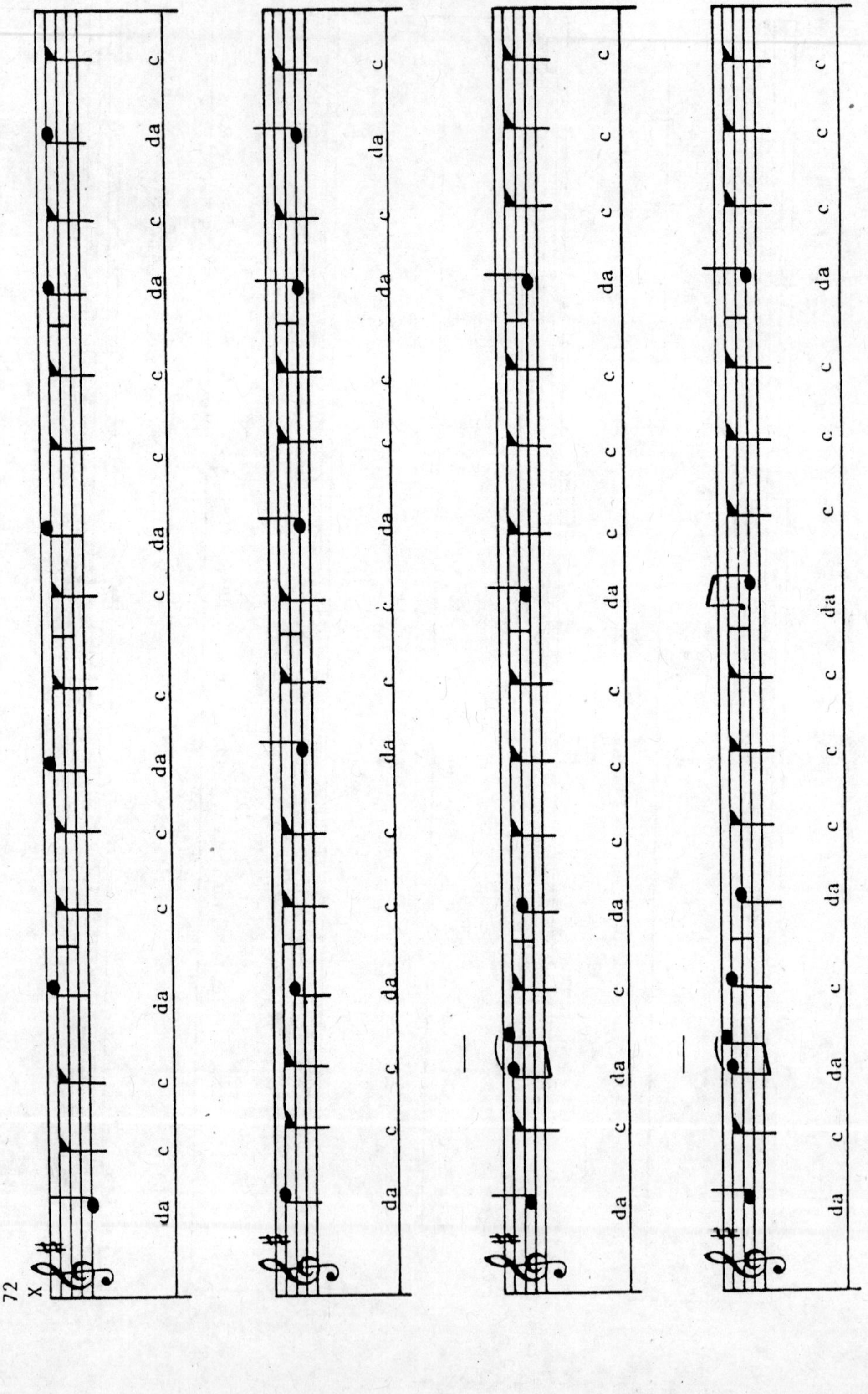
72
X
da c c da c c da c c da c c da c da c
da c c da c c da c c da c c da c da c
da c da c da c c c da c c c da c c c
da c da c da c c c da c c c da c c c

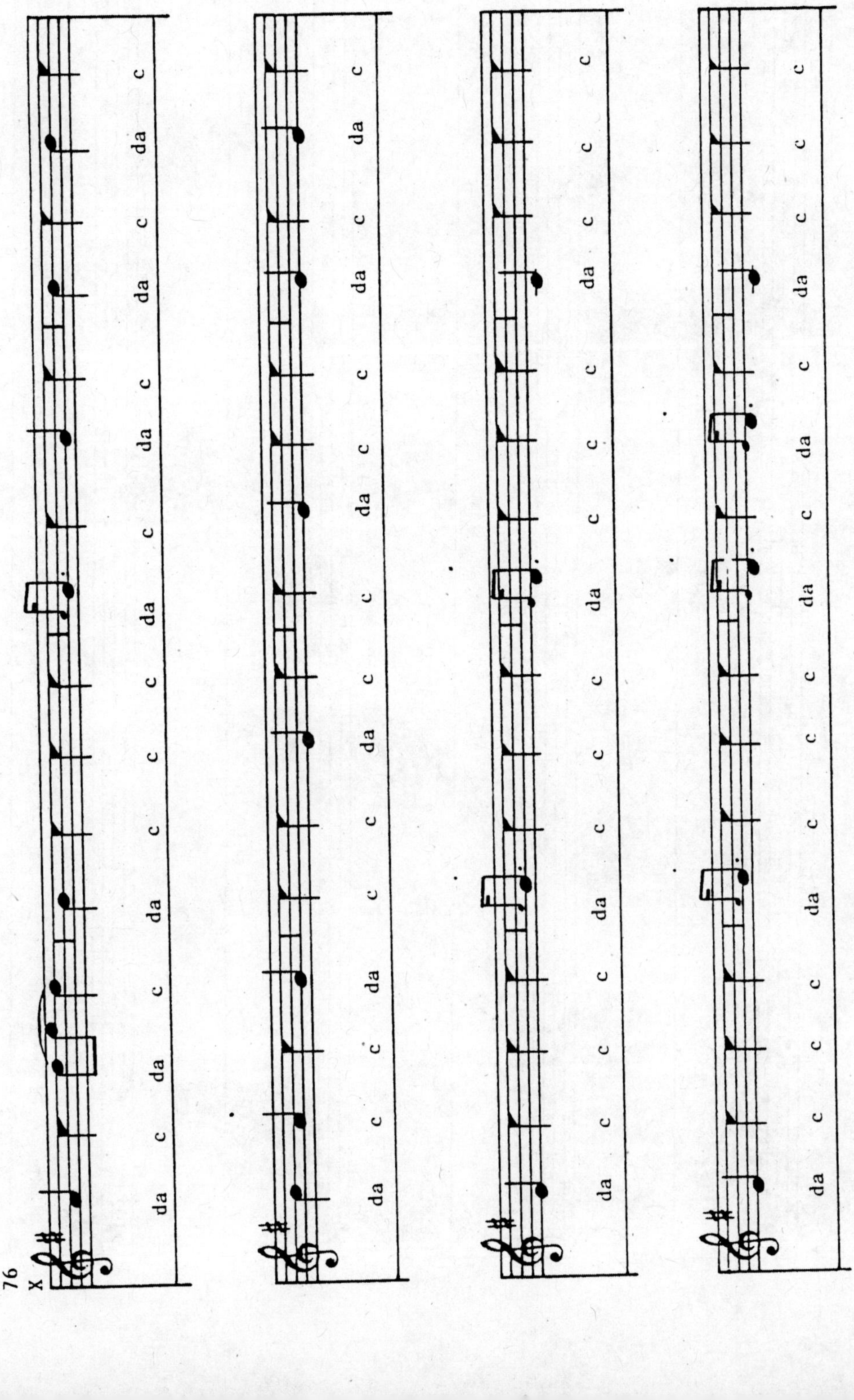
X 76
da c da c da c c c da c da c da c da c
da c c da c c da c c da c c da c da c
da c c c da c c c da c c c da c c c
da c c c da c c c da c da c da c c c

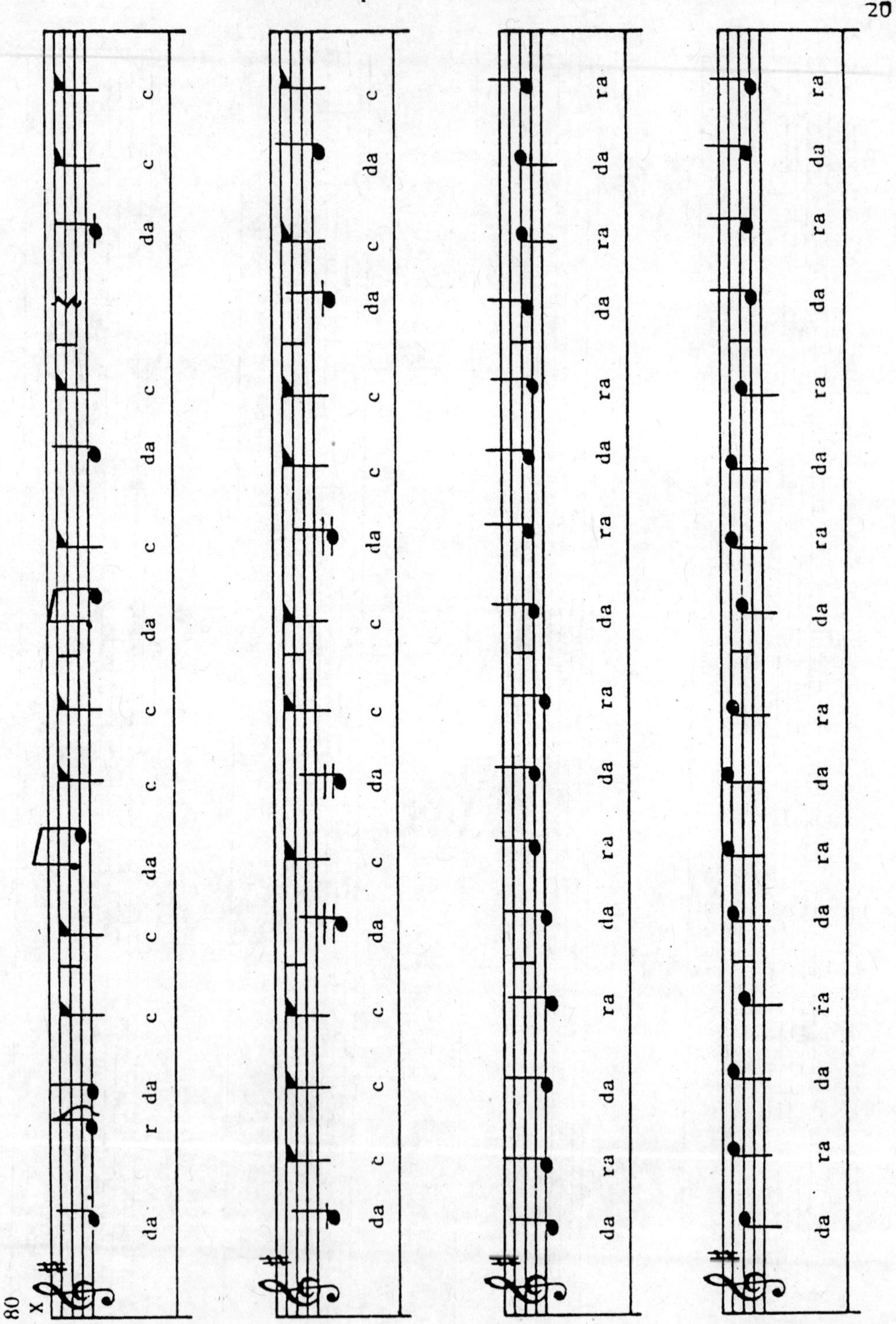
20
80
x
da r da c c da c c da c da c da c c
da c c c da c da c c da c c da c da c
da ra da ra da ra da ra da ra da ra da ra da ra
da ra da ra da ra da ra da ra da ra da ra da ra

84

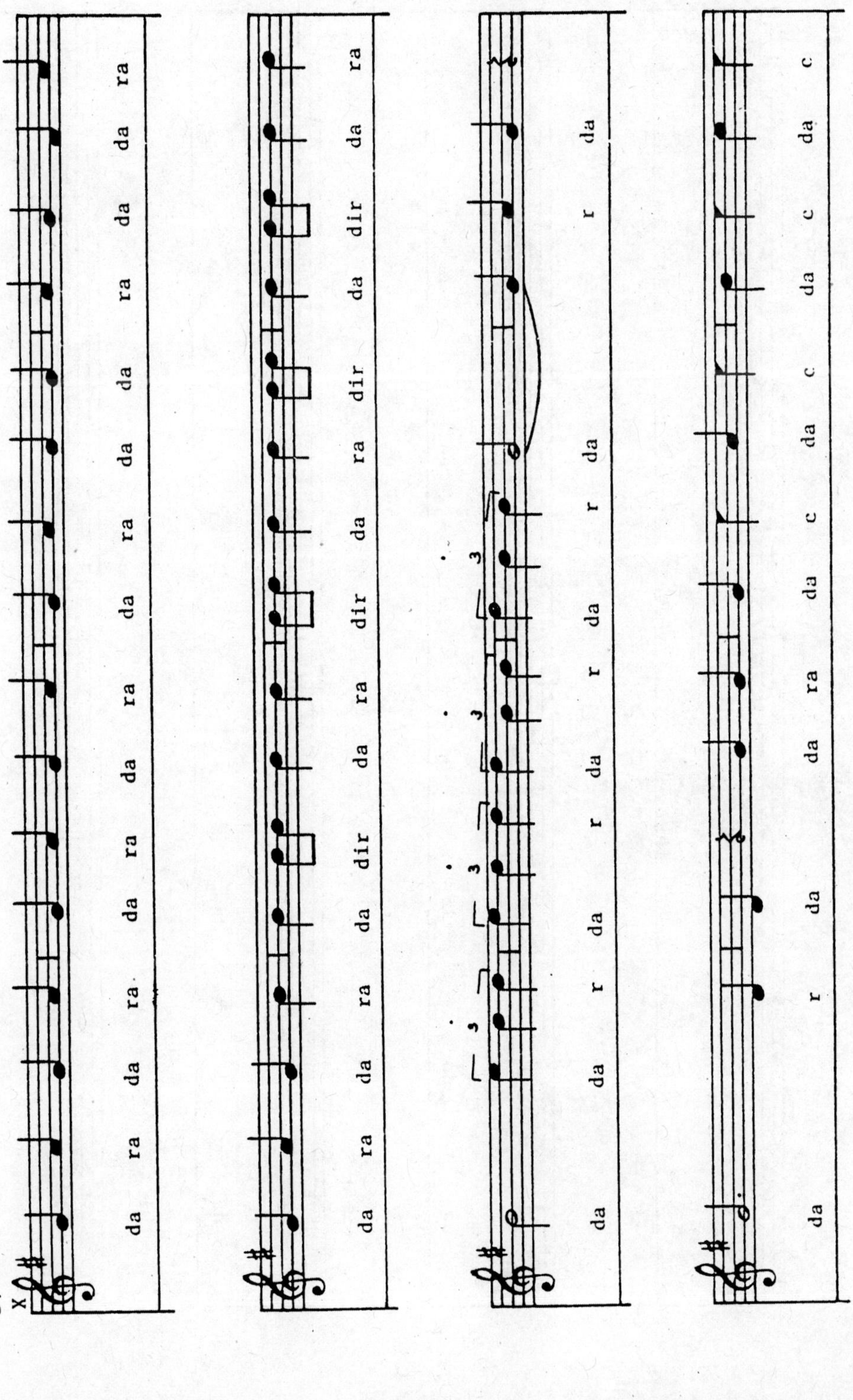
X
da ra da ra da ra da ra da ra da da ra da da ra
da ra da ra da dir da ra dir da ra dir da dir da ra
3 3 3 3
da da r da r da r da r da
da r da da ra da c da c da c da c

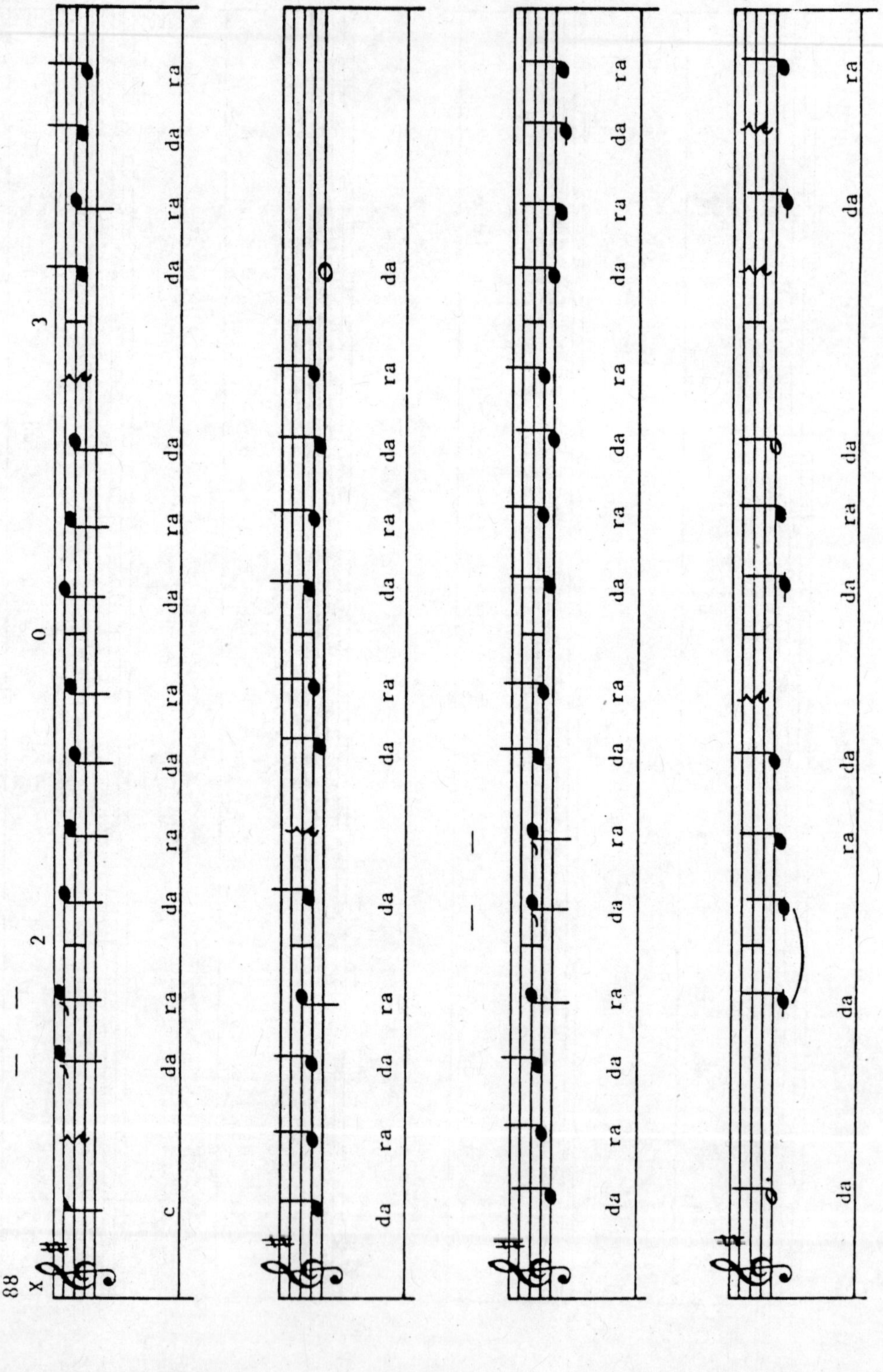
88
X
2
0
3
c da ra da ra da ra da ra da da ra da ra
da ra da ra da da ra da ra da ra da
da ra da ra da ra da ra da ra da ra da ra da ra
da da ra da da ra da da ra

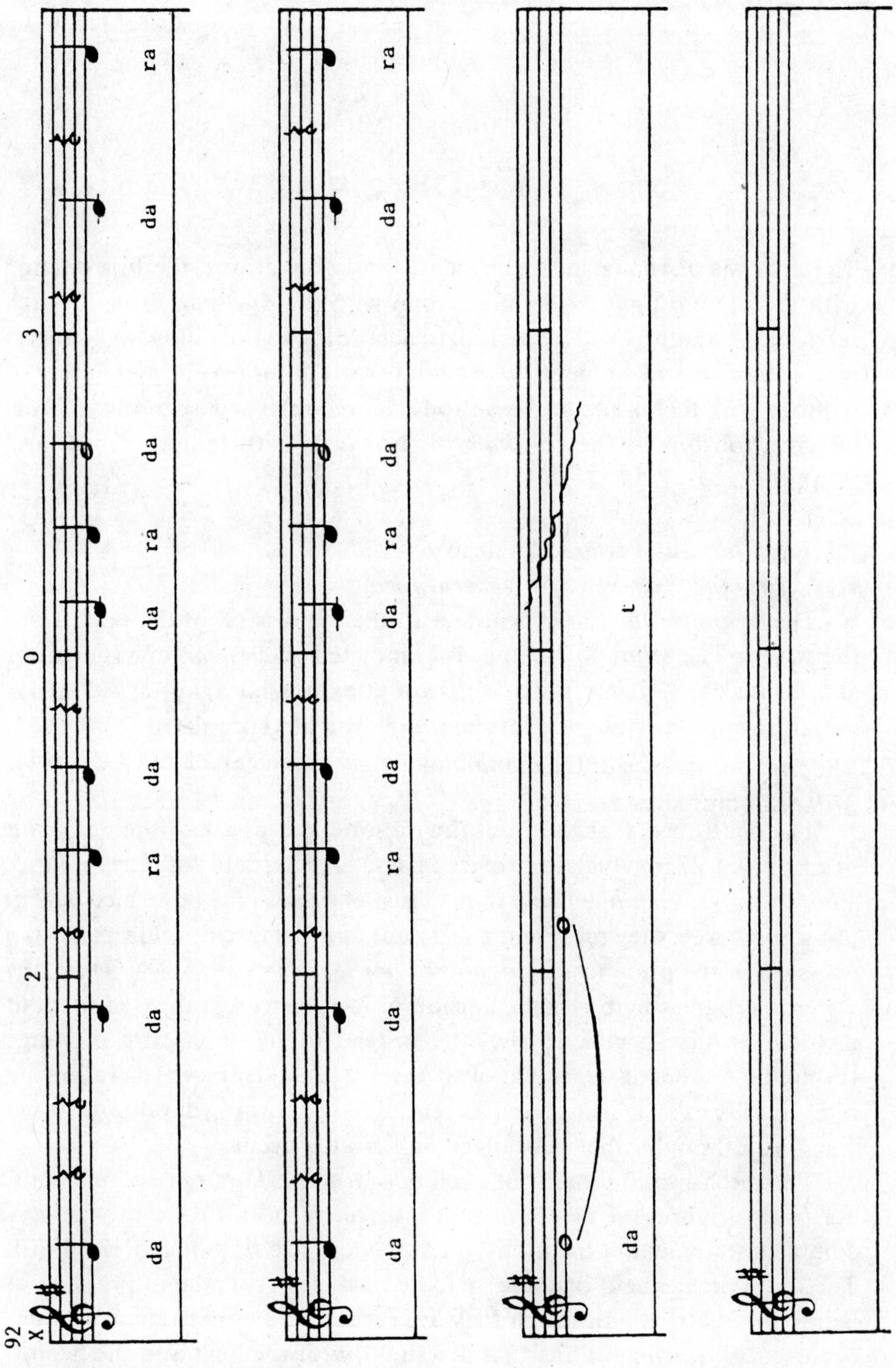
92
X
2
0
3
da da ra da da ra da da ra
da da ra da da ra da da ra
da
t

CHAPTER VII

ANALYSIS

The analysis of the corpus is presented in two sections, the first dealing with the *vilambit gat vistār*, the second with the *drut gat vistār*. In each section, the analysis will be presented according to the following parameters: (1) structural elements in general form, (2) context of precomposed sections, (3) technique in variation of precomposed sections, (4) the interrelationship of the *śṛṅkhalā* of the *vistār* with tempo, range, and technique.

7.1 *Vilambit Gat Vistār*—Analysis

7.1.1 *Structural elements in general form*

The *vilambit gat vistār* begins with the expression of the *mukhṛā* of the *sthāyī*. The *sthāyī* of the *gat* is completed in *āvartan* one (hereafter abbreviated to ā 1, etc.). The *mukhṛā* is expressed again at ā 1 m 12, initiating another statement of the *sthāyī* which is completed at ā 2 m 11. The first occurrence of the *manjhā* of the *gat* is seen at ā 2 m 12-ā 3 m 11. *Mukhrā* completes ā 3.

The continued realization of the *rāg*-oriented phase of the *gat vistār* occurs in ā 4-27 in which improvised passages alternate with the *mukhṛā, sthāyī*, and/or *manjhā*. These improvised passages may be termed *baṛhat tān*-s. However, they represent a different approach to development than was seen in the previous discussion of *baṛhat* tān-s (see 5.2.1). Here, the *vistār* is progressing by the expansion of range through the treatment of melodic motifs specific to the *rāg*, instead of by expansion of range through the ordered treatment of successive scale-degrees. The following pitch-motifs may be considered as central to the ensuing development (see Ex. 7-1) although other subsidiary motifs also occur.

The pitch-motif content of each *baṛhat tān* is summarized in Figure 16. In this figure, the listing of a specific pitch-motif may imply either a complete statement of the motif or a statement of a fragment of the motif. The rhythmic element of these melodic passages gives the impression of being non-metrical, although they are set to *tāl*, owing to the persistent occurrence of articulations that are slightly off the beat and the prominent use of *mīṇḍ* that fills spaces of large duration.

Ex. 7-1 Pitch-motifs of *Rāg Rasiyā*

Two more expressions of the *sthāyī* occur in ā 28, 29 before the commencement of the *layakārī*-oriented phase of the *vistār*. From ā 30 to ā 38, *tān*-s of *chaḥ guṇ layakārī* alternate with *mukhṛā*. There is one instance in which the *sthāyī* is fully restated (ā 35). While these *tān*-s begin from different *mātrā*-s, they all end immediately before the *mukhṛā* (m 12). Those *chaḥ guṇ tān*-s beginning in ā 31, 34, and 36 are concluded with *tihāī*-s. The motivic units of these *tihāī*-s are indicated in brackets on the transcription.

Following the *chaḥ guṇ tān*-s there are two more statements of the *sthāyī* (ā 38 m 12-ā 40 m 11), one of the *manjhā* (ā 40 m 12-ā 41 m 11), and a return to the *mukhṛā* (ā 41 m 12). The remaining portion of the *vilambit gat vistār* is comprised of *āṭh guṇ tān*-s and *tihāī*-s occasionally interrupted by the *mukhṛā* (ā 50, 51) and four more statements of the *sthāyī* (ā 46 m 12-ā 48 m 11, ā 54 m 12-ā 56 m 11). The *tān* occurring in ā 42 utilizes *krintan* and *sparś* as articulatory devices. This *tān*, for the most part, is comprised of a tonal sequence [*alaṅkār*]. These same components occur in the next *tān* (ā 43 m 3-11), which serves as a bridge to the *bol tān* extending from ā 43 m 15 to ā 46 m 11 (the *bol tān* is so named because it utilizes *mizrāb bol*-s as an essential structural device). *Gamak* is interspersed as an articulatory and embellishing device throughout the *bol tān*. A short *tān* occurs in ā 49 m 11-16. It includes a *tihāī* (m 14-16) constructed in such a way that *sam* is realized by antistress. This tech-

Āvartan	*Motif (s)*
4	a,e,f
5	f
6	a,b
7	a,f
10	a,d,e
11	(b,f) a,b,c
12	e,f,a,f
15	a,b,e
16	a,b,c,d,e
17	a,f
18	b,a,c,d,e
19	f
20	a,f
21	f,a,f
23	a,f,e, (f,e)
24	a,b,f,
25	d,f,e,f
26	a,d,e,f
27	a,f

Figure 16: Motivic Content of *Baṛhat Tān*-s

nique is known as *visam* (H. 'opposite of *sam*'). The *tān* occurring in ā 50 m 3-11 incorporates what is known as *mīṇḍ* in *tān*-s. After an introductory *sapāṭ* passage and its rearticulation, the *tān* in ā 51 is structured as a tonal sequence. Following a return to *mukhṛā* is an extended *tān* comprised of four phrases occurring in the following places: (1) ā 52 m 4-13, (2) ā 52 m 13-a 53 m 2, (3) ā 53 m 3-9, (4) ā 53 m 10-14. These phrases are centered around the motifs presented above in Example 7-1. The *tān* is concluded by a *tihāī* ending on the *sam* of ā 54. A *tān* based on a tonal sequence follows that incorporates repetitions of *sparś* and *krintan* in m 4-8. The *tān* is concluded by a *tihāī* (m 9-11) and the *sthāyī* is then restated twice, following which is another *tān* (ā 57 m 1-11) and *tihāī* (m 10-11). *Mukhṛā*, varied by a *tihāī* (m 13-16), terminates the *vistār* of the *vilambit* gat. A summary of the super-structural analysis appears in Figure 17.

7.1.2 *Contexts of precomposed sections*

The precomposed elements of this *gat* are *mukhṛā* of the *sthāyī*, the *sthāyī*, and the *manjhā*. *Mukhṛā* is given a separate status because it reappears isolated from the *sthāyī* many times. The *gat* in this performance does not have an *antarā*, possibly because the *manjhā* extends well into the *tār saptak* (H. 'upper octave').

The *mukhṛā* is stated forty-two times, the *sthāyī* fifteen, and the *manjhā* three during the *gat vistār* (see Fig. 18). Fourteen of the statements of the *sthāyī* (note that in Fig. 18, *mukhṛā* is considered as the beginning of the *sthāyī*) are during those periods when the *tablā* accompanist is improvising at a relatively high density referent. In that there are no other instances of extended improvisation on the *tablā*, it may be inferred that the *sthāyī* functions primarily as a structural basis by which the *tablā* accompanist may gauge the progression of the *tāl* cycle.

The *manjhā* appears to be of relatively less significance than the *sthāyī*. In this performance, its main function appears to be as an element of variety, providing a variant route by which the melodic line can avoid a return to the *sthāyī* or *mukhṛā*.

Of the forty-two statements of the *mukhṛā*, twenty-two are independent of the *sthāyī*. Fifteen statements of the *mukhṛā* are preceded and followed by improvisation (on the *sitār*); eight are preceded by improvisation and followed by the remainder of the *sthāyī*; nine are preceded by the *sthāyī* and followed by improvisation (see Fig. 19). The following observations concerning the function of *mukhṛā* in gat *vistār* may be made on the basis of the data presented in Figure 19 (in all cases, *mukhṛā* serves as a structural marker indicating the imminence of *sam*):

Āvartan	*Activity*
0	mukhṛā (m 12-16)
1	sthāyī, mukhṛā (m 12-16)
2	sthāyī, manjhā (m 12-...)
3	manjhā (m...-11), mukhṛā (m 12-16)
4	baṛhat tān (m 4-16)
5	baṛhat tān (m 4-11), mukhṛā (m 12-16)
6	baṛhat tān (m 3-11), mukhṛā (m 12-16)
7	baṛhat tān (m 3-10), tihāī (m 10-12), mukhṛā (m 13-16)
8	sthāyī (m 1-11), manjhā (m 12-...)
9	manjhā (m...-11), mukhṛā (m 12-16)
10	baṛhat tān (m 3-11), mukhṛā (m 12-16)
11	baṛhat tān (m 6-...)
12	baṛhat tān (m...-11), mukhṛā (m 12-16)
13	sthāyī (m 1-11), mukhṛā (m 12-16)
14	sthāyī (m 1-11), mukhṛā (m 12-16), varied by tihāī (m 14-16)
15	baṛhat tān (m 6-11), mukhṛā (m 12-14)
16	baṛhat tān (m 1-11), mukhṛā (m 12-16) varied by tihāī (m 14-16)
17	baṛhat tān (m 3-...)
18	baṛhat tān (m...-11), including a tihāī (m 10-11), mukhṛā (m 12-16)
19	baṛhat tān (m 4-11), including a tihāī (m 8-11), mukhṛā (m 12-16) with tihāī (m 15-16)
20	baṛhat tān (m 5-...)
21	baṛhat tān (m...-11), including a tihāī (m 10-11), mukhṛā (m 12-16)
22	sthāyī (m 1-11), mukhṛā (m 12-16),
23	baṛhat tān (m 1-12), mukhṛā (m 12-16)
24	baṛhat tān- approaches cau gun layakārī (m 5-11), with tihāī (m 10-11), mukhṛā (m 12-16)
25	baṛhat tān (m 1-6, 9-...)
26	baṛhat tān (m......)
27	baṛhat tān (m...-11) including a tihāī (m 8-11), mukhṛā (m 12-16)
28	sthāyī (m 1-11), mukhṛā (m 12-16)
29	sthāyī (m 1-11), mukhṛā (m 12-16) varied by cau guṇ tān (m 14-16)

30 chah guṇ tān (m 5-12), mukhṛā (m 12-16)
31 chah guṇ tān (m 1-11) with tihāī (m 9-11), mukhṛā (m 12-15), chah guṇ tān (m 16)
32 chah guṇ tān (m...-11) with tihāī (m 8-11), mukhṛā (m 12-16) varied by tihāī (m 15-16)
33 chah guṇ tān (m 4-12), mukhṛā (m 12-16)
34 chah guṇ tān (m 1-11) with tihāī (m 9-11), mukhṛā (m 12-16)
35 sthāyī (m 1-11), mukhṛā (m 12-16)
36 chah guṇ tān (m 4-...)
37 chah guṇ tān (m...-11) with tihāī (m 9-11), mukhṛā (m 12-16)
38 chah guṇ tān (m 3-12) with tihāī (m 8-12), mukhṛā (m 12-16)
39 sthāyī (m 1-11), mukhṛā (m 12-16)
40 sthāyī (m 1-11), manjhā (m 12-...)
41 manjhā (m...-11), mukhṛā (m 12-16) varied by tihāī (m 14-16)
42 āṭh guṇ tān (m 5-16) with tihāī (m 13-16)
43 āṭh guṇ tān (m 3-....)
44 āṭh guṇ tān (m...-16) including a tihāī (m 13-16)
45 āṭh guṇ tān (m 1-....)
46 āṭh guṇ tān (m...-11) including a tihāī (m 9-11), mukhṛā (m 12-16)
47 sthāyī (m 1-11), mukhṛā (m 12-16)
48 sthāyī (m 1-11), mukhṛā (m 12-16)
49 āṭh guṇ tān (m 11-16) including a tihāī (m 14-16)
50 āṭh guṇ tān (m 3-11), mukhṛā (m 12-16)
51 āṭh guṇ tān (m 1-11), mukhṛā (m 12-16) varied by tān (m 14-16)
52 āṭh guṇ tān (m 4-...)
53 āṭh guṇ tān (m...-16) including a tihāī (m 14-16)
54 āṭh guṇ tān (m 1-11) including a tihāī (m 9-11), mukhṛā (m 12-16)
55 sthāyī (m 1-11), mukhṛā (m 12-16)
56 sthāyī (m 1-11), mukhṛā (m 12-16)
57 āṭh guṇ tān (m 4-11) including a tihāī (m 10-11), mukhṛā (m 12-16) with a concluding tihāī (m 13-16)

Figure 17: Structural Elements in the *Vilambit Gat Vistār*

Sthāyī

# Āvartan	# Āvartan	# Āvartan
1) ā 0-1	6) ā 21 m 12- ā 22 m 11	11) ā 39 m 12- ā 40 m 11
2) ā 1 m 12- ā 2 m 11	7) ā 27 m 12- ā 28 m 11	12) ā 46 m 12- ā 47 m 11
3) ā 7 m 13- ā 8 m 11	8) ā 28 m 12- ā 29 m 11	13) ā 47 m 12- ā 48 m 11
4) ā 12 m 12- ā 13 m 11	9) ā 34 m 12- ā 35 m 11	14) ā 54 m 12- ā 55 m 11
5) ā 13 m 12- ā 14 m 11	10) ā 38 m 12- ā 39 m 11	15) ā 55 m 12- ā 56 m 11

manjhā

Āvartan
1) ā 2 m 12- ā 3 m 11
2) ā 8 m 12- ā 9 m 11
3) ā 40 m 12- ā 41 m 11

mukhṛa (m 12-16)

# Āvartan	# Āvartan	# Āvartan
1-2) ā 0, ā 1	10-13) ā 12, 13, 14, 15, 16	29-32) ā 37, 38, 39, 41
3) ā 3	14-15) ā 18, 19	33-35) ā 46, 47, 48
4-6) ā 5, 6, 7 (m 13-16)	16-19) ā 21, 22, 23, 24	36-37) ā 50, 51
7-8) ā 9, 10	20-28) ā 27, 28, 29, 30, 31, 32, 33, 34, 35	38-41) ā 54, 55, 56, 57

Figure 18: Precomposed Sections in the *Vilambit Gat Vistār*

A	B	C
Āvartan	*Āvartan*	*Āvartan*
5	7	3
6	12	9
10	21	14
15	27	22
16	34	29
18	38	35
19	46	41
23	54	48
24		56
30		
31		
32		
33		
37		
50		
51		

A = mukhṛā preceded and followed by improvisation

B = mukhṛā preceded by improvisation, followed by sthāyī

C = mukhṛā preceded by sthāyī or manjhā, followed by improvisation

Figure 19: Contexts of *Mukhṛā*

	Āvartan-(s)
Basic mukhṛā	0, 1, 12, 13, 21, 27, 34, 39, 46, 47, 48, 54, 55
Variation by:	
a) krintan	6, 23, 41
b) sparś	10
c) giṭkiṛī	19, 24, 32, 38
d) mīṇḍ	3, 5, 9, 14, 22, 28, 37, 56
e) gamak	16, 35
f) tān	18, 29, 51, 57
g) compression	7
h) deletion	15, 30, 31, 33, 50

Figure 20: Variation of *Mukhṛā*

(a) *Mukhṛā* serves as an introductory statement indicating that the *gat* beginning. At this point, the *sitār* is not yet accompanied by the *tablā*.

(b) *Mukhṛā* serves as a point of departure from a precomposed section (in the present case, *sthāyī* or *manjhā*; however, *antarā* may also be inferred).

(c) *Mukhṛā* serves as a point of departure from an improvised section, leading the melodic line back to the *sthāyī*.

(d) *Mukhṛā* serves as a point of departure from an improvised section, leading to another separate improvised section.

Basic mukhṛā
a) Krintan
b) Sparś
c) Giṭkiṛī

Figure 21: Technique in Variation of *Mukhṛā*

7.1.3 *Technique in variation of mukhṛā*

The concept of variation of the *gat* as a developmental process has been discussed earlier (see 5.2). Here, specific examples of one section of the *gat*, the *mukhṛā*, are presented in order to illustrate the importance of technique in the procedure of variation.

The statements of the *mukhṛā* grouped according to the technique of variation are presented in Figure 20. Examples of each category have been extracted and arranged in parsed notation in Figure 21. To facilitate this arrangement, after the complete basic *mukhṛā* has been presented, only the last four *mātrā*-s in each of the remaining examples are notated. The category listed as 'basic *mukhṛā*' in Figure 20 contains some instances of variation within it, however, the degree of variation is so slight that the writer has chosen to group them together.

The importance of technique as an essential method of variation on precomposed structures is made evident by the mere fact that the above categorization can be made. Categories (a), (b), (c), (d), and (e) are based purely on the occurrence of specific techniques altering specific motifs.

7.1.4 *Śṛṅkhalā of the vistār*

In section 7.1.1, the general structure of the performance was discussed. By referring to Figure 17, a summary of the order of events in the *vistār* (i.e., the *śṛṅkhalā*) may be detailed. Such a summary appears in Figure 22.

sthāyī
↓
manjhā
↓
baṛhat tān-s
↓
cau guṇ tān-s
↓
sthāyī
↓
chah guṇ tān-s
↓
sthāyī
↓
manjhā
↓
āṭh guṇ tān-s

Figure 22: *Śṛṅkhalā* of the *Vilambit Gat Vistār*

By comparing Figure 22 with Figure 13 (see 5.2.1), it is apparent that the *śṛṅkhalā* of the *vilambit gat vistār* of the corpus fits the model of the *śṛṅkhalā* of the *tālīm*. The only difference is that certain stages are omitted (e.g., *antarā*, and *vilambit, du guṇ, ti guṇ, pañc guṇ*, and *sāt guṇ tān*-s). The omissions may possibly have resulted from the limitation of melodic freedom in this *rāg*. Available time for the performance could have been another contributing factor. Whatever the cause, the result provides insight into one method of variation upon the *tālīm śṛṅkhalā*—deletion of certain stages—in order to adapt to a particular performance situation.

An *āvartan* by *āvartan* account of tempo progression is given in Table 2. The data presented in the table appears in graphic form in Figure 23.

TABLE 2

TEMPO VARIATION IN THE *VILAMBIT GAT VISTĀR*

Ā	Mātrā-s per min.	Ā	Mātrā-s per min.	Ā	Mātrā-s per min.
1	43	20	52.5	39	65
2	41	21	51	40	68
3	43	22	56.5	41	58
4	43	23	52.5	42	61
5	43	24	53	43	62
6	45	25	53	44	61
7	45	26	52	45	61
8	47	27	51	46	65
9	47	28	58	47	67
10	48	29	63	48	68
11	46	30	59.5	49	65.5
12	45	31	60.5	50	67
13	51	32	61	51	68
14	57	33	60	52	68
15	51	34	65	53	68
16	51	35	62	54	68
17	51.5	36	60.5	55	71
18	50.5	37	62	56	76
19	52.5	38	61	57	68

Ā = Āvartan

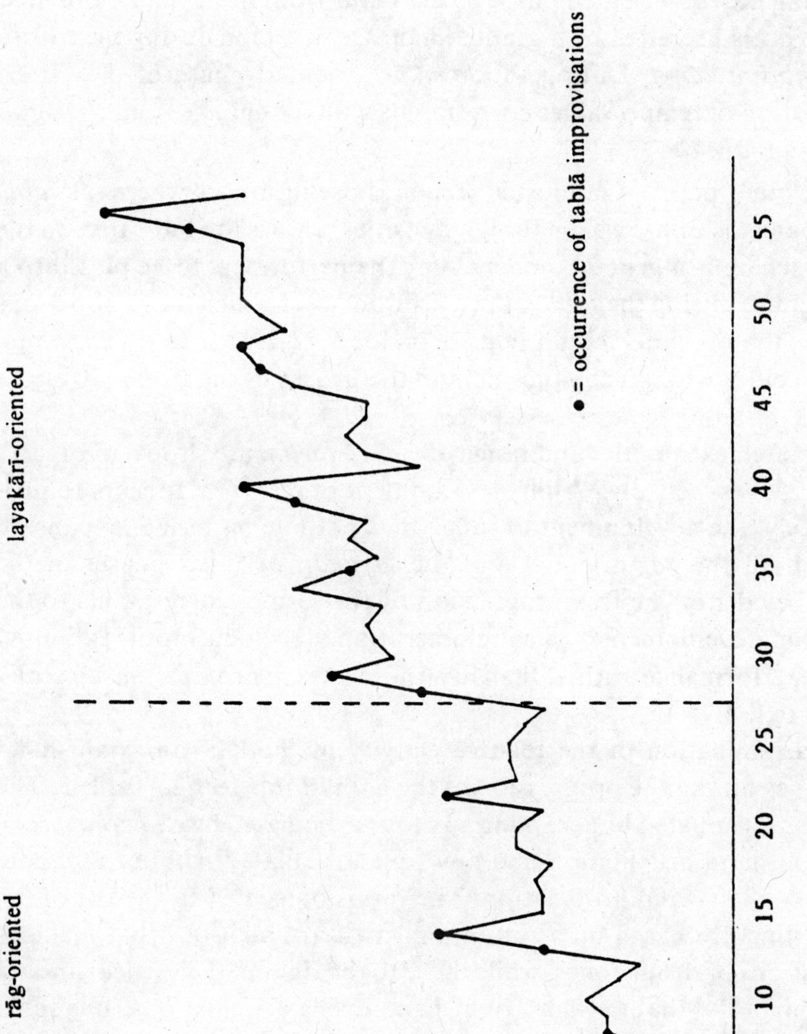

Figure 23: Tempo Variation in the *Vilambit Gat Vistār*

The graph clearly illustrates the close relationship between the *śṛṅkhalā* and tempo progression. There is a dramatic increase in tempo (ā 28-29) separating the *rāg*-oriented phase of the *vistār* from the *layakārī*-oriented phase. This is preceded by a gradual increase in tempo during the course of the *baṛhat tān*-s. During the *layakārī*-oriented phase of the *vistār*, stratification of tempo values corresponds with the change from *chah guṇ* to *āṭh guṇ layakārī*.

One other point of interest is seen in those instances where the *tablā* accompanist is improvising at high densities (values are indicated on the graph). There is a general tendency for the performers to be pulled to a faster tempo during the *tablā* improvisation, after which the tempo drops down to the previous tempo (e.g., ā 14-15; ā 22-23), or to a new tempo that coincides with an advancement in the phases of the *śṛṅkhalā* (e.g., ā 29-30; ā 48-50).

The pitch extremities and range of each *āvartan* are shown in Figures 24 and 25, respectively. While development of *tessitura* appears to proceed freely, the development of range by a definite pattern of expansion during both the *rāg*-oriented and the *layakārī*-oriented phases of the *vistār* is evident. The free progression of the former corresponds to the method of development by a conglomeration of melodic motifs exhibited in this performance rather than by the ordered progression of scale-degrees (c.f. 5.2.1).

An examination of the relative activity of the left- and right-hand techniques during the progression of the *gat vistār* is seen in Table 3. The table was formulated by accepting any tone articulated by a *mizrāb* stroke as a right-hand articulation and any tone articulated without a *mizrāb* stroke as a left-hand articulation. The ratios presented to the left of the vertical line are based on a total number of articulations that includes articulations of drone tones, while those to the right of the vertical line are based on a total that excludes right-hand drone articulations. It is sufficient to graph the data regarding only one hand in order to illustrate relative activity of both hands. The data of the ratios of the left-hand articulations with the total number of articulations minus the drone articulations is seen in Figure 26. The graph reveals that the ratio of left-hand articulations to right-hand articulations tends to decrease during the course of the *vistār*.

From the above results, it may be concluded that left-hand techniques play a greater role during the *rāg*-oriented phase of the *vistār* than in the *layakārī*-oriented phase.

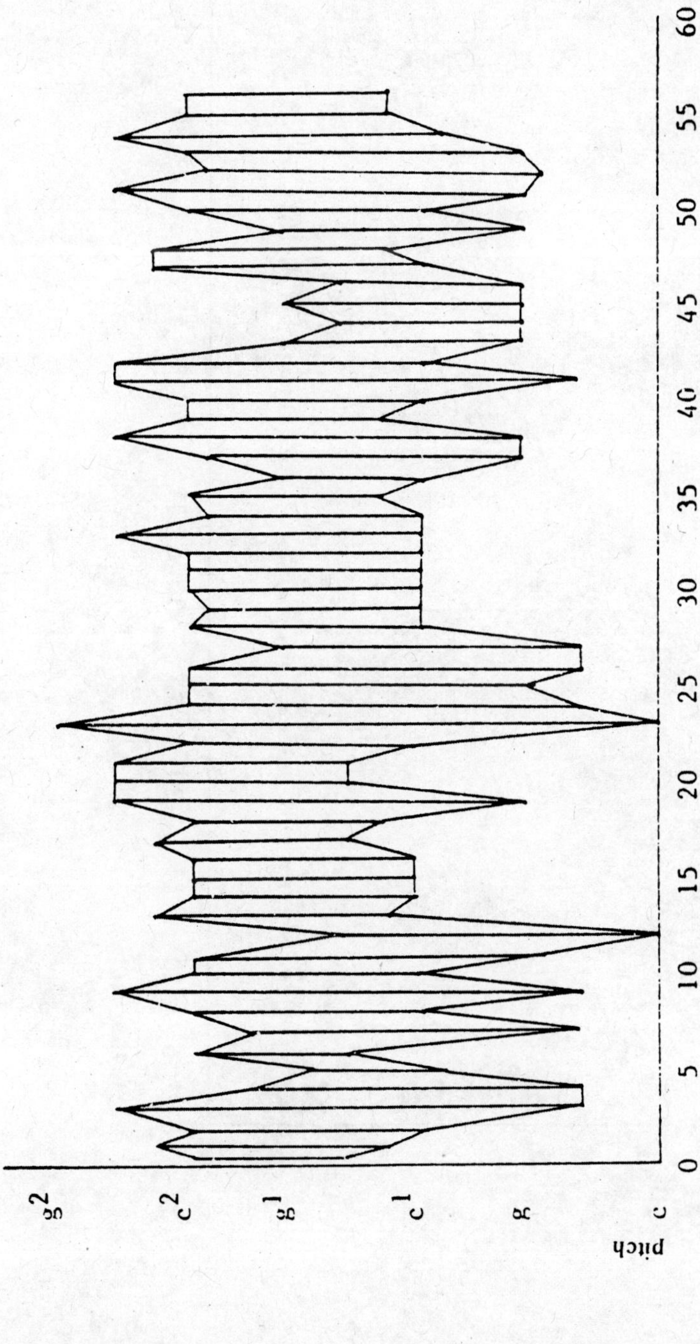

Figure 24: Pitch Extremities in the *Vilambit Gat Vistār*

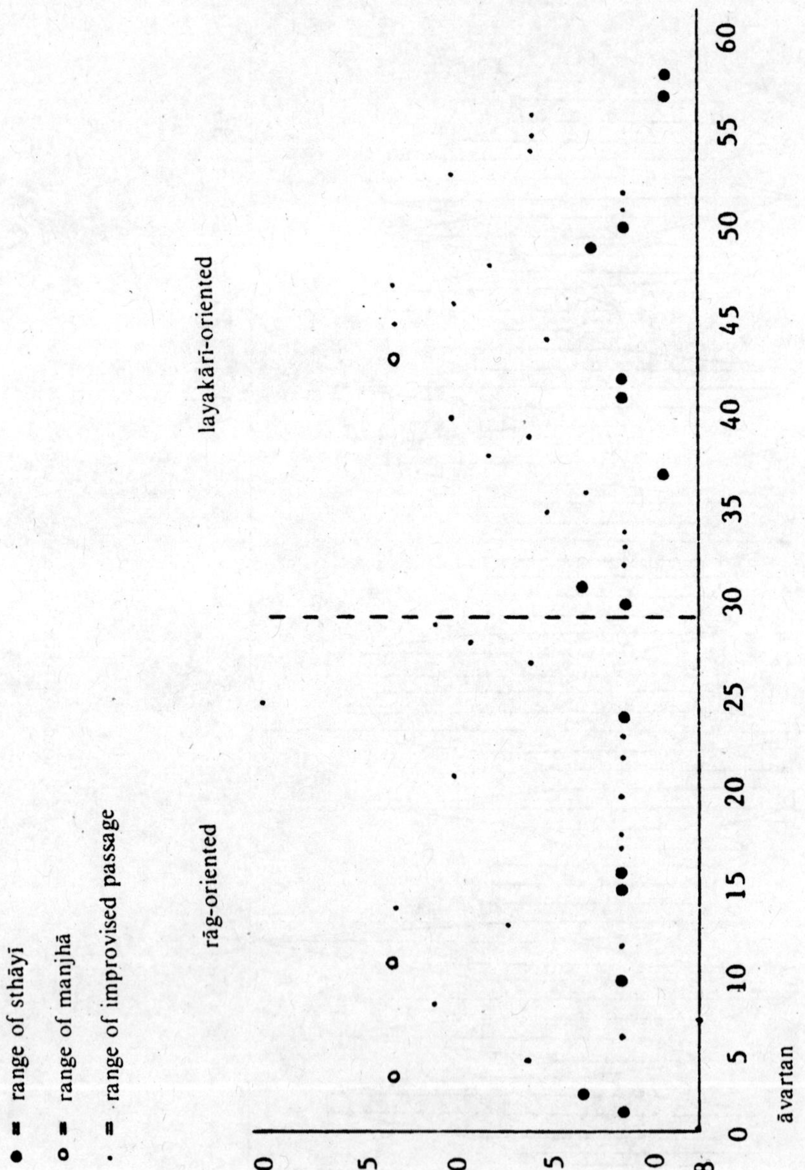

Figure 25: Range Progression in the *Vilambit Gat Vistār*

TABLE 3

RATIOS OF LEFT- AND RIGHT-HAND ARTICULATIONS IN THE *VILAMBIT GAT VISTĀR*

Ā	T	R.H.	L.H.	R.H./T	L.H./T	T-D	R.H.-D	R.H.-D/T-D	L.H./T-D
M	21	15	6	.714	.285	15	9	.600	.400
1*	69	50	19	.724	.275	43	24	.558	.441
2*	91	45	46	.494	.505	68	22	.323	.676
3*	75	41	34	.546	.453	61	27	.442	.557
4	54	43	11	.796	.203	30	19	.633	.366
5	59	46	13	.779	.220	39	26	.666	.333
6	67	48	19	.716	.283	44	25	.568	.431
7	60	45	15	.750	.250	45	30	.666	.333
8*	74	44	30	.594	.405	49	19	.387	.612
9*	72	46	26	.638	.361	54	28	.518	.481
10	57	44	13	.771	.228	44	31	.704	.295
11	69	39	30	.565	.434	56	26	.464	.535
12	59	41	18	.694	.305	46	28	.608	.391
13*	71	45	26	.633	.366	49	23	.469	.530
14*	72	47	25	.652	.347	50	25	.500	.500
15	42	36	6	.857	.142	23	17	.739	.260
16	78	44	34	.564	.435	74	40	.540	.459
17	55	39	16	.709	.290	39	23	.589	.410
18	83	55	28	.662	.337	68	40	.588	.411
19	69	44	25	.637	.362	56	31	.553	.446
20	49	29	20	.591	.408	37	17	.459	.540
21	56	40	16	.714	.285	44	28	.636	.363
22*	65	42	23	.646	.353	46	23	.500	.500
23	57	39	18	.684	.315	42	24	.571	.428
24	62	45	17	.725	.275	44	27	.613	.386
25	68	39	29	.573	.426	52	23	.442	.557
26	69	42	27	.608	.391	58	31	.534	.465
27	58	43	15	.741	.258	45	30	.666	.333
28*	67	44	23	.656	.343	45	22	.488	.511
29*	64	47	16	.734	.262	46	28	.608	.347
30	58	52	6	.896	.103	43	37	.860	.139
31	79	64	15	.810	.189	66	51	.772	.227
32	78	55	23	.705	.294	66	43	.636	.348

TABLE 3 (CONTINUED)

Ā	T	R.H.	L.H.	R.H. / T	L.H. / T	T-D	R.H.-D	R.H.-D / T-D	L.H. / T-D
33	63	51	12	.810	.190	39	27	.692	.307
34	75	58	17	.773	.226	60	43	.716	.116
35	61*	46	15	.754	.245	36	21	.583	.416
36	75	70	5	.933	.066	67	62	.925	.074
37	77	60	17	.779	.220	67	50	.746	.253
38	71	50	21	.704	.295	51	30	.588	.411
39*	72	47	25	.652	.347	47	22	.468	.531
40*	85	48	37	.564	.435	57	20	.350	.649
41*	74	42	32	.567	.432	61	29	.475	.524
42	67	51	16	.761	.239	47	31	.660	.340
43	85	61	24	.717	.283	61	37	.607	.393
44	121	111	10	.917	.083	121	111	.917	.083
45	125	102	23	.816	.184	104	81	.778	.283
46	98	79	19	.806	.193	98	79	.806	.193
47*	65	42	23	.646	.353	65	42	.646	.353
48*	70	45	25	.642	.357	47	22	.468	.531
49	63	63	0	1	0	27	27	.100	.000
50	84	77	7	.916	.083	55	48	.872	.127
51	85	81	4	.952	.047	63	59	.936	.063
52	82	79	3	.963	.036	58	55	.948	.051
53	94	85	9	.904	.095	74	65	.878	.121
54	97	74	23	.763	.237	86	63	.732	.263
55*	70	49	21	.700	.300	43	22	.511	.488
56*	58	37	21	.637	.362	47	26	.553	.446
57	79	77	2	.975	.025	64	62	.969	.031

Ā = Āvartan
T = Total # Articulations
R.H. = Right-hand Articulations
L.H. = Left-hand Articulations
D = Drone Strokes
* = Sthāyī or Manjhā

A comparison of the relative importance of the techniques comprising the left-hand articulations is seen in Table 4. In the table, since right-hand articulations are of no statistical concern, those articulations that utilize any left-hand technique (other than the basic fretting techniques) are included in the totals, regardless of whether or not there is a *mizrāb* stroke. A cursory examination of the chart reveals that: (1) techniques incorporating pulling of the wire occur much more often than the other techniques examined, and (2) there is no indication that the mixture of these techniques varies in accordance with the progression of the *vistār*. Relatively stable proportions of these techniques appear throughout the performance.

7.2 *Drut Gat Vistār*—Analysis

7.2.1 *Structural elements in general form*

The *drut gat* is introduced by a short *tān*, after which the *sthāyī* is stated twice. The *sthāyī* begins on *sam*, hence precluding a *mukhṛā* in the *gat*, and is divided in correspondence with the *tāl* sections (i.e., four groups of four). The first expression of the *sthāyī* is actually a variant form in that the tones of the first four *mātrā*-s are different than in any other statement of the *sthāyī*. The entire *manjhā* follows a second statement of the *sthyāyī*, and is three *āvartan*-s long (ā 3-5). The first half of the first and second of these (ā 3-4) and the second half of the third (ā 5) are divided in syncopation with the *tāl*. The division 3-3-2 occurs in the former, 3-2-3 in the latter. The *manjhā* is followed by another statement of the *sthāyī*, concluding the first complete expression of the precomposed section of the *vistār*.

A *tihāī* in *du guṇ layakārī* occurs in the seventh *āvartan* (m 8-16). The *tihāī* ends on the last *mātrā* of the *tāl* instead of the *sam*. This practice (i.e., showing *sam* before the actual sum arrives) is known as *anāgat* (H. 'that not yet arrived'). Following the *tihāī* is a short improvisation that carries the rhythmic flow of the line back into *sam* (and the *sthāyī*) at ā 9. A *thā guṇ tān* follows (ā 10-12), concluded by a *tihāī* (ā 13) showing *anāgat* (m 15). Another statement of the *sthāyī* (ā 14) is followed by a *du guṇ tān* (ā 15 m 9-ā 18 m 5) and a *tihāī* (ā 18 m 6-15) showing *anāgat*.

Two restatements of the *sthāyī* (ā 19-20) and a cycle of rhythmic pacing on the drone wires precede the beginning of a series of *toṛā*-s (see 5.2.2). The first *toṛā* (ā 22-28) consists of four subsections concluded by a *tihāī* (ā 29). The first two subsections (ā 22-23; ā 24-25) are comprised of an initial statement and a slightly varied restatement of a phrase, while the last two subsections (ā 26-27; ā 28) are through-composed on the basis of motifs derived from the *manjhā*.

Three statements of the *sthāyī* (ā 30, 32, 33), an abbreviated restatement of the *manjhā* (ā 34), and rhythmic pacing (ā 31, 35, 36) occur

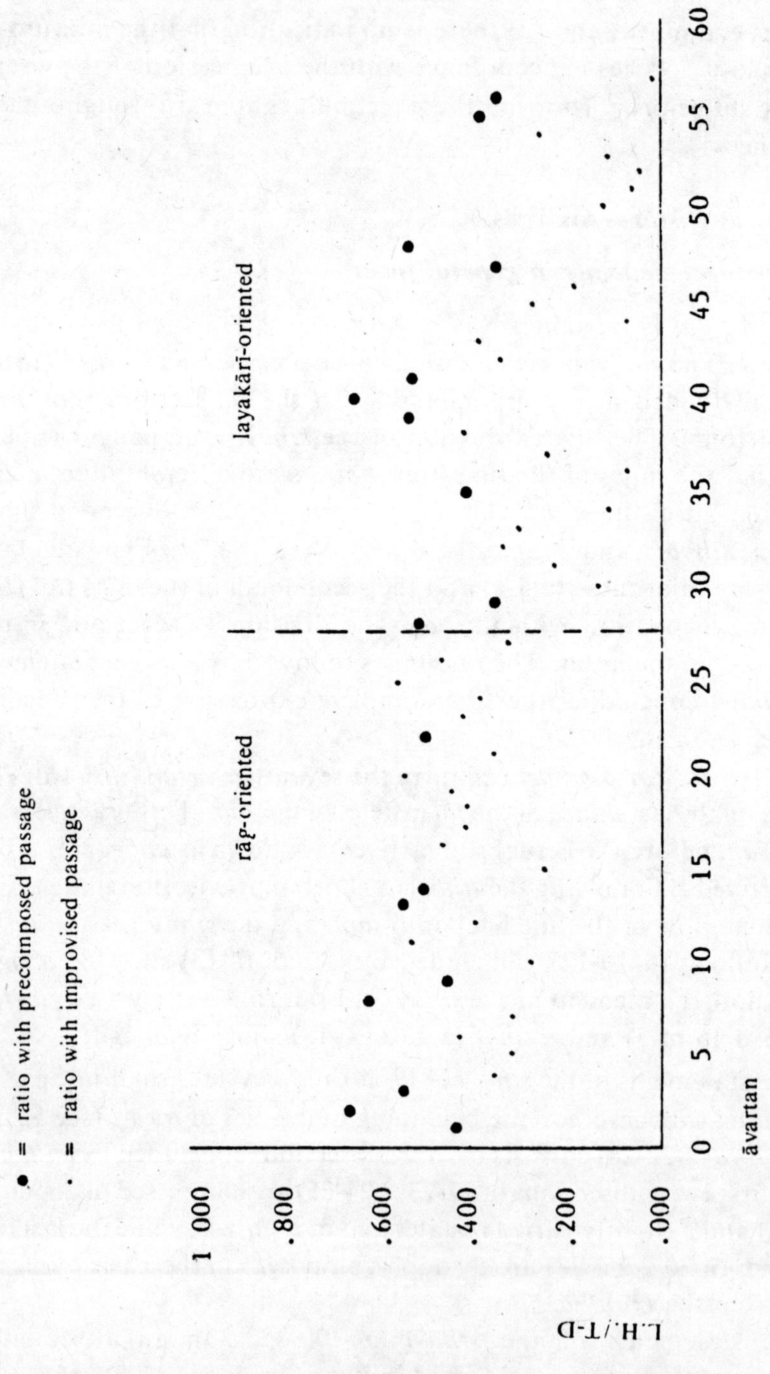

Figure 26: Left-hand Articulation in the *Vilambit Gat Vistār* (L.H./T—D)

TABLE 4

RATIOS OF PARALLEL AND PERPENDICULAR LEFT-HAND TECHNIQUES IN THE *VILAMBIT GAT VISTĀR*

Ā	L.H.T.	|	Gharṣaṇ	Sparś	Krintan	||	| / L.H.T.	|| / L.H.T.
M	8	5	0	1	2	3	.625	.375
1	29	22	1	2	4	7	.758	.241
2	54	35	4	5	10	19	.648	.351
3	36	27	2	3	4	9	.750	.250
4	13	10	1	1	1	3	.769	.231
5	22	20	0	1	0	1	.909	.091
6	22	16	0	0	6	6	.727	.273
7	18	14	3	0	1	4	.778	.222
8	35	22	4	3	6	13	.629	.371
9	36	29	2	3	2	7	.806	.194
10	14	7	0	2	5	7	.500	.500
11	30	16	2	4	8	14	.533	.467
12	21	16	2	1	2	5	.762	.238
13	30	18	2	4	6	12	.600	.400
14	26	18	3	2	3	8	.692	.308
15	9	8	0	0	1	1	.889	.111
16	42	29	4	3	6	13	.690	.310
17	28	25	0	0	3	3	.893	.107
18	28	13	5	5	5	15	.464	.535
19	25	15	3	4	3	10	.600	.400
20	28	24	0	1	3	4	.857	.143
21	19	15	0	0	4	4	.789	.211
22	26	16	4	3	3	10	.615	.385
23	21	16	0	1	4	5	.762	.238
24	21	13	4	2	2	8	.619	.380
25	34	24	2	3	3	8	.750	.250
26	27	9	5	6	7	18	.333	667
27	17	12	1	1	3	5	.706	.294
28	30	19	4	3	4	11	.633	.367
29	16	3	4	5	4	13	.188	.812
30	6	2	0	0	4	4	.333	.667
31	16	11	0	0	5	5	.688	.312
32	23	8	4	3	8	15	.348	.652
33	13	3	0	0	10	10	.231	.769
34	25	11	0	7	7	14	.611	.389

TABLE 4 *(CONTINUED)*

Ā	L.H.T.	|	Gharṣaṇ	Sparś	Krintan	||	| / L.H.T.	|| / L.H.T.
35	19	13	2	2	2	6	.684	.316
36	6	0	0	0	6	6	0	1
37	17	7	0	0	10	10	.412	.588
38	23	8	3	1	11	15	.348	.652
39	26	17	3	3	3	9	.654	.346
40	41	24	7	5	5	17	.585	.415
41	36	26	1	4	5	10	.722	.278
42	16	0	0	11	5	16	0	1
43	24	6	0	9	9	18	.250	.750
44	10	10	0	0	0	0	1	0
45	26	26	0	0	0	0	1	0
46	27	18	0	4	5	9	.667	.333
47	26	19	1	3	3	7	.731	.269
48	29	20	3	3	3	9	.690	.310
49	0	0	0	0	0	0	0	0
50	18	15	1	0	2	3	.833	.167
51	4	2	0	0	2	2	.500	.500
52	3	2	0	0	1	1	.667	.333
53	12	8	0	0	4	4	.667	.333
54	24	7	0	9	8	17	.292	.708
55	24	15	3	3	3	9	.625	.375
56	24	14	4	3	3	10	.583	.417
57	4	4	0	0	0	0	1	0
	1228	745	94	140	249	483	.689	.311

Ā = Āvartan
L.H.T. = # of tones produced by pulling, sliding on, hammering on, or plucking the wire.
| = # of tones produced with pulling.
|| = # of tones produced by the parallel techniques: Gharṣaṇ Sparś, and Krintan.

during a *tablā* improvisation in *du guṇ layakārī* (ā 30-35). Following this passage, a *thā guṇ tān* (ā 37 m 11-ā 41 m 5) introduces a *du guṇ toṛa* (ā 41 m 6-ā 44) that also is derived from a motif of the *manjhā*. A restatement of the *sthāyī* (ā 45) and two *āvartan*-s of rhythmic pacing follow (ā 46, 47). A *tān* (ā 48), a *toṛa* (a 49 m 9-ā 50 m 8) joined to a *du guṇ tān* (ā 50 m 9-ā 51 m 6), and a *tihāī* (ā 51 m 8-ā 52 m 2) follow. The *tihāī* ends on the second *mātrā* of ā 52, expressing *sam* after the actual *sam* has passed. This practice is known as *atit* (H. 'that which has passed'). This *tihāī* also elides with another *tihāī* (ā 52 m 2-16) in which the third statement of motivic unit is altered (ā 52 m 14-16) in order to express *anāgat* and also provide a motif for the development of the *thā guṇ tān* that follows (ā 53-55).

Two *āvartan*-s of pacing with strokes on the drone wires (ā 56, 57), two restatements of the *sthāyī* (ā 58, 59), and an abbreviated restatement of the *manjhā* (ā 60) precede the introduction of the *jhālā* (ā 61). The *jhālā* is developed in ā 62-81. The *jhālā* is comprised of ten units, each two *āvartan*-s long. Each unit is either a through-composed phrase (ā 66-67, 68-69, 72-73, 76-77, 80-81) or a motif one *āvartan* in length followed by a restatement (ā 62-63, 64-65, 70-71, 74-75, 78-79). Two *thā guṇ tān*-s (ā 82-87, ā 88-90) and *tihāī* (ā 91 m 4-ā 93) conclude the *drut gat vistār*.

7.2.2 *Contexts of precomposed sections*

The precomposed elements contained in the *drut gat vistār* are *sthāyī* and *manjhā*. There is no *antarā*, possibly because the *manjhā* is very extensive in duration and range. The *sthāyī* is stated thirteen times, the complete *manjhā* once, and an abbreviated form of the *manjhā* twice. The places and contexts of the occurrences of the *sthāyī* and *manjhā* are presented in Figure 28. It is evident from the contexts in which the *sthayī* occurs that it is serving a similar purpose as did the *mukhṛā* in the *vilambit gat*, that is, a ground base from and to which improvised sections are constructed. In contrast, the *manjhā* never occurs as a point of return for improvised sections. *Manjhā* always occurs after the *sthāyī*.

7.2.3 *Technique in variation of the sthāyī*

Of the thirteen occurrences of the *sthāyī* only two are played in exactly the same way (ā 32, 33). The other eleven statements of the *sthāyī* incorporate *krintan, krintan*$_1$ *zamzamā, gamak, giṭkiṛī, bol,* and *tān* as methods of variation. Four particular statements of the *sthāyī* have been isolated and arranged in parsed notation to facilitate the illustration of these variation techniques in Figure 29. *Krintan* occurs at m 9 of ā 1 and ā 45. *Krintan*$_1$ occurs on m 14 of ā 1, *zamzamā* at ml of ā 9. *Gamak* occurs in m 6-7, and a *tān* in m 14-15, of ā 45. The *bol* of the *sthāyī* is varied considerably in ā 58, while *giṭkiṛī* occurs on m 14-15 in the same cycle.

7.2.4 *Śṛṅkhalā of the drut gat vistār*

The progression of the *drut gat vistār* is virtually the same as that which was discussed in section 5.2.2, excepting that the *gat* of the corpus lacks an *antarā*. A condensed summary of the *vistār* yields the progression presented in Figure 30.

Āvartan	*Activity*	*Āvartan*	*Activity*
0	introductory tān (m 14-16)	32, 33	sthāyī
1, 2	sthāyī	34	manjhā (abbreviated)
3-5	manjhā	35, 36	pacing
6	sthāyī	37-40	thā guṇ tān (m 11-...)
7	tihāī (m 8-16) anāgat (m 16)	41-44	toṛā (m 6....)
8	bridge	45	sthāyī
9	sthāyī	46, 47	pacing
10-12	thā guṇ tān (m 11-...)	48	du guṇ tān
13	tihāī (m 14-15) anāgat (m 15)	49, 50	toṛā (ā 49 m 9...)
14	sthāyī, anāgat (m 16)	51	tihāī (m 8-...)
15-18	du guṇ tān anāgat (m 9)	52	atīt (m 2); tihāī (m 12-16) anāgat (m 16)
18	tihāī (m 6-15) anāgat (m 15)	53-55	thā guṇ tān
19, 20	sthāyī	56, 57	pacing
21	pacing	58, 59	sthāyī
22-28	toṛā	60	manjhā (abbreviated)
29	tihāī (m 1-16)	61-81	jhālā
30	sthāyī	82-90	thā guṇ tān-s (ā 82-87; 88-90)
31	pacing	91-93	tihāī
		94	concludes on *sam* (articulation of taraf)

Figure 27: Structural Elements in the *Drut Gat Vistār*

sthāyī			manjhā		
#	Āvartan	Context	#	Āvartan	Context
1)	ā 1	B	1)	ā 3 -ā 5	D
2)	ā 2	D	2)	ā 34	A
3)	ā 6	A	3)	ā 60	A
4)	ā 9	C			
5)	ā 14	C			
6)	ā 19	B			
7)	ā 20	A			
8)	ā 30	C			
9)	ā 32	B			
10)	ā 33	D			
11)	ā 45	C			
12)	ā 58	B			
13)	ā 59	A			

A = preceded by sthāyī or manjhā, followed by improvisation

B = preceded by improvisation, followed by sthāyī or manjhā

C = preceded by improvisation, followed by improvisation

D = preceded by sthāyī or manjhā, followed by sthāyī or manjhā

Figure 28: Occurrences and Contexts of Precomposed Sections in the *Drut Gat Vistār*

A graphic representation of the tempo variation during the progression of the *drut gat vistār* appears in Figure 31. A gradual increase in tempo during the section of the *vistār* preceding *jhālā*, and a sharp increase in tempo during *jhālā* is illustrated by the graph. One other facet of the tempo development becomes evident if this graph is compared with the analysis of general form presented above in Figure 27, that is the function of the drone wire in maintaining a steady tempo. The occurrences of rhythmic pacing on the drone wires at ā 21, 35-36, and 46-47 are all at a slower tempo than the preceding and following *āvartan*-s. This suggests that the performer is attempting to restrain the tempo from increasing at too fast a rate. The opposite occurs in *jhālā*, where the tempo

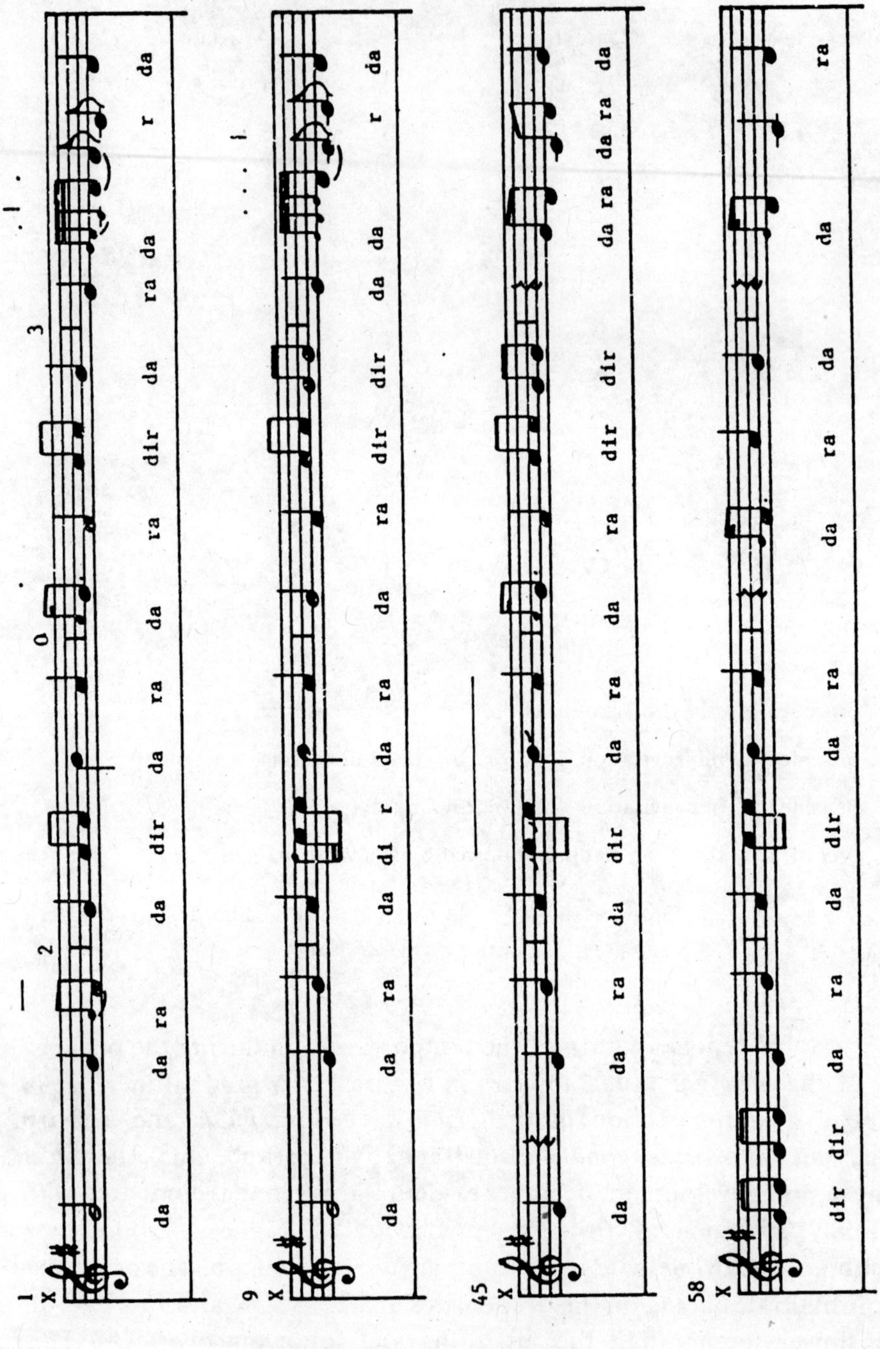

Figure 29: **Technique in Variation of *Sthāyī***

sthāyī

↓

manjhā

↓

tān-s and tihāī-s

↓

toṛā-s and tihāī-s

↓

jhālā

Figure 30: Sṛṅkhalā of the Drut Gat Vistār

is steadily pushed higher in order to reach a speed which creates an exciting climax and conclusion to the performance.

An examination of the transcription of the left-hand techniques reveals that there is far less utilization of left-hand articulatory techniques in the *drut gat vistār* than was evidence in the *vilambit gat vistār*. There is a greater emphasis on pre-fabricated *mizrāb bol*-s and fretted tones (referred to as 'cut notes' by practitioners) than on the maintenance of a sound continuum through articulation by pulling the wire. Whatever left-hand articulations do occur function primarily as auxiliary tones. Correlations of right-hand technique with the progression of the *vistār* are seen at the places of the introduction of *toṛā*-s and *jhālā*. The former becomes evident only if precomposed sections are excluded from the examination, because the *gat* itself is a form of *toṛā*. The first *toṛā* in the improvisational sense occurs at ā 22. From that point on, there is a greater variety of *mizrāb bol*-s occurring in the improvised sections of the *vistār* than had been evidenced in the preceding events of the *vistār*. The common feature of these *bol*-s is the inclusion of '*dir*', the identifying factor of *toṛā*.

A completely different approach to right-hand technique is exhibited in the *jhālā*. Strokes on the *cikārī* wires, which had been of little significance previously, become a principal factor in defining rhythmic motifs. They comprise a substantial portion of the aural experience during this phase of the *vistār*. This particular *jhālā* is an example of *śuddh jhālā*. There is one occurrence of a '*r*' stroke on the *bāj* wire (ā 80 m 2), but this is not sufficient to warrant being termed *ṭhoṅk jhālā*. The common *bol*-s occurring in this *jhālā*, along with the *āvartan*-s in which they occur, are listed in Figure 32.

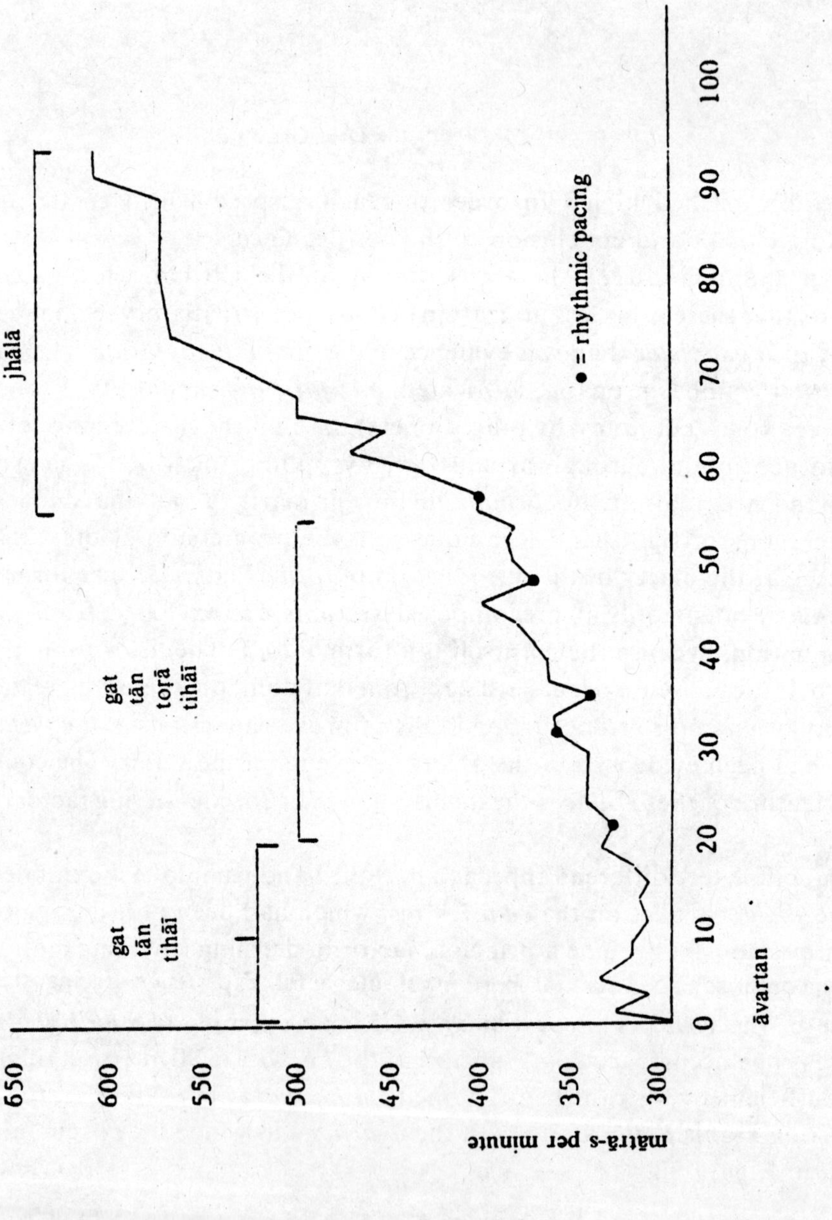

Figure 31: Tempo Variation in the *Drut Gat Vistār*

Bol				Āvartan—(s)
X	2	0	3	
da c c c	da c c c	da c c c	da c c c	62, 63, 65, 78
da c da c	da c c c	da c c c	da c c c	64, 74, 75
da c c da	c c da c	c da c c	da c da c	68, 69, 72, 73, 77
da c da c	da c da c	da c c da	c c da c	71
da c c c	da c da c	c da c c	da c da c	81

Figure 32: *Jhālā Bol*-s in the *Drut Gat Vistār*

CHAPTER VIII

SUMMARY AND CONCLUSIONS

In the preceding discussions, it has been shown that although the origins of the *sitār* are obscured by myth and controversy, the development of *sitār* technique may be traced to a number of donating sources: the *bīn*, *rabāb*, *dhrupad aṅg* and *khyāl aṅg* vocal music, and percussion instruments. Of these sources, the actual physical maneuvers of technique have been largely derived from the *bīn*, and to a lesser extent, *rabāb*, while stylized formal elements of music have been derived from all of the sources. It was also shown that the *sitār* was the instrument of choice through which a totally new and unique system of *rāg prastār* was developed during the eighteenth and nineteenth centuries—the *gat śailī*. The development of the *gat śailī* centered on the reorganization of the previously acquired techniques and stylized formal elements within the context of the expansion of a nuclear melodic theme—the *gat*.

Gat-s are archetypal forms that are generated primarily through right-hand technique. Their rhythmic structure is dictated by the *mizrāb bol* underlying the melodic line. While there do exist a number of standardized *bol* patterns for complete *gat*-s, there has been a great deal of creative composition during the last forty years that has led to the formation of an extensive repertory of compositions for the *sitār*. However, these compositions retain the practice of basing rhythmic structure on right-hand technique, and the extended *bol*-s underlying their construction are the result of permutation and combination of a basic set of right-hand *mizrāb bol*-s.

The development of the *gat* by improvisation is known as *gat vistār*. The improvisational procedures employed in *gat vistār* are of two general types: (1) variations on precomposed elements, and (2) spontaneous compositions based on an ordered series of stylized formal elements. It has been shown that the *vilambit gat vistār* provides a greater potential for *rāg* development than other *gat* forms. The *vistār* of the *vilambit gat* was viewed as consisting of two phases: (1) *rāg*-oriented, and (2) *layakārī*-oriented. The progression of both of these phases, and the role of technique in that progression, was examined in the analysis (see 7.1). On the basis of that analysis, the following conclusions may be offered:

(a) Of the precomposed elements of a *vilambit gat, mukhṛā* is the most essential. It reappears more often than other precomposed elements, and serves a number of functions. *Mukhṛā* acts as a structural marker indicating: (1) the beginning of the *gat*, (2) the imminence of the *sam*, (3) the departure from a precomposed element of the *gat* to an improvisational passage, and *vice versa*, and (4) the departure from one improvisational passage leading to another independent improvisation.

(b) Right- and left-hand techniques are essential elements in the improvisational procedure based on variation of a precomposed element. Often, a specific technique is utilized as the factor of variation in such an improvisation.

(c) The order of the progression of the *vistār* [*śṛṅkhalā*], while being flexible in content, adheres to the following practices: (1) a correlation of tempo increases with the progressive stages of the *vistār*, (2) an expansion of range during both the *rāg*-oriented and *layakārī*-oriented phases of the *śṛṅkhalā*, and (3) a greater emphasis on left-hand articulatory techniques during the *rāg*-oriented phase of the *vistār* than the *layakārī*-oriented phase.

Many of the above statements may also be applied to the *drut gat vistār*. However, some require modification while others do not apply at all. In *drut gat*-s lacking a *mukhṛā*, the *sthāyī*, or a portion of the *sthāyī*, may function as the *mukhṛā* functions in the *vilambit gat*. Regarding the involvement of technique in *vistār*, it has been shown above that the right-hand technique is the focus of attention in regards to correlating technique with the progressive stages of the *vistār*.

These conclusions are subject to verification by similar studies of other performances of the artist examined in this study in order to determine the extent to which they are applicable to this complete repertory, and performances by other artists in order to determine the extent to which they are applicable to *sitār*-ists in general.

APPENDIX A

Guide to Transliteration

Devanāgarī script	*Romanization*	*Pronunciation*
अ	a	hut
आ	ā	hot
इ	i	hit
ई	ī	meet
उ	u	good
ऊ	ū	food
ऋ	ṛ	rich
ए	e	ate
ऐ	ai	bait
ओ	o	oats
औ	au	now
क	ka	kin (unaspirated)
ख	kha	kin (aspirated)
ग	ga	get
घ	gha	get (aspirated)
ङ	ṅa	sing
च	ca	chin (unaspirated)
छ	cha	chin (aspirated)
ज	ja	jet
ज़	za	zoo
झ	jha	jut (aspirated)
ञ	ña	crunch
ट	ṭa	tin (retroflex)
ठ	ṭha	tin (retroflex, aspirated)
ड, ड़	ḍa, ṛa	done (retroflex), no equivalent-rla
ढ, ढ़	ḍha, ṛha	done (retroflex, aspirated no equivalent-rhla)
ण	ṇa	fern (retroflex)
त	ta	tuck
थ	tha	tuck (aspirated)
द	da	duck
ध	dha	duck (aspirated)
न	na	nut
प	pa	pun
फ	pha	pun (aspirated)
ब	ba	but

भ	bha	but (aspirated)
म	ma	mother
य	ya	yard
र	ra	rust
ल	la	lung
व	va	volume (with a hint of 'w')
श	śa	shut
ष	ṣa	shut
स	sa	sun
ह	ha	hat
ँ	˜	(nasalization)
:	ḥ	final 'h'

For a more detailed explanation of the romanization and pronunciation of *Devanāgarī* script, see the Central Hindi Directorate's *A Basic Grammar of Modern Hindi* (New Delhi: Government of India, 1975).

APPENDIX B

Hastavyāpāra of the *Eka-tantrī Vīṇā*

The following information is a paraphrase of the passages in the *Saṅgīta Ratnākara* that describe the playing techniques of the *eka-tantrī vīṇā*. (1951:238-243)

Before describing the particular techniques of the right and left hands, Śāraṅgadeva states that a wooden stick, *kamrikā*, is used at times to press the wire of the *vīṇā*. The *kamrikā* is held in the left hand, and its actions are referred to as *sāraṇā*, of which there are four:

	sāraṇā	*Manner of performance*
(1)	*utkṣiptā*	Having first maintained continuous contact of the *kamrikā* with the wire, pluck the wire from inside (with the *kamrikā*) and then hurl it upward to a far distance (arm's length). Finally, again place the *kamrikā* in contact with the wire and rub it slowly back and forth.
(2)	*saṁniviṣṭā*	Having first touched the wire lightly with the *kamrikā*, move it to a different place (on the wire).
(3)	*ubhayī*	Combine the first two *sāraṇā*-s.
(4)	*Kampitā*	Place the *kamrikā* at the place of the tone and shake it.

Techniques of the right hand

	Technical term	*Manner of performance*
(1)	*ghāta*	Joining the middle finger with the index finger, strike the wire with the inside of the index finger.
(2)	*pāta*	Strike outward with the index finger.
(3)	*saṁlekha*	Strike inward with the index finger.
(4)	*ullekha*	Strike inward with the middle finger.
(5)	*avalekha*	Strike outward with the middle finger.
(6)	*bhramara*	Strike inward with all four fingers successively and quickly.
(7)	*saṁdhita*	Strike outward with the middle and ring fingers.
(8)	*cchinna*	Keeping the index near the wire, strike outward with the ring finger.
(9)	*nakhakartarī*	Strike outward with all four nails, successively and quickly.

Techniques of the left hand

	Technical term	*Manner of performance*
(1)	*sphurita*	Shake the wire with the index finger.
(2)	*khasita*	Rub the wire gently.

Techniques combining the left and right hands

	Technical term	*Manner of performance*
(1)	*ghoṣa*	Pressing the wire with the left little finger, keep the right thumb near the wire and hit as in *kartarī*.
(2)	*refa*	Strike inward with the right ring finger and outward with the left middle finger.
(3)	*bindu*	After striking the wire with the right ring finger, press the wire with the left index finger.
(4)	*ardhakartarī*	While the right hand performs *kartarī*, the left presses the wire.
(5)	*kartarī*	All fingers of both hands strike outward quickly and successively.
(6)	*niṣkoṭa*	Having abandoned *sārāṇa*, strike the wire with the index and middle fingers of both hands.
(7)	*skhalita*	The left hand performs *utkṣiptā sārāṇā* while the right performs as in *kartarī*.
(8)	*śukawaktraka*	Having joined the tips of the right thumb and index, strike the wire.
(9)	*mūrcchanā*	While striking with the right hand, the left hand performs *kampita* with the *kamrikā*.
(10)	*talahasta*	Strike the wire with the palm of the right hand and then touch the wire with the left index and middle fingers.
(11)	*ardhacandra*	While touching the wire with the thumb and little finger of the left hand, strike it with the right hand.
(12)	*prasāra*	(unclear) Having contracted the left thumb under *ardhacandra*, the fingers are joined and touch the wire.
(13)	*kuhara*	The right-hand fingers and thumb, slightly contracted, strike the wire while the left little finger and thumb touch it.

APPENDIX C

Tape-recorded Examples

An accompanying tape containing a recording of the corpus and also a recording of examples of *laṛī, laṛ lapeṭ, laṛ guthāv,* and *tār paran* played by *Paṇḍit* Ravi Shankar and Dr. Lalmani Misra are on deposit at the Archive of Ethnic Music and Dance at the Music (Ethnomusicology) Department, University of Hawaii at Manoa.

APPENDIX D

Glossary

The glossary is alphabetized according to the Roman alphabet with the exception that those characters requiring diacritical marks are placed after the non-marked version of the same character. Thus *atīt* precedes *āndolan, tīn-tāl*, precedes *ṭhumrī*, etc.

abhyās	practice, preparation
alaṅkār	an exercise incorporating tonal sequence
Amīrkhānī bāj	an instrumental style of composition no longer extant attributed to Amir Khan
anāgat	not yet arrived; showing sam before the actual *sam* occurs
anibaddh	non-metrical; not set to rhythm
anibaddh tānpurā	see *tānpurā*
antarā	a section of a composition usually emphasizing the upper octave tonic
aṅg	literally limb, but in music, there are several meanings: (a) upper or lower part of an octave; (b) a style of music; (c) a classification of melody types; (d) a section of a musical form
atīt	passed; showing *sam* after the actual *sam* has occurred
aṛa cautāl	a rhythmic cycle fourteen *mātrā*-s in length
aṛī	literally 'slanted'; in music, referring to those rhythms of three against two, four against three, etc.
ālāp	the introductory, non-metrical exposition of a *rāg*
āndolan	a slow shaking ornament
āṭh guṇ	division of the *mātrā* into eight equal parts
āvartan	one revolution of a *tāl* cycle
baṛā khyāl	a vocal form sung in a slow tempo developed by Nyamat Khan in the eighteenth century
baṛhat tān	a melodic phrase emphasizing development of the character of one particular tone
bāj tār	the first playing wire on the *sitār*; tuned a perfect fourth above the tonic pitch
bīn	a fretted stick zither with gourd resonators
bīnkār	one who plays *bīn*; belonging to a school of musicians established by descendants of Tansen
bol	mnemonic device by which drum strokes and right-hand strokes of plucked string instruments are taught

bol banāv	an improvisational procedure in light classical music
cau guṇ	division of the *mātrā* into four equal parts
chaḥ guṇ	division of the *mātrā* into six equal parts
choṭā khyāl	a vocal form sung in a medium or fast tempo
cikārī	the side drone wires on the *sitār*
daṇḍ	the neck of the *sitār*
dā	an inward stroke by the right index finger
dādrā	(a) a rhythmic cycle six *mātrā*-s in length; (b) a light-classical vocal form composed in *dādrā tāl*
dāṛh	the supporting posts for the *cikārī* wires on the *sitār*
dār	a composite *mizrāb bol: dā* followed by a shortened *rā*
dhrupad	a medieval vocal style known for its devotional character and austere ornamentation
dhrupad aṅg	a style of music based on the forms and ornamentation found in *dhrupad* vocal music
dhun	a light-classical form in instrumental music
dir	a composite *mizrāb bol: dā* and *rā* played in quick succession
dirā	a composite *mizrāb bol:* a shortened *dā* followed by *rā*
drut gat	an instrumental composition played in a fast tempo
du guṇ	division of the *mātrā* into two equal parts
ek-tāl	a rhythmic cycle twelve *mātrā*-s in length
eka-tantrī vīṇā	a one-stringed stick zither described in the *Saṅgīta Ratnākara*
gamak	(a) any ornament; (b) any shaking ornament; (c) a specific heavy shaking ornament
gat	an instrumental composition with an underlying *mizrāb bol*
gat śailī	a style of instrumental componsition developed by *sitār*-ists of the eighteenth century.
gat vistār	the orderly progression of development of the *gat* by stylized improvisational techniques
gharānā	a school of musicians
gharṣaṇ	an ornamental technique on string instruments: a slide
ghasīṭ	see *gharṣaṇ*
ghazal	a light-classical vocal form with an Urdu text
ghuṛac	the bridge of the *sitār*
giṭkiṛī	an ornament incorporating three tones of different pitches
gīt	a modern song form
gulū	the wooden section connecting the gourd resonator to the neck of the *sitār*
guru	teacher
hastavyāpāra	the collective term of techniques used on the *eka-tantrī vīṇā*

Hindustānī — pertaining to North India

jantra — (a) any instrument;
(b) an instrument believed to have been the predecessor of the modern *sitār*

javārī — the curvature of the bridge which has a large role in determining timbre of Indian stringed instruments

jhap-tāl — a rhythmic cycle ten *mātrā*-s in length

jhālā — an improvisatory climaxing section played after *joṛ* and at the end of drut *gat vistār*

jhūmrā — a rhythmic cycle fourteen *mātrā*-s in length

joṛ — a solo instrumental movement incorporating a recurring pulse played after *ālāp*

joṛ ālāp — see *joṛ*

joṛī tār — the second playing wire on the *sitār*, tuned to the tonic pitch

kachuā — tortoise; tortoise-shaped

kampan — an ornament; tremolo

kamrikā — the wooden slide used to alter pitch on the *eka-tantrī vīṇā*

kaṇ — a grace tone

katar jhār — an improvisatory procedure incorporating various melodic and rhythmic motifs

kavvālī — a Muslim devotional song believed to have been developed by Amir Khusrau in the thirteenth century

khasiṭa — a *glissando* technique used on the *eka-tantrī vīṇā*

khaṭkā — crushed note; *acciaccatura*

khālī — a wave of the hand when showing *tāl*; a section of a *tāl* cycle indicating antistress; empty

khū̃ṭī — a tuning peg

khyāl — a vocal form; see *baṛā khyāl* and *choṭā khyāl*

khyāl aṅg — a style of music based on the forms and ornamentation in *khyāl* vocal music

kinnarī vīṇā — a fretted stick zither described in the *Saṅgīta Ratnākara*

krintan — an articulation by a pluck of the left middle finger

kūṭ bāj — a style of instrumental composition set to *tāl*-s other than *tīn-tāl*

laṛ guthāv — an improvisatory procedure on *sitār* incorporating rearticulations of unisons and transposition of melodic motifs

laṛ lapeṭ — an improvisatory procedure on *sitār* incorporating rearticulations of unisons and turns around a prominent tone

laṛī — an improvisatory procedure on *sitār* incorporating rearticulations of primes

laṅgoṭ — the bone piece attached to the bottom of the main gourd resonator which serves to anchor the wires of the *sitār*

lay — the space between rhythmic pulses which defines the duration of the *mātrā*; tempo

layakārī	usually refers to the division of the *mātrā*, but may also denote other aspects of rhythm including syncopation motifs, and tempo changes
madhya	middle
madhya spatak	central octave
mandra saptak	lower octave
manjhā	the second line, or section, of a gat that usually extends to a lower *tessitura* than the other sections
mankā	tuning bead
Masikhānī bāj	a style of *sitār* playing incorporating *Masītkhānī gat-s* as nuclear melodies; a school of musicians following the style of *sitār* playing created by Masit Khan
Masītkhānī gat	a compositional form in instrumental music created by Masit Khan during the eighteenth century
mātrā	the basic durational units of a *tāl*
mizrāb	a wire plectrum used in playing the *sitār, surbahār, bīn,* and other stringed instruments in India and West Asia a glide between two or more tones performed on the *sitār* by pulling the wire across the fret
mukhṛā	the opening section of a composition that serves to emphasize the arrival of the first *mātrā* of the *tāl* cycle
murkī	an ornament incorporating a turn around a tone
mūrcchanā	octave species
nibaddh	metrical; set to rhythm
nibaddh tānpurā	see *sitār*
niṣād	the seventh scale-degree in the Indian octave
pacīsā	the secondary nut of the *sitār* neck
pakhāvaj	a barrel-shaped drum used to provide rhythmic accom paniment to *dhrupad aṅg* music
palṭā	see *alaṅkār*
pañcam savārī	a rhythmic cycle fifteen *mātrā*-s in length
paramparā	tradition
pardā	fret
pāñc guṇ	division of the *mātrā* into five equal parts
prakṛti	elemental nature
prastār	expansion; spreading out; development
rabāb	a short-necked lute used to play *dhrupad aṅg* music during the latter part of the medieval period and early part of the modern period
rabābiyā	one who plays *rabāb;* belonging to a school of musicians established by descendants of Tansen
radā	a composite *mizrāb bol;* a shortened *rā* stroke followed by a *dā* stroke
Razākhānī bāj	a style of *sitār* playing incorporating *Razākhānī gat-s* as nuclear melodies; a school of musicians following the style of *sitār* playing created by Gulam Raza Khan

Razākhānī gat	a compositional form in instrumental music created by Gulam Raza Khan in the late eighteenth century
rā	an outward stroke by the right index finger
rāg	the basis of melody in Indian music
rūpak tāl	a rhythmic cycle seven *mātrā*-s in length
sam	the beginning point of a *tāl* cycle; the point of most emphasis in a *tāl*
saṅgīt	originally the threefold art of instrumental music, vocal music, and dance; presently, music
sapāṭ	straight up and down; a type of *tān* incorporating such a melodic line
saptak	octave
sargam	a simple composition in a *rāg*, regarded as an exercise
sāt guṇ	division of the *mātrā* into seven equal parts
silsillā	see *śṛṅkhalā*
sitār	a long-necked lute with gourd resonators and raised frets popular in North India
Sitārkhānī gat	a compositional form in instrumental music developed by members of the *Razākhānī bāj*
sparś	an articulation by a striking action of the left middle finger
sphurita	a technique used in playing the *eka-tantrī vīṇā* producing a tremolo effect
sthāyī	the first line of a composition, usually emphasizes the central octave
surbahār	an instrument similar to the *sitār* but larger in size and deeper in pitch
sūt	a technique derived from the *rabāb* performed by sliding the finger along the playing wire
svar	tone; signifies a particular scale-degree and the way it is approached
svatantra	independent; a term used to signify that contemporary instrumental music in North India has achieved sufficient originality to be distinguished from vocal forms
ṣaḍja	the tonic pitch: the first scale-degree in the Indian octave
śailī	style
śiṣya	student
śṛṅkhalā	the ordered progression of improvisatory procedures in *gat vistār*
śuddh	pure; unaltered
śuddh jhālā	a type of *jhālā* using only '*dā* strokes in the melodic line
tablā	a set of drums consisting of a cone-shaped wooden drum tuned to a specific pitch and a kettle-shaped metal drum of indefinite pitch used to accompany *khyālaṅg* music and music of the *gat śailī*

tablī	the soundboard of the *sitār*
taraf	a set of sympathetically resonating wires that are housed under the frets of the *sitār*
tarafdār	having a *taraf*; a *sitār* equipped with sympathetically resonating wires
tarāna	a vocal form similar to the *choṭā khyāl* but incorporating nonsense syllables as a text believed to have been the inspiration for the *Razākhānī gat*
tāl	the basis of rhythm in Indian music; a rhythmic cycle
tālī	a clap of the hand when showing *tāl*; a section of a *tāl* cycle
tālīm	education; the rigorous training given to a student of music
tān	a musical phrase; a melodic passage
tānpurā	an Indian long-necked lute similar to the *sitār* in construction, but unfretted
tār	(a) wire; (2) upper
tār gahan	the nut on the *sitār*
tār paran	an improvisational procedure on string instruments in which the rhythm is set to a drum composition
tār saptak	upper octave
thā guṇ	division of the *mātrā* by one
ṭhāṭ	(a) fret setting on the *sitār* (b) one of ten parent scales that serve as a basis of *rāg* classification in North Indian music
ti guṇ	division of the *mātrā* into three equal parts
tihāī	a cadence technique in which a phrase played three times ends either on *sam* or just before *mukhṛā*
tīn-tāl	a rhythmic cycle sixteen *mātrā*-s in length
toṛā	an improvised passage including varied *bol* patterns and the *bol* '*dir*'
tritantrī vīṇā	**a three-stringed instrument mentioned in the *Saṅgīta Ratnākara* thought to be the prototype of the *sitār* and *tānpurā***
tumbā	the gourd resonator on the *sitār*
ṭappā	a vocal form distinguished by flurries of fast melodic passages
ṭhoṅk jhālā	a type of *jhālā* using '*dā*' strokes and other strokes in the melodic line
ṭnumrī	a light-classical vocal form noted for its romantic song texts and expressive performance
ṭhumrī aṅg	a style of music incorporating the form and ornamentation of the *ṭhumrī* vocal form
vilambit	slow
vilambit gat	an instrumental composition played in a slow tempo
vilambit tān	a melodic improvisatory procedure using few right-hand articulations, and an abundance of *mīṇḍ*